Adobe® Illustrator® CS6

ILLUSTRATED

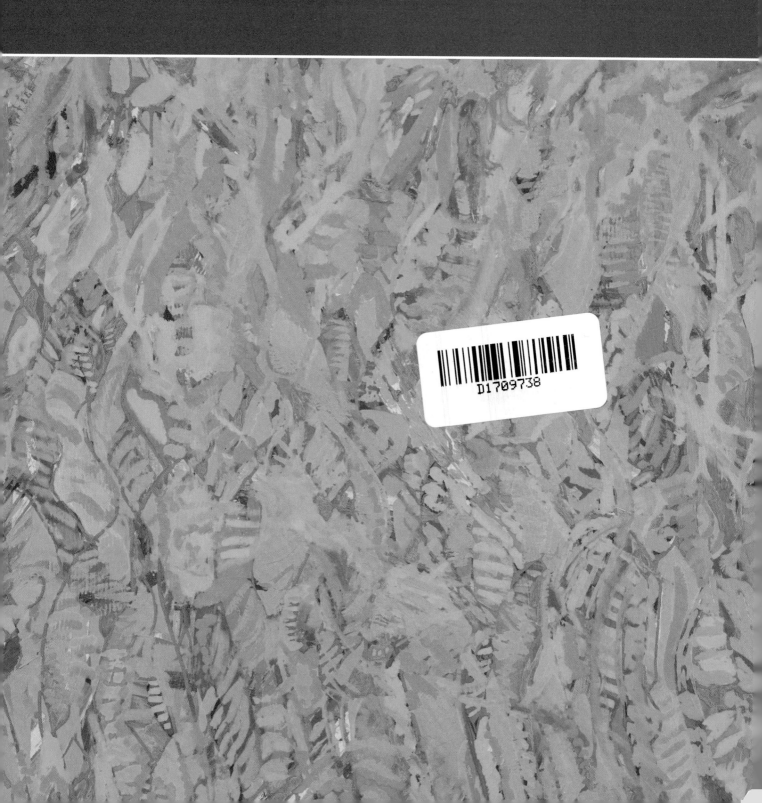

Adobe® Illustrator® CS6

ILLUSTRATED

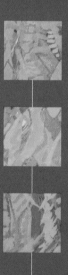

Chris Botello

COURSE TECHNOLOGY
CENGAGE Learning·

Australia · Brazil · Japan · Korea · Mexico · Singapore · Spain · United Kingdom · United States

COURSE TECHNOLOGY
CENGAGE Learning·

Adobe® Illustrator® CS6—Illustrated
Chris Botello

Editor-in-Chief: Marie Lee

Executive Editor: Marjorie Hunt

Senior Product Manager: Christina Kling-Garrett

Product Manager: Kim Klasner

Associate Acquisitions Editor: Amanda Lyons

Editorial Assistant: Brandelynn Perry

Developmental Editor: Ann Fisher

Content Project Manager: Jennifer Feltri-George

Art Director: GEX Publishing Services

Print Buyer: Fola Orekoya

Text Designer: GEX Publishing Services

Proofreader: Harold Johnson

Indexer: BIM Indexing

QA Reviewers: Jeff Schwartz, John Freitas, Susan Whalen, Ashlee Welz Smith

Cover Designer: GEX Publishing Services

Cover Artist: Mark Hunt

Composition: GEX Publishing Services

For product information and technology assistance, contact us at
Cengage Learning Customer & Sales Support, 1-800-354-9706
For permission to use material from this text or product, submit all requests online at **www.cengage.com/permissions**
Further permissions questions can be emailed to
permissionrequest@cengage.com

Library of Congress Control Number: 2012948805

ISBN-13: 978-1-133-52640-7

ISBN-10: 1-133-52640-3

International Student Edition:

ISBN-13: 978-1-133-52639-1

ISBN-10: 1-133-52639-X

Cengage Learning
20 Channel Center Street
Boston, MA 02210
USA

Cengage Learning is a leading provider of customized learning solutions with office locations around the globe, including Singapore, the United Kingdom, Australia, Mexico, Brazil, and Japan. Locate your local office at:
international.cengage.com/region

Cengage Learning products are represented in Canada by Nelson Education, Ltd.

To learn more about Course Technology, visit **www.cengage.com/coursetechnology**

To learn more about Cengage Learning, visit **www.cengage.com**

Purchase any of our products at your local college store or at our preferred online store **www.cengagebrain.com**

Printed in the United States of America
1 2 3 4 5 6 7 18 17 16 15 14 13 12

Brief Contents

Contents

Illustrator CS6

Preface

Welcome to *Adobe® Illustrator® CS6—Illustrated*. The unique page design of the book makes it a great learning tool for both new and experienced users. Each skill is presented on two facing pages so that you don't have to turn the page to find a screen shot or finish a paragraph. See the illustration on the right to learn more about the pedagogical and design elements of a typical lesson.

This book is an ideal learning tool for a wide range of learners—the "rookies" will find the clean design easy to follow and focused with only essential information presented, and the "hot shots" will appreciate being able to move quickly through the lessons to find the information they need without reading a lot of text. The design also makes this a great reference after the course is over!

Coverage

Eight units offer the essential skills, tips, tricks, and techniques to work with vector graphics. Through a thorough exploration of vector graphics, students are able to apply their knowledge to all of the Illustrator tools, features and special effects, allowing them to create fun and interesting artwork. Coverage includes working with drawing techniques, type, layers, patterns, gradients, effects, and 3D objects.

Written by Chris Botello, a professional designer who works on movie posters and theatrical campaigns for the entertainment industry, Illustrator CS6 Illustrated offers a real-world perspective with exercises designed to develop the practical skills and techniques necessary to work effectively in a professional graphic arts environment.

Each two-page spread focuses on a single skill.

Introduction briefly explains why the lesson skill is important.

A case scenario motivates the the steps and puts learning in context.

Tips and troubleshooting advice, right where you need it—next to the step itself.

Sidebars provide useful information related to the lesson skill.

Large screen shots keep students on track as they complete steps.

Brightly colored tabs indicate which section of the book you are in.

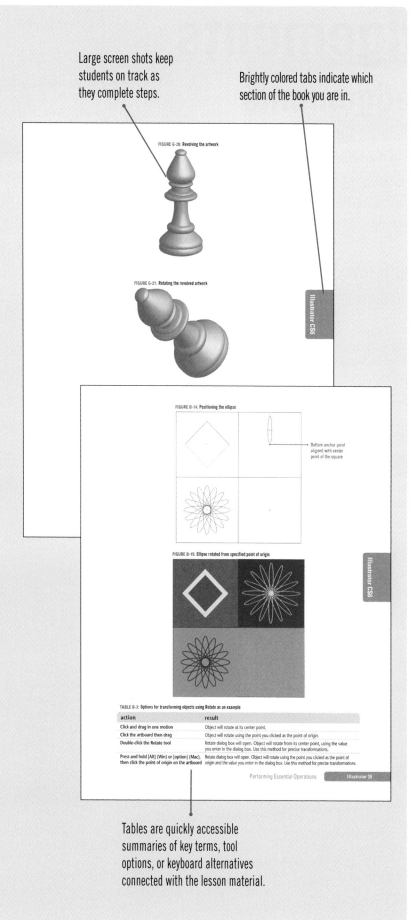

FIGURE G-20: Revolving the artwork

FIGURE G-21: Rotating the revolved artwork

Illustrator CS6

FIGURE B-14: Positioning the ellipse

Bottom anchor point aligned with center point of the square

FIGURE B-15: Ellipse rotated from specified point of origin

Illustrator CS6

TABLE B-2: Options for transforming objects using Rotate as an example

action	result
Click and drag in one motion	Object will rotate at its center point.
Click the artboard then drag	Object will rotate using the point you clicked as the point of origin.
Double-click the Rotate tool	Rotate dialog box will open. Object will rotate from its center point, using the value you enter in the dialog box. Use this method for precise transformations.
Press and hold [Alt] (Win) or [option] (Mac), then click the point of origin on the artboard	Rotate dialog box will open. Object will rotate using the point you clicked as the point of origin and the value you enter in the dialog box. Use this method for precise transformations.

Performing Essential Operations   Illustrator 39

Tables are quickly accessible summaries of key terms, tool options, or keyboard alternatives connected with the lesson material.

Assignments

The lessons use MegaPixel, a graphic arts design agency, as the case study. The assignments on the light yellow pages at the end of each unit increase in difficulty. Additional case studies provide a variety of interesting and relevant exercises for students to practice skills.

Assignments include:

- **Concepts Reviews** consist of multiple choice, matching, and screen identification questions.
- **Skills Reviews** provide additional hands-on, step-by-step reinforcement.
- **Independent Challenges** are case projects requiring critical thinking and application of the unit skills. The Independent Challenges increase in difficulty, with the first one in each unit being the easiest. Independent Challenges 2 and 3 become increasingly open-ended, requiring more independent problem solving.
- **Real Life Independent Challenges** are practical exercises to help students with their everyday lives by focusing on important and useful essential skills, including creating photo montages for scrapbooks and photo albums, retouching and color-correcting family photos, applying layer styles and getting Illustrator Help online.
- **Advanced Challenge Exercises** set within the Independent Challenges provide optional steps for more advanced students.
- **Visual Workshops** are practical, self-graded capstone projects that require independent problem solving.

Acknowledgements

Author Acknowledgements

This book is the definition of a team effort. Thank you to Ann Fisher, the development editor and my longtime friend, for guiding the book through to completion. Special thanks to the technical editors, John Freitas and Susan Whalen, who took great care to be sure that the exercises all worked. Thank you guys for having my back.

I would also like to thank Marie Lee, Editor-in-Chief at Course Technology, Marjorie Hunt, Executive Editor, and Amanda Lyons, Associate Acquisitions Editor. I would also like to thank our Content Project Manager, Jennifer Feltri-George, and Christina Kling-Garrett, our Product Manager.

Finally, thank you to the production and editorial teams for their hard work in putting it all together.

Chris Botello

Advisory Board Acknowledgements

We would like to thank our Advisory Board for their honest feedback and suggestions that helped guide our development decisions for this edition. They are as follows:

Rich Barnett, Wadsworth High School

Lisa Cogley, James A. Rhodes State College

Trudy Lund, Smoke Valley School District

Diane Miller, James A. Rhodes State College

Charles Schneider, Red Clay Consolidated School District

Read This Before You Begin

This book assumes the following:

1. The software has been registered properly. If the product is not registered, students must respond to registration and dialog boxes each time they start the software.
2. Default tools in the Tools panel might differ, but tool options and other settings do not carry over to the End-of-Unit exercises or between units.
3. Students know how to create a folder using a file management utility.
4. After introduction and reinforcement in initial units, the student will be able to respond to the dialog boxes that open when saving a file. Later units do not provide step-by-step guidance.
5. Panels, windows, and dialog boxes have default settings when opened. Exceptions may occur when students open these elements repeatedly in a lesson or in the unit.
6. The few exercises that do contain live type were created using commonly available fonts. Nevertheless, it is possible, that students may run into a missing font issue when opening a data file. In that case, students should use an available font that is similar to the size and weight of the type shown in the lesson.

Frequently Asked Questions

What are the Minimum System Requirements (Windows)?

- Intel® Pentium® 4 or AMD Athlon® 64 or faster processor with 1GB RAM (2GB recommended)

- Microsoft® Windows Vista or Windows 7

- 1.6GB of available hard disk space (2 GB recommended)

- Color monitor with 16-bit color video card

- DVD-ROM

- Adobe Flash Player 10 (for exporting SWF files)

What are Data Files and where are they located?

Your instructor will provide the Data Files to you or direct you to a location on a network drive from which you can download them. As you download the files, select where to store them, such as a hard drive, a network server, or a USB drive. The instructions in the lessons refer to "the drive and folder where your Data Files are stored" when referring to the Data Files for the book.

What software was used to write and test this book?

This book was written and tested with Adobe Illustrator CS6 using a typical installation of Microsoft Windows 7 with Aero turned on.

Do I need to be connected to the Internet to complete the steps and exercises in this book?

Some of the exercises in this book assume that your computer is connected to the Internet. If you are not connected to the Internet, see your instructor for information on how to complete the exercises.

What do I do if my screen is different from the figures shown in this book?

This book was written and tested on computers with monitors set at a resolution of 1280 × 1024. If your screen shows more or less information than the figures in the book, your monitor is probably set at a higher or lower resolution. If you don't see something on your screen, you might have to scroll down or up to see the object identified in the figures.

CourseMate

ENGAGING. TRACKABLE. AFFORDABLE

Cengage Learning's CourseMate for Adobe Illustrator CS6 Illustrated brings course concepts to life with interactive learning, study, and exam preparation tools that support the printed textbook. Watch student comprehension soar as your class works with the printed textbook and the textbook-specific website. CourseMate goes beyond the book to deliver what you need!

FOR STUDENTS:

Interactive eBook that you can read, highlight, or annotate on your computer.

Total Training videos with audio-visual, step-by-step instructions reinforce concepts you learn about Adobe Illustrator.

Glossary and Flashcards to help you master key terms.

Interactive exercises give you immediate feedback to help you learn.

FOR INSTRUCTORS:

Engagement Tracker, a first-of-its-kind tool that monitors student engagement in the course.

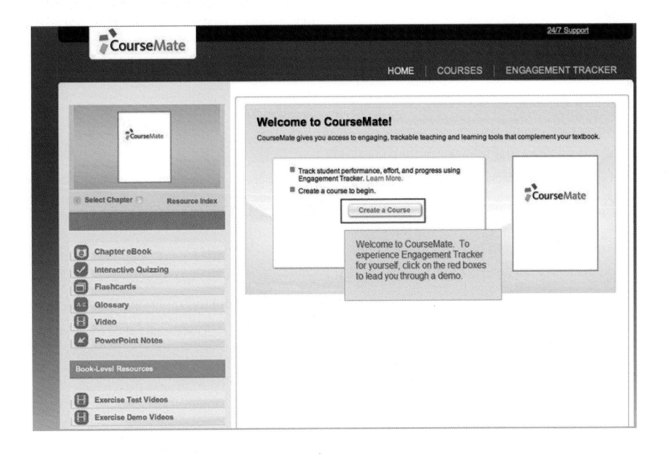

Instructor Resources

The Instructor Resources CD is Course Technology's way of putting the resources and information needed to teach and learn effectively into your hands. With an integrated array of teaching and learning tools that offer you and your students a broad range of technology-based instructional options, we believe this CD represents the highest quality and most cutting edge resources available to instructors today. The resources available with this book are:

- **Instructor's Manual**—Available as an electronic file, the Instructor's Manual includes detailed lecture topics with teaching tips for each unit.

- **Sample Syllabus**—Prepare and customize your course easily using this sample course outline.

- **PowerPoint Presentations**—Each unit has a corresponding PowerPoint presentation that you can use in lecture, distribute to your students, or customize to suit your course.

- **Figure Files**—The figures in the text are provided on the Instructor Resources CD to help you illustrate key topics or concepts. You can create traditional overhead transparencies by printing the figure files. Or you can create electronic slide shows by using the figures in a presentation program such as PowerPoint.

- **Solutions to Exercises**—Solutions to Exercises contains files students are asked to create or modify in the lessons and end-of-unit material. Also provided in this section is a document outlining the solutions for the end-of-unit Concepts Review, Skills Review, and Independent Challenges.

- **Data Files for Students**—To complete the units in this book, your students will need Data Files. You can post the Data Files on a file server for students to copy. The Data Files are available on the Instructor Resources CD-ROM, the Review Pack, and can also be downloaded from cengagebrain.com. For more information on how to download the Data Files, see the inside front cover.

- **ExamView**—ExamView is a powerful testing software package that allows you to create and administer printed, computer (LAN-based), and Internet exams. ExamView includes hundreds of questions that correspond to the topics covered in this text, enabling students to generate detailed study guides that include page references for further review. The computer-based and Internet testing components allow students to take exams at their computers, and also saves you time by grading each exam automatically.

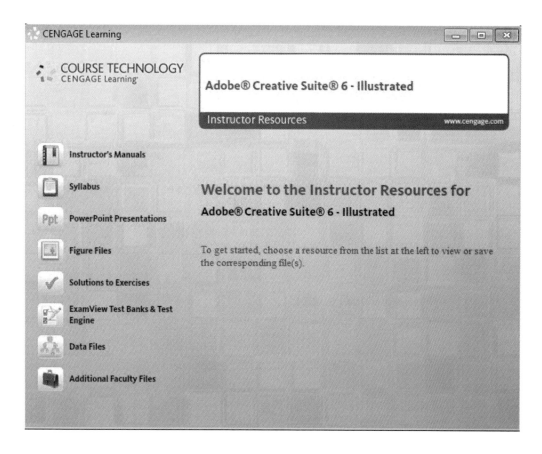

Other Adobe® CS6 Titles

Adobe® Dreamweaver® CS6—Illustrated
Sherry Bishop (9781133526025)

Eleven units provide essential training on using Adobe Dreamweaver CS6 to create websites. Coverage includes creating a web site, developing web pages, formatting text, using and managing images, creating links and navigation bars using CSS to layout pages, and collecting data with forms.

Adobe® Flash® Professional CS6—Illustrated
Barbara M. Waxer (9781133526001)

Eight units provide essential training on using Adobe Flash Professional CS6, including creating graphics, text, and symbols, using the Timeline, creating animation, creating buttons and using media, adding interactivity, and integrating Flash projects with other CS6 programs.

Adobe® Illustrator® CS6—Illustrated
Chris Botello (9781133526407)

Eight units cover essential skills for working with Adobe Illustrator CS6 including drawing basic and complex shapes, using the Pen tool, working with blends, compound paths and clipping masks, creating pattern fills and gradient fills for objects, and designing stunning 3D effects.

Adobe® InDesign® CS6—Illustrated
Ann Fisher (9781133187585)

Eight units provide essential training on using Adobe InDesign CS6 for designing simple layouts, combining text, graphics, and color, as well as multi-page documents, layered documents, tables, and InDesign libraries.

Adobe® Photoshop® CS6—Illustrated
Chris Botello (9781133190394)

Eight units offer thorough coverage of essential skills for working with Adobe Photoshop CS6 from both the design and production perspective, including creating and managing layer masks, creating color effects and improving images with adjustment layers, working with text and combining text and imagery, and using filters and layer styles to create eye-popping special effects.

Adobe® Creative Suite 6 Web Tools: Dreamweaver, Photoshop, Flash Illustrated
(9781133629740)

Covers essential skills for working with Adobe Dreamweaver® CS6, Adobe Photoshop® CS6, and Adobe Flash® CS6 with ten Dreamweaver units, one Bridge unit, four Photoshop units, five Flash units, and one unit on integration.

Adobe® Creative Suite 6 Design Tools: Photoshop, Illustrator, InDesign Illustrated
(9781133562580)

Covers essential skills for working with Adobe Photoshop® CS6, Adobe Illustrator® CS6, and Adobe InDesign® CS6 with seven Photoshop units, seven Illustrator units, six InDesign units, and one unit on integration.

For more information on the Illustrated Series, please visit:
www.cengage.com/ct/illustrated

UNIT A
Illustrator CS6

Getting Started with Adobe Illustrator CS6

Files You Will Need:

To view a list of files needed for this unit, see the Data Files Grid in the back of the book.

Adobe Illustrator CS6 is a professional illustration software application created by Adobe Systems Incorporated. With Illustrator, you can create everything from simple graphics, icons, and text to complex and multilayered illustrations. You can use these elements within a page layout, in a multimedia presentation, or on the web. Illustrator offers dozens of essential tools. Using them in combination with various menu commands gives you the potential to create any illustration that your imagination can dream up. With experience, you will find that your ability to create complex graphics is based on your ability to master simple, basic operations. MegaPixel is a graphic arts service bureau and design agency. Laura Jacobs, the owner of MegaPixel, has hired you as a production artist. Part of your job includes using Illustrator to produce high-quality illustrations.

OBJECTIVES

Define illustration software

Start Adobe Illustrator CS6 and change preference settings

View the workspace

Create and save a document

Change the artboard size and close a document

Open a document and change views

Get help

Work with ruler guides

Work with Smart Guides and exit Illustrator

Defining Illustration Software

Graphics that you create in Illustrator are called vector graphics. **Vector graphics** are created with lines and curves and are defined by mathematical objects called **vectors**, which use geometric characteristics to define an object. Vector graphics consist of **anchor points** and **line segments**, together referred to as **paths**. Vector graphics render bold graphics with clean, crisp lines that can be scaled to various sizes. Figure A-1 shows an example of a vector graphic. Vectors are often used to create logos or line art and are the best choice for typographical work, especially small or italic type. Laura stops by your office and asks you to give her a brief overview of Illustrator's capabilities.

DETAILS

You can use Illustrator to:

- **Create illustrations**

  Illustrator has a variety of simple shape tools and drawing tools that you can use to create anything from a very simple logo to a complex, sophisticated illustration.

QUICK TIP

Swatch libraries such as Nature and Skintones are helpful when you need to use a very specific color, such as a specific skin type or for something found in nature. The swatches are carefully mixed to give you just the color you need.

- **Apply process and spot colors**

  You can create your own process colors, name them, and then save them in the Swatches panel. You can also choose spot colors from hundreds of swatch libraries, including color books such as Pantone and Trumatch, as well as custom swatch libraries by category such as Nature and Skintones.

- **Create type**

  Illustrator includes everything you need to create and format type. You can create large blocks of text or large bold headlines. You can type along a path and even fill an object with text. Using the Character panel, you can change the font, size, leading, baseline shift, tracking, and kerning values to achieve the exact look you want.

- **Create gradient fills**

  Gradient fills are multicolor blends that fill Illustrator objects and outlines. You can create and name gradients and then save them in the Swatches panel for future use. Once applied, you can manipulate gradients using the Gradient tool.

- **Transform and distort objects**

  Transform tools, such as Scale, Rotate, Reflect, and Shear, allow you to change the physical appearance of an object. The Effect menu contains many special effects, such as Distort & Transform, Stylize, Warp, and 3D, that you can apply to Illustrator objects.

- **Export documents**

  Illustrator documents can be exported in other file formats, such as Flash movies (*.swf), Photoshop documents (*.psd), and JPEGs (*.jpg).

- **Work with multiple artboards**

  You can work with multiple artboards, allowing you to work on the front and back of a design in one document, or design differently sized components of a project, like letterhead, business cards, and envelopes. You can choose the number of artboards you want when you create a new document or you can add them as you go using the Artboard tool.

FIGURE A-1: Vector graphic

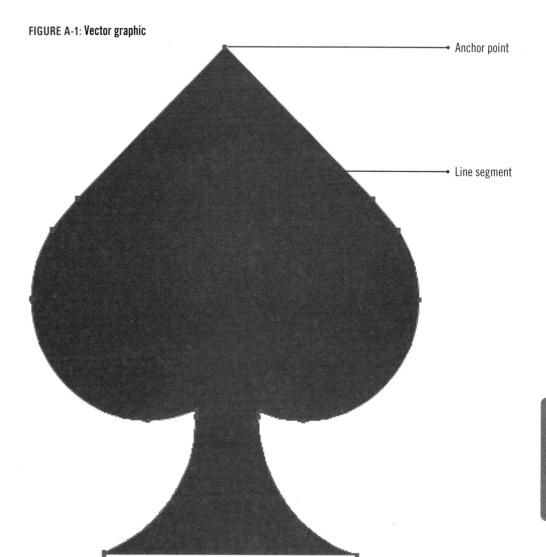

Anchor point

Line segment

Illustrator CS6

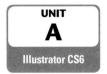
Starting Adobe Illustrator CS6 and Changing Preference Settings

Depending on your operating system, you can start Illustrator by selecting the program application icon or by double-clicking it. When you install Illustrator, the installation program may place an Illustrator shortcut icon on your desktop (Win) or in the dock (Mac). You can double-click (Win) or single-click (Mac) the icon to open the program. However, you can also always start the program using the Start menu (Win). In Illustrator, you can change the application's settings, such as the color of guides or the units of measure. These settings are also known as preferences, and are accessed in the Preferences dialog box. You start Illustrator and change the preference settings for the units of measure.

STEPS

WIN

TROUBLE

Adobe Illustrator CS6 may be in a folder named Adobe Design Premium CS6 or Adobe Master Collection CS6.

1. Click the Start button 🔘 on the Windows taskbar, point to All Programs, then click Adobe Illustrator CS6 or Adobe Illustrator CS6 (64 Bit) as shown in Figure A-2

2. Click Edit on the Menu bar, point to Preferences, then click Units

3. In the Preferences dialog box, click the General list arrow, then click Inches, verify that Stroke is set to Points, that Type is set to Points, then click OK

MAC

TROUBLE

Adobe Illustrator CS6 may be in a folder named Adobe Design Premium CS6 or Adobe Master Collection CS6.

1. Open the Finder, click the hard drive icon, click Applications, click the Adobe Illustrator CS6 folder, then double-click the Adobe Illustrator CS6 or the Adobe Illustrator CS6 (64 Bit) icon

2. Click Illustrator on the Menu bar, point to Preferences, then click Units

3. In the Preferences dialog box, click the General list arrow, then click Inches if necessary, verify that Stroke is set to Points, that Type is set to Points, then click OK

Setting preferences

You can make changes to Illustrator based on your personal preferences. For example, you can change the color of guides and Smart Guides, and specify whether documents are opened as tabbed or not. These settings and many more are available in the Illustrator Preferences dialog box. To open the Preferences dialog box, click Edit (Win) or Illustrator (Mac) on the Menu bar, point to Preferences, then click a preference category, such as

Guides & Grid, to open the dialog box. Click a category name in the box on the left side of the dialog box to switch categories. Keep in mind that in order for the settings you change to stick to all future documents, no documents can be open while you make changes in the Preferences dialog box. If a document is open when you change preference settings, the changes will only affect the currently open document.

Adobe
Illustrator CS6
(64 Bit)

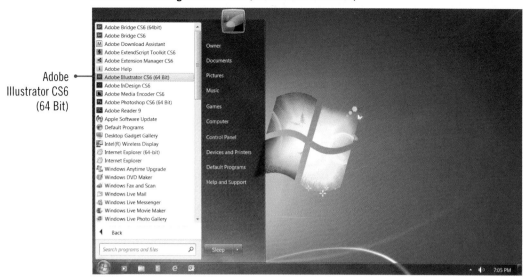

Using Adobe Illustrator CS6 templates

Templates are predesigned Illustrator drawings that you can open and modify to meet your needs. Templates can really help you jump-start a project if you're running out of time or need some creative guidance. For example, there is a template called Stationery.ait which could be a starting point for creating your own personal stationery. There is a placeholder for your name and other contact information. There are six categories of templates: Blank Templates, Film, Japanese Templates, Club, FlexSkins, and

Tech. Within those folders are the actual templates, such as Banner Ads, Business Cards, and CD Cases. You can access templates by clicking the Go to Bridge button on the Menu bar. The Adobe Bridge window opens with the six categories of template folders in the Content pane. Double-click the template you want to open in Illustrator. You can also access templates in the New Document dialog box by expanding the Advanced section in the dialog box, then clicking the Templates button.

Viewing the Workspace

The workspace includes the Tools panel along the left side, additional panels along the right side, the status bar along the bottom, and the Menu bar and Control panel along the top. The default workspace, Essentials, is one of many predefined workspaces that you can choose to work in. It includes the basic tools and panels you need to perform essential tasks. 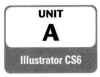 You create a new document and explain the workspace elements to Laura.

STEPS

1. **Click File on the Menu bar, click New, then click OK, to accept default settings and close the New Document dialog box**

   The Illustrator window opens, as shown in Figure A-3, displaying the Essentials workspace, and a new Untitled-1 document, as shown in the document tab. Illustrator documents have tabs that include their name, magnification level, and color mode. When more than one document is open, each document tab is arranged horizontally below the Control panel. Clicking a document tab activates that document in the Illustrator workspace. On a Macintosh, document tabs only appear when more than one document is open. Also, the Minimize, Maximize, and Close buttons are on the document title bar.

QUICK TIP

Press and hold a tool to expose hidden tools. Click the Tearoff icon to the right of a tool group to create a floating toolbar.

2. **Locate the Tools panel along the left side of the workspace**

   The Tools panel contains tools that let you create, select, and manipulate objects in Illustrator. Some tool icons include a small white triangle. This triangle indicates that there are more hidden tools behind that tool.

TROUBLE

The appearance of your Menu bar may differ depending on your monitor size and resolution setting.

3. **Locate the Menu bar at the top of the workspace**

   The Menu bar includes the program menus, the Go to Bridge and Arrange Documents buttons, the Workspace switcher, the Help text box, and the Minimize, Maximize, and Close buttons.

4. **Click the workspace switcher, then click Painting**

   The Essentials workspace changes to the Painting workspace, which opens a number of color panels and the Brushes panel specific to painting.

5. **Click the workspace switcher, then click Essentials**

   The Essentials workspace replaces the Painting workspace.

6. **Locate the Control panel below the Menu bar**

   The Control panel describes the characteristics of the selected object on the artboard. The **artboard** is the area on which you create artwork. You may have more than one artboard in a document. The space surrounding the artboard is called the **pasteboard**. You can place objects on the pasteboard until you're ready to place them on the artboard.

7. **Locate the group of collapsed panels along the right side, then click the Swatches panel button** ⊞

   The Swatches panel opens. It contains preset colors, along with gradients, pattern swatches, and shades of gray.

QUICK TIP

You can also open and close panels using the Window menu.

8. **Click the Collapse to icons button** ▸▸ **on the Swatches panel to minimize the panel**

   The panel is collapsed in its original panel group.

QUICK TIP

You can drag a document tab in a downward direction to convert a tabbed document to a floating window.

9. **Click the Close button** ✖ **on the document tab named Untitled-1 to close the document**

FIGURE A-3: The Illustrator workspace

Menu bar

Control panel

Tools panel

Workspace switcher

Panels dock

Your page size and number of artboards may differ

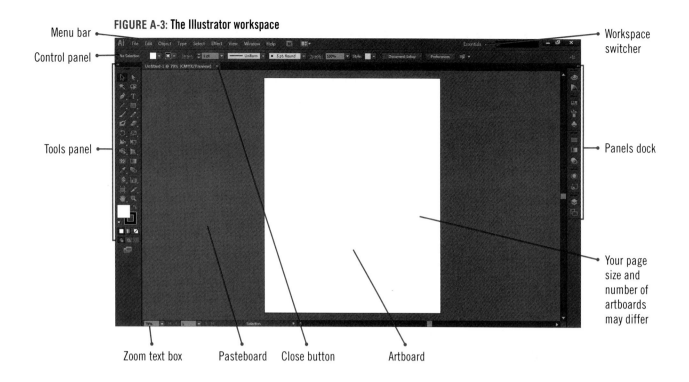

Zoom text box   Pasteboard   Close button   Artboard

Creating custom workspaces

Illustrator offers custom workspaces for specific types of projects. For example, the Typography workspace displays the Character, Paragraph, and OpenType panels, all of which can be useful when creating a text-intensive document. To choose a custom workspace, click Window on the Menu bar, point to Workspace, and then click one of the eight workspace names. You can also create your own custom workspace with a unique name. For example, you may prefer to hide all of the panels in order to maximize the Document window, or you may want the Tools panel to be a lot closer to the artboard. Illustrator makes it very easy to create the workspace you want and then save it. Once the workspace is set up as you like it, click Window on the Menu bar, point to Workspace, then click New Workspace. In the New Workspace dialog box, name the workspace, then click OK. Your custom workspace will be added to the list of custom workspaces.

Creating and Saving a Document

To create a new Illustrator document, you start out by making choices in the New Document dialog box, such as the name and size of the artboard. You can also decide to work with more than one artboard by changing the number of artboards in the Number of Artboards text box. It is very important to save your work often so that you don't lose any of it. Using the Save As command allows you to save a document with a new name. Using the Save command saves your most recent changes. ▨▨▨ You show Laura how to create a new document using multiple artboards and then how to save the document.

STEPS

1. **Click File on the Menu bar, then click New**

   The New Document dialog box opens. Here, you name the document, choose the unit of measure, such as inches or picas, and choose a size for the artboard as well as an orientation for the artboard. The default orientation, **portrait**, is taller than it is wide. A **landscape** orientation is wider than it is tall—in other words, its orientation is the opposite from portrait.

2. **Type double artboards_AI-A in the Name text box, then verify that the Portrait orientation is selected**

3. **Click the Size list arrow, click Letter, click the Units list arrow, then click Inches**

   The Size options include many default page sizes. The Letter size is 8.5" × 11".

4. **Click the Number of Artboards up arrow once to change the number to 2, then click the Arrange by Row button** ⇥

   The Document window will have two 8.5" × 11" artboards arranged as a row. Multiple artboards are useful when you want to work on multiple illustrations simultaneously.

5. **Double-click the Spacing text box, type .25, press [Tab] compare your screen to Figure A-4, then click OK**

   The Spacing value represents the spacing between the artboards. The new document named Double Artboards.ai appears in the workspace. Notice the two artboards are arranged in a row.

> **QUICK TIP**
> Once you make changes to a document, you can use the Save command to save changes.

6. **Click the Selection tool** ▶, **click the artboard on the right, then click the artboard on the left**

   Only one artboard can be active at a time. The double artboards_AI-A document has been named but it has not yet been saved to a location. Because you have not yet modified the document, you use the Save As command to save the document to your hard drive.

7. **Click File on the Menu bar, then click Save As**

   The Save As dialog box opens, as shown in Figure A-5.

> **TROUBLE**
> You may have to click Save twice, depending on how filename extensions are applied on your system.

8. **Click the Save in list arrow (Win) or the Save As expand arrow (Mac), navigate to the location where you store your Data Files, then click Save**

   The Illustrator Options dialog box opens. This dialog box also allows you to save the Illustrator document as an older version of Illustrator, such as CS4 or CS5, using the Version list arrow.

9. **Click OK**

   The Illustrator Options dialog box closes, and the double artboards_AI-A.ai document remains open. It is now stored on the hard drive.

FIGURE A-4: New Document dialog box

Spacing text box

Arrange by Row button

Landscape orientation

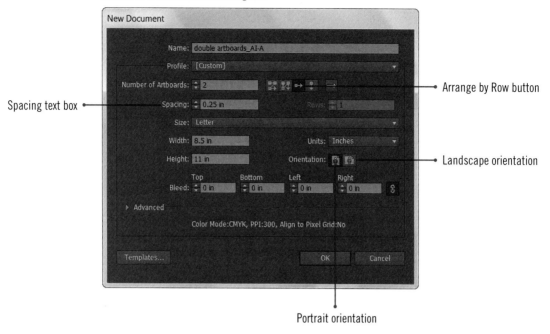

Portrait orientation

FIGURE A-5: Save As dialog box

Save in list arrow

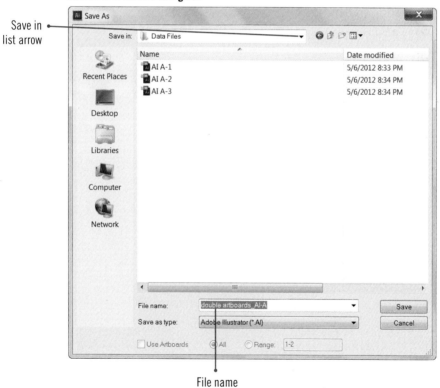

File name

Creating document profiles

The Profile menu in the New Document dialog box allows you to specify the type of document you need. You can choose Print, Web, Devices, Video and Film, Basic RGB, and Flash Builder. The dialog box options available depend on which profile you choose. For example, if you choose Devices, the Color Mode changes to RGB, the unit of measure changes to pixels, and the Size changes to iPad; these are some of the default settings for the Devices profile.

Changing the Artboard Size and Closing a Document

Once you create a document, you may need to change the artboard size. To do so, simply click the Artboard tool on the Tools panel. Dotted lines and handles appear around the selected artboard, indicating that it can be resized. You can resize an artboard manually by dragging an edge or by changing the width and height values on the Control panel. To exit artboard mode, click any tool on the Tools panel. You close a document by clicking the Close button on the document tab (Win) or the document title bar (Mac). When you close a document, Illustrator remains open. You show Laura how to edit an artboard size, and then close the double artboards_AI-A.ai document.

STEPS

QUICK TIP
You can also edit the artboard when the Selection tool is selected by clicking the Document Setup button on the Control panel, then clicking the Edit Artboards button in the Document Setup dialog box.

1. **Click the Artboard tool 🎬 on the Tools panel**

   The artboard on the left becomes editable, as indicated by the dotted line surrounding it.

2. **Position the mouse pointer at the top of the artboard; when the pointer changes to a double-sided arrow ↕, click and drag downward to change the height of the artboard as shown in Figure A-6, then release the mouse button**

   The height of your artboard may vary from the figure. As you drag the mouse pointer, you may see W and H values appear next to the cursor. These are called Measurement Labels. To turn this feature off, click Edit (Win) or Illustrator (Mac), point to Preferences, click Smart Guides, then remove the check mark in the Measurement Labels check box.

3. **Double-click the W Value text box on the Control panel, type 6, press [Tab] to highlight the H Value text box, type 4, then press [Enter] (Win) or [return] (Mac)**

   As shown in Figure A-7, the left artboard is now six inches wide by four inches tall.

QUICK TIP
You can click any tool on the Tools panel to return to the normal workspace view when you are finished editing the artboard(s).

4. **Click the Selection tool ▶ on the Tools panel**

   The workspace returns to its normal appearance; the artboard is resized and no longer editable. You're done editing the artboards and are ready to save the document.

5. **Click File on the Menu bar, then click Save**

QUICK TIP
If you click the Close command before saving, Illustrator will prompt you to save changes to the document.

6. **Click File on the Menu bar, then click Close**

   The double artboards_AI-A.ai document is closed and the Illustrator program remains open.

FIGURE A-6: Manually resizing the artboard

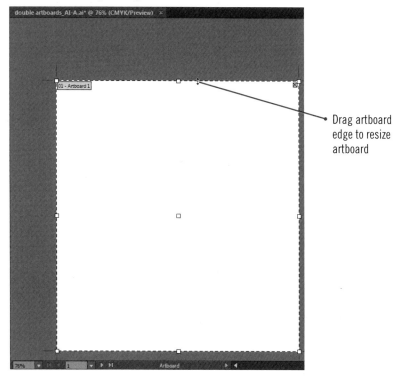

Drag artboard
edge to resize
artboard

FIGURE A-7: Left artboard is resized

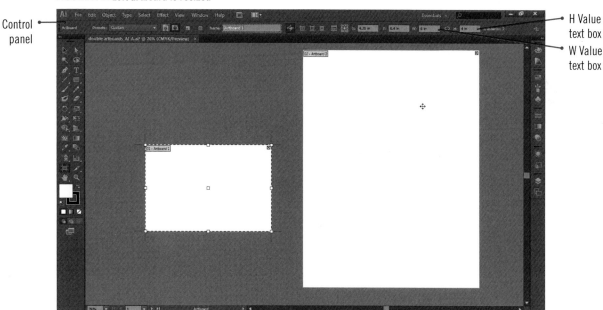

Control
panel

H Value
text box

W Value
text box

Working in artboard mode

There are many ways to work with multiple artboards. You can change the size and location of them, and you can add or delete them. Click the Artboard tool on the Tools panel to enter artboard mode. When you click an individual artboard, handles appear around the selected artboard, indicating that it can be modified. You can move the artboard to a different location and change its size. When you drag an artboard, the art on the artboard will move with it. If you do not want the art on the artboard to move, click the Move/Copy Artwork with Artboard button on the Control panel to deselect it. At any time, you can create a new artboard simply by clicking and dragging in the gray canvas area. It's just as easy to delete an artboard. Simply click it to select it, then press [Delete]. To exit artboard mode, click another tool on the Tools panel.

Opening a Document and Changing Views

You can easily open existing Illustrator documents, including documents that you closed earlier, and you can have multiple Illustrator documents open at the same time. Illustrator documents open in Preview mode, or you can view them in Outline mode. You open an Illustrator document and show Laura the difference between Preview and Outline modes. You also show her some keyboard shortcuts that are useful for working in either mode.

STEPS

1. **Click File on the Menu bar, then click Open**
   The Open dialog box opens.

2. **Navigate to the location where you store your Data Files, then click AI A-1.ai**
   A preview of the document appears in the Open dialog box, as shown in Figure A-8.

> **TROUBLE**
> If you do not see all of the document, click View on the Menu bar, then click Fit Artboard in Window.

3. **Click Open, save the document as workspace basics_AI-A, then click OK to close the Illustrator Options dialog box**
   The document opens in the workspace in Preview mode. **Preview mode** shows artwork with its fill and stroke colors. It also shows how each object is layered or "stacked" from the bottom of the artboard upward.

4. **Click the Selection tool ▶ on the Tools panel if necessary, then click the star in the center of the artboard**
   The star is positioned in front of the four squares. If you see a square with handles around the selected star, click the View menu, then click Hide Bounding Box. The **bounding box** is a selection box which appears when you select an object. It contains resize handles which you can use to resize the object.

> **QUICK TIP**
> You can switch between Preview and Outline modes by pressing [Ctrl][Y] (Win) or ⌘ [Y] (Mac).

5. **Click View on the Menu bar, then click Outline**
   The objects appear as vector outlines, as shown in Figure A-9. **Outline mode** shows only the vector outline of objects without fills or strokes applied, so you cannot easily determine whether the star is in front of or behind the four squares. All objects are on the same level vertically; it is not obvious how they overlap each other. Outline mode is useful when you want to select an object that may be partially or fully blocked by another, or if you want to view an object's center point.

6. **Click the edge of the diamond in the upper-left corner**
   The diamond's anchor points and line segments are visible. In Outline mode, you can only select objects by clicking their edges.

7. **Click View on the Menu bar, then click Preview**
   The workspace returns to Preview mode.

8. **Click the Zoom tool 🔍 on the Tools panel, then click anywhere on the artboard twice**
   The Zoom tool increases the magnification level. The new magnification level appears on the status bar and on the document tab. You can also press and hold [Alt] (Win) or [option] (Mac) while clicking the Zoom tool to zoom out and decrease the magnification level.

9. **Click the Hand tool ✋ on the Tools panel, then when the pointer turns to 🖐, drag the artboard to see a different view of the artwork**
   Using a combination of the Zoom and Hand tools is a great way to view part of your illustration up close.

> **QUICK TIP**
> If you have multiple artboards, use the Fit All in Window option to view all artboards in the Document window.

10. **Deselect all, double-click ✋ on the Tools panel to fit the artboard in the window, then save your work**

Illustrator 12

Getting Started with Adobe Illustrator CS6

FIGURE A-8: Open dialog box

Preview of document

FIGURE A-9: Outline mode

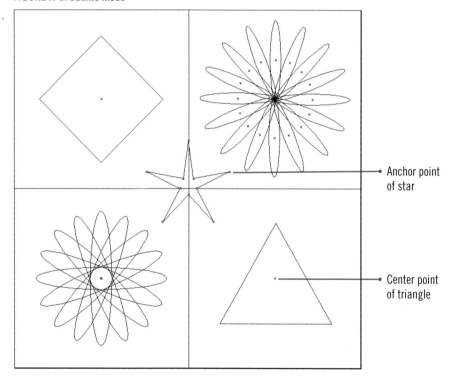

Anchor point
of star

Center point
of triangle

Creating new views

In Illustrator, you can define an area of the artboard and save it as a named view, which you can then select from the View menu. The New View feature allows you to make window views of specific sections of the artboard. For instance, if you were working on an illustration of a map, you may want to create four views of the North, East, South, and West regions. To create a new view, you define the area of the artboard that you want to see by zooming in on it with the Zoom tool or Navigator panel. Click View on the Menu bar, then click New View. Name the view in the Name text box of the New View dialog box, then click OK. The named view appears as an option on the View menu. You can change the name of a view or delete a view using the Edit Views command, also on the View menu.

Getting Help

Illustrator is a very sophisticated drawing program. It will take some time to learn everything there is to know about Illustrator. In the meantime, if you are curious about a feature or if you are stuck along the way, you can access Illustrator's Help feature while working in Illustrator. The Help feature provides articles on specific Illustrator topics as well as many videos and tutorials. You demonstrate Illustrator's Help feature to Laura and find information about Illustrator's new improved user interface.

STEPS

TROUBLE
If Adobe Help Manager opens (Mac), click Cancel to close it.

1. **Click Help on the Menu bar, then click Illustrator Help**

   The Illustrator Help page of the Adobe.com website opens in your browser, as shown in Figure A-10. At the top of the page are help categories, such as What's New, Reshaping objects, and Web graphics. Clicking a category brings you to that section of help and offers more specific topics within the chosen category. Clicking a topic opens a new web page with information about the chosen topic.

2. **Click the What's New category at the top of the page**

   The screen refreshes to show the What's New category at the top of the page with a list of topics related to it below.

3. **Click Improved User Interface in the list of topics**

   As shown in Figure A-11, there are three subtopics available in the Improved user interface category.

4. **Click Panels, then compare your screen to Figure A-12**

5. **Read the information about panels**

6. **Close the Help window**

7. **Keep the document open for the next lesson**

Working with Adobe Bridge

Adobe Bridge is a content management application that is accessible from the Menu bar in Illustrator. Clicking the Go to Bridge button on the Menu bar opens the Bridge application. In Bridge, you can open and preview all files that Adobe programs can open. The main job of Bridge is to help you organize and view your content. In the Bridge window, you will see a list of your folders on your hard drive. Clicking a folder displays the contents of the folder in the Content pane. When you select a file in the Content pane, information about the file appears in the File Properties pane. You can view file properties, such as size, date created, date modified, and resolution. You can assign the same keyword or keywords to all of the files that are used for the same purpose. In Bridge, you can then search for files by sorting them by their keywords. Labels and ratings are two other ways to sort files in Bridge. These are just some of the basic uses of Bridge. Bridge has many advanced uses too, such as viewing and applying metadata to files. Metadata is file information that is applied to files using tags. Use the Metadata panel to view metadata and the File Info dialog box (File menu) to add metadata to a file.

FIGURE A-10: Illustrator Help window

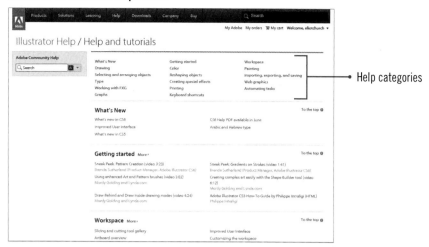

Help categories

FIGURE A-11: Improved user interface page

Improved user
interface topic

Panels subtopic

Three subtopics

FIGURE A-12: Panels information

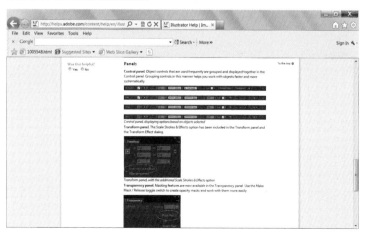

Working with Ruler Guides

Ruler guides are vertical and horizontal lines that are useful for aligning objects on the artboard. You create ruler guides from the horizontal and vertical rulers in the workspace. Ruler guides can be locked or unlocked. You can move them to new locations and delete them as necessary. You can also hide them temporarily and then show them again. 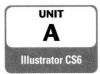 You display the rulers and then show Laura how easy it is to create horizontal and vertical ruler guides.

STEPS

1. **Click** View **on the Menu bar, point to** Rulers, **then click** Show Rulers

   A horizontal ruler appears at the top of the window, and a vertical ruler appears along the left side of the window, as shown in Figure A-13.

2. **Position the mouse pointer over the horizontal ruler, click and drag in a downward direction until the new guide appears, drag it below the diamond, as shown in Figure A-14, then release the mouse button**

   A new horizontal guide appears on the artboard.

3. **Click** View **on the Menu bar, point to** Guides, **then click** Lock Guides **to remove the check mark, if necessary**

   Selecting Lock Guides removes the check mark next to Lock Guides and, therefore, unlocks the guides.

4. **Click the** Selection tool 🔲 **on the Tools panel, drag the guide up and down, then align the horizontal guide with the** 4" mark **on the vertical ruler**

5. **Position the mouse pointer over the vertical ruler, then drag a** vertical guide **to the center of the star so that the ruler guide is aligned with the** 4" mark **on the horizontal ruler, as shown in Figure A-15**

   The vertical guide is a darker shade of blue than the horizontal guide because it is still selected.

6. **Save your work**

> **QUICK TIP**
> To change the color and style of guides, click Edit (Win) or Illustrator (Mac) on the Menu bar, point to Preferences, then click Guides & Grid.

FIGURE A-13: Viewing the rulers in Illustrator

Rulers ●──

FIGURE A-14: Viewing the horizontal guide

Horizontal ●──
guide

FIGURE A-15: Viewing the vertical guide

──● Vertical
guide

Working with Smart Guides and Exiting Illustrator

The Smart Guides feature is a visual aid that works alongside ruler guides. Smart Guides are useful when you need to be very precise about the alignment of objects. **Smart Guides** appear as you drag the mouse pointer over the artboard. Words such as *center*, *anchor*, *path*, and *intersect* appear when the mouse pointer touches one of those items. Smart Guides are also useful for moving objects in Illustrator. If you want to align two objects by their center points, the word *center* will appear once the two are aligned. You turn the Smart Guides feature on by selecting Smart Guides on the View menu. 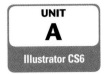 To complete your demonstration about ruler guides to Laura, you show her how Smart Guides work, and then you exit Illustrator.

1. Click View on the Menu bar, then click Smart Guides to add a check mark to it, if necessary

2. Drag the mouse pointer over the white flower graphic in the upper-right corner, then notice the word *path* as you drag along the flower petals, as shown in Figure A-16

3. Drag the mouse pointer near the center of the flower where the petals overlap and notice the word *intersect*

   You can use the Smart Guides to align an object over another. You want to move the blue-and-white diamond on top of the white flower.

4. Position the mouse pointer over the center of the blue-and-white diamond, then drag the center point to the right over the white flower; then when it is aligned with the center of the white flower and the word *intersect* appears, as shown in Figure A-17, release the mouse button

   When the center of the diamond is aligned with the center of the flower, the word *intersect* appears, and the mouse pointer changes from black to white. An outline of the diamond appears, indicating its new location when you release the mouse.

5. Click the pasteboard to deselect the diamond

   The two shapes appear to be one shape.

6. Save your work

   The diamond is aligned perfectly over the flower, as shown in Figure A-18. You've completed your work in the document.

7. Click File on the Menu bar, then click Close

8. Click File on the Menu bar, then click Exit (Win); or click Illustrator on the Menu bar, then click Quit Illustrator (Mac)

FIGURE A-16: Viewing Smart Guides

Smart Guide •———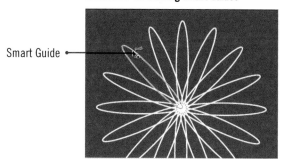

FIGURE A-17: Aligning the center of the two objects

Smart Guides •———
indicate that
two centers are
aligned

Outline of •———
bounding box

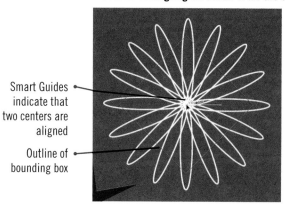

FIGURE A-18: Result of moving the diamond

Practice

Concepts Review

Label the elements of the Illustrator screen shown in Figure A-19.

FIGURE A-19

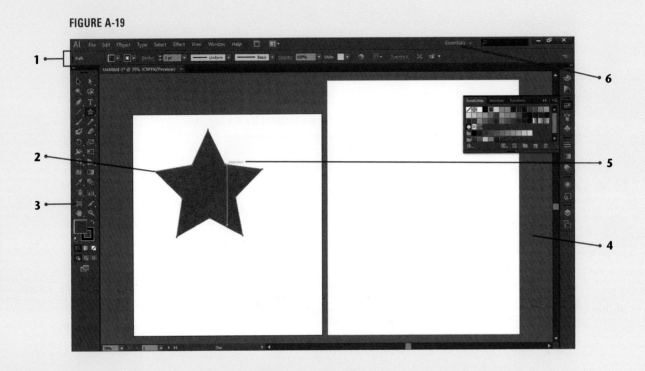

Match each term with the statement that best describes it.

7. **Anchor point**
8. **Vector graphic**
9. **Smart Guides**
10. **Hand tool**
11. **Preview mode**
12. **Landscape**

a. Allows you to move the view of the artboard
b. Shows objects in color
c. Is a type of artboard orientation
d. Is created with lines and curves
e. Visual clues that display words, such as *intersect*
f. Is an element of a vector graphic

Select the best answer from the list of choices.

13. **Another name for a vector graphic is a(n)** _____.
    - **a.** bitmap
    - **b.** path
    - **c.** anchor point
    - **d.** template

14. **To return to the normal view of Illustrator after editing an artboard, click** _____.
    - **a.** the Selection tool
    - **b.** any tool on the Tools panel
    - **c.** the pasteboard
    - **d.** the status bar

15. **The name of the view that displays only the vector shapes without colors applied is called** _____.
    - **a.** Preview
    - **b.** Profile
    - **c.** Portrait
    - **d.** Outline

Skills Review

1. **Define illustration software.**
   - **a.** List two elements of a vector graphic.
   - **b.** List three tasks you can perform in Illustrator.
   - **c.** List two formats in which you can export Illustrator documents.
   - **d.** List two transform tools.

2. **Start Illustrator and change preference settings.**
   - **a.** Start Illustrator.
   - **b.** Click Edit (Win) or Illustrator (Mac) on the Menu bar, point to Preferences, then click Units.
   - **c.** In the Preferences dialog box, click the General list arrow, then click Inches, verify that Stroke is set to Points, that Type is set to Points, then click OK.

3. **View the workspace.**
   - **a.** Click File on the Menu bar, click New, then click OK to close the New Document dialog box.
   - **b.** Locate the Tools panel along the left side of the workspace.
   - **c.** Locate the Menu bar at the top of the workspace.
   - **d.** Click the workspace switcher, then click Typography.
   - **e.** Click the workspace switcher, then click Essentials.
   - **f.** Locate the Control panel below the Menu bar.
   - **g.** Locate the group of collapsed panels along the right side, then click the Graphic Styles panel button.
   - **h.** Collapse the Graphic Styles panel.
   - **i.** Locate the status bar at the bottom of the window.
   - **j.** Click the close box on the document tab named Untitled-1 to close the document.

4. **Create and save a document.**
   - **a.** Click File on the Menu bar, then click New.
   - **b.** Type **four artboards_AI-A** in the Name text box.
   - **c.** Click the Size list arrow, click Letter, if necessary, click the Units list arrow, then click Inches, if necessary.
   - **d.** Click the Number of Artboards up arrow until the value changes to 4, click the Arrange by Row button, if necessary, then click OK.
   - **e.** Click the Selection tool, click the second artboard, click the third artboard, then click the first artboard.
   - **f.** Click File on the Menu bar, then click Save As.
   - **g.** Click the Save in list arrow (Win) or the Save As expand arrow (Mac), navigate to the location where you store your Data Files, then click Save.
   - **h.** Click OK in the Illustrator Options dialog box.

Skills Review (continued)

5. **Change the artboard size and close a document.**
   a. Click the Artboard tool on the Tools panel.
   b. Position the mouse pointer at the top of the first artboard; when the pointer changes to a double-sided arrow, click and drag downward to change the height of the artboard, then release the mouse button.
   c. Double-click the W Value text box on the Control panel, type **5**, press [Tab] to highlight the H Value text box, type **7**, then press [Enter] (Win) or [return] (Mac).
   d. Click the Selection tool on the Tools panel.
   e. Click File on the Menu bar, then click Save.
   f. Click File on the Menu bar, then click Close.

6. **Open a document and change views.**
   a. Click File on the Menu bar, then click Open.
   b. Navigate to the location where you store your Data Files, click AI A-2.ai, then click Open.
   c. Click File on the Menu bar, click Save As, save the document as **workspace review_AI-A**, then click OK to close the Illustrator Options dialog box.
   d. Click the Selection tool on the Tools panel if necessary, then click the star in the center of the artboard.
   e. Click View on the Menu bar, then click Outline.
   f. Click the edge of the hexagon in the lower-right corner.
   g. Click View on the Menu bar, then click Preview.
   h. Click the Zoom tool on the Tools panel, then click anywhere on the artboard three times.
   i. Click the Hand tool on the Tools panel; then drag the artboard with the Hand pointer to see a different view of the artwork.
   j. Double-click the Hand tool on the Tools panel to fit the artboard in the window, then save your work.

7. **Get help.**
   a. Click Help on the Menu bar, then click Illustrator Help.
   b. Click the Drawing category, then click Drawing basics.
   c. Click About vector graphics.
   d. Read the article, then close the Help window.
   e. Save the document, but do not close it.

8. **Work with ruler guides.**
   a. Click View on the Menu bar, point to Rulers, then click Show Rulers, if necessary.
   b. Position the mouse pointer over the horizontal ruler, click and drag in a downward direction until the new guide appears, drag it to the center of the star (the 4" mark on the vertical ruler), then release the mouse button.
   c. Click View on the Menu bar, point to Guides, then click Lock Guides to remove the checkmark, if necessary.
   d. Click the Selection tool on the Tools panel, drag the guide up and down, then align the horizontal guide with the 2" mark on the vertical ruler.
   e. Position the mouse pointer over the vertical ruler, then drag a vertical guide to the 2" mark on the horizontal ruler.
   f. Save your work.

9. **Work with Smart Guides and exit Illustrator.**
   a. Click View on the Menu bar, then click Smart Guides to select it if necessary.
   b. Drag the mouse pointer over the hexagon in the lower-right corner, then notice the word *path* as you drag along the edges.
   c. Position the mouse pointer over the approximate center of the pink star, drag the center point over the green and white rotated diamond in the upper-left corner until it is aligned with the center of the diamond and the word *intersect* appears, then release the mouse. Click the pasteboard to deselect the star, then save your work.

Skills Review (continued)

d. Compare your screen to Figure A-20, then close the document.

e. Click File on the Menu bar, then click Exit (Win) or click Illustrator on the Menu bar, then click Quit Illustrator (Mac).

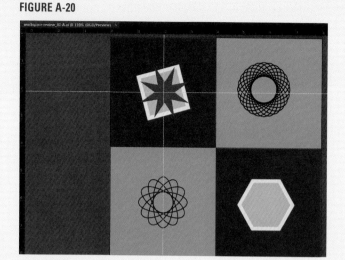

Independent Challenge 1

You and three friends have just opened a clothing consignment shop. You are responsible for designing the business cards for each employee. The only thing that will change on each card is the employee name. You decide to create the cards in Illustrator using four artboards.

a. Create a new document named **consignment cards_AI-A** with four artboards, arranged by row.

b. Change the document width to 3 inches and the height to 2.5 inches, verify that the Landscape orientation button is selected (second button in Orientation section), then click OK.

c. Save the consignment cards_AI-A.ai document in the location where you store your Data Files.

FIGURE A-21

d. Click the Selection tool on the Tools panel, then click the second artboard in the row.

e. Click View on the Menu bar, then click Fit Artboard in Window.

f. Click View on the Menu bar, then click Fit All in Window.

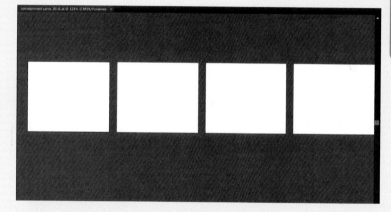

g. Save your work in the location where you store your Data Files, compare your screen to Figure A-21, then close consignment cards_AI-A.ai.

Independent Challenge 2

You are preparing an exercise for the Illustrator class that you teach. The exercise will support a lecture on Illustrator's preview and outline modes and the use of Smart Guides. You review the steps that you'll use in class to make sure everything works correctly.

a. Open the file AI A-3.ai from the location where you store your Data Files, then save it as **exercise_AI-A**.

b. Click View on the Menu bar, then click Smart Guides to activate the feature, if necessary.

c. Click View on the Menu bar, then click Outline.

d. Click the Selection tool, then drag the pointer over each object, locating anchor points, paths, and centers.

e. Click View on the Menu bar, then click Preview.

Illustrator CS6

Independent Challenge 2 (continued)

f. Drag each object on top of the purple square in the upper-left artboard in an arrangement that you choose. Compare your screen to the sample shown in Figure A-22.

g. Deselect all, then save your work in the location where you store your Data Files.

Advanced Challenge Exercise

- Click the Zoom tool, then click four times on your shape arrangement.
- Click the Hand tool, then move the artboard to improve the view, if necessary.
- Click View on the Menu bar, then click New View.
- Type **Close Up** in the Name text box, then click OK.

h. Close exercise_AI-A.ai.

FIGURE A-22

Independent Challenge 3

You are planning a special dinner party. Your first job is to design an invitation and name cards for the table. You decide to use Illustrator so that you can see both documents at the same time during the creation process.

a. Create a new document named **dinner party_AI-A** with two artboards, arranged by row.

b. Set the document width to 4 inches and the height to 8 inches, verify that the Portrait orientation button is selected (first button in Orientation section), then click OK.

c. Save the dinner party_AI-A.ai document in your Data Files folder.

d. Click the Selection tool, if necessary, then click the second artboard in the row.

e. Click View on the Menu bar, point to Rulers, then click Show Rulers, if necessary.

FIGURE A-23

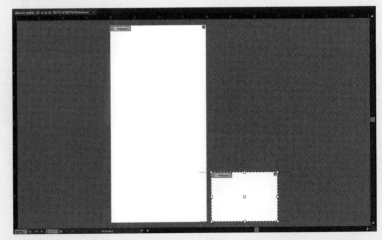

f. Click the Artboard tool, then drag the top edge of the second artboard in a downward direction until the top of the artboard is lined up with the 2" mark on the vertical ruler.

g. Type **2.75** in the W text box on the Control panel, then compare your screen to Figure A-23.

h. Click any tool on the Tools panel to return to the normal view of Illustrator.

i. Save your work in the location where you store your Data Files.

Independent Challenge 3 (continued)

Advanced Challenge Exercise

- Click Edit (Win) or Illustrator (Mac), point to Preferences, then click Guides & Grid.
- In the Guides section, click the Color list arrow, then click Light Red.
- Click OK to close the Preferences dialog box, then create a new horizontal ruler guide that rests on the top edge of the right artboard. Return to the Preferences dialog box and change the guide color back to Cyan.

j. Close dinner party_AI-A.ai.

Real Life Independent Challenge

You would like to apply for a part-time job teaching an introductory course in Illustrator at your local library. After reviewing the syllabus, you realize that you had better brush up on some of the new features that you are not familiar with in Illustrator CS6, especially the new patterns feature. You start Illustrator and use the online Help system to do some research.

a. Start Illustrator.
b. Click Help on the Menu bar, then click Illustrator Help.
c. Click What's New in the list of categories.
d. Click What's new in CS6, then click Patterns.
e. Read the Patterns topic.
f. Close the browser window.

Visual Workshop

Start Illustrator and create a new 8.5" × 11" document with four artboards and a .25-inch space in between them, arranged in a row. Save the document as **guides_AI-A** in the location where you store your Data Files. Using Figure A-24 as a guide, create the same ruler guides shown in the figure. Save your work, then close guides_AI-A.ai.

FIGURE A-24

Getting Started with Adobe Illustrator CS6

Performing Essential Operations

Files You Will Need:

To view a list of files needed for this unit, see the Data Files Grid in the back of the book.

Adobe Illustrator was first developed in 1986, exclusively for the Apple Macintosh computer. The product first shipped in January 1987 as a showcase for Adobe Systems' in-house font development software and PostScript file format. In 1988, Adobe released Illustrator 88, which introduced many of the basic tools and features that we still use today. Illustrator CS6 is the 16th version of Illustrator. Over the last 24 years, Adobe has done an admirable job in finding ways for Illustrator to evolve in smart, effective ways while still maintaining its simple, essential core capabilities. In this chapter, you'll explore Illustrator's three essential operations: creating objects, applying color to objects, and transforming objects. While exploring these essential operations, you'll focus on what an Illustrator graphic actually is, and you'll incorporate basic skills that include selecting and moving objects. MegaPixel has offered you a promotion: you will be in charge of training the design team in Adobe Illustrator CS6.

OBJECTIVES

Create an object

Resize an object

Duplicate an object

Transform and color an object

Use the Transform Again command

Specify a point of origin

Use the Star and Reflect tools

Use the Polygon tool

Creating an Object

Illustrator is all about creating objects: circles, squares, rectangles, triangles, stars, polygons, and other free-form shapes. Illustrator offers many different ways of achieving the same goal. When creating objects, for instance, you'll find that you can use a number of different techniques; some of them take a freehand approach, while others are very specific. ██████ MegaPixel has a new client, a toy manufacturer. Work for this client will involve producing many basic, childlike illustrations for the client's products. Jon Schenk, the creative director at MegaPixel, asks you to create a training exercise that involves creating basic shapes.

STEPS

QUICK TIP
Click OK in the
Illustrator Options
dialog box after
clicking Save.

1. **Open the file AI B-1.ai from the location where you store your Data Files, save it as basic shapes_AI-B, click Window on the Menu bar, point to Workspace, then click Reset Essentials**

   Verify that guides are not showing. Note the current fill and stroke colors at the bottom of the Tools panel. Any new object you create will be created with the current fill and stroke colors on the Tools panel.

   QUICK TIP
   Press [X] repeatedly
   to toggle between
   activating the Fill
   button and activat-
   ing the Stroke
   button on the
   Tools panel.

2. **Click the Stroke button ⬜ on the Tools panel so that it is in front of the Fill button, click the Swatches panel icon ▦ to open the Swatches panel, then click [None] on the Swatches panel**

3. **Click the Fill button ⬜ on the Tools panel so that it is in front of the Stroke button, then click the CMYK Red swatch on the Swatches panel**

   The Fill and Stroke buttons on your Tools panel should resemble Figure B-1.

   QUICK TIP
   This is a freehand
   method for creating
   an object. You used
   the mouse to create
   an object of an
   unspecified size.

4. **Click the Rectangle tool ▦ on the Tools panel, position the mouse pointer anywhere on the artboard, then drag and release to create a rectangle of any size**

   Objects remain selected after they are created. As shown in Figure B-2, the selected rectangle has four paths, four anchor points, and a center point.

5. **Click Edit on the Menu bar, click Cut to remove the rectangle from the artboard, press and hold [Shift], then draw a new rectangle of any size**

   Pressing and holding [Shift] when drawing a rectangle or an ellipse constrains the rectangle to a perfect square and the ellipse to a perfect circle.

6. **Press [Ctrl][X] (Win) or ⌘[X] (Mac) to cut the object, note that the Rectangle tool is still active on the Tools panel, then click anywhere on the artboard**

   The Rectangle dialog box opens, offering you the ability to enter specific values for the width and height of the rectangle you are about to create.

7. **Type 5 in the Width text box, press [Tab], type 3 in the Height text box, press [Tab], then compare your dialog box to Figure B-3**

   Using the tool's dialog box is the quickest and easiest method for creating an object at a specific size.

8. **Click OK**

   The rectangle is created on the artboard with the dimensions you entered.

   QUICK TIP
   Remember to press
   [Shift] to create
   a square.

9. **Create a square of any size that is smaller than the rectangle, anywhere on the artboard, then save your work**

FIGURE B-1: Fill and Stroke buttons on the Tools panel

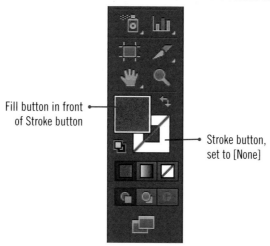

Fill button in front
of Stroke button

Stroke button,
set to [None]

FIGURE B-2: Points and paths on a selected object

Path

Anchor
point

Center
point

FIGURE B-3: Rectangle dialog box

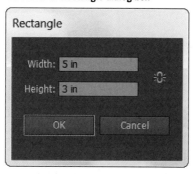

Hiding and showing edges and guides

By default, when an object is selected, its paths and anchor points become visible. These components are called edges. Sometimes you will want to select and work with objects without their edges showing. You can hide edges using the View menu. Click View on the Menu bar, then click Hide Edges. Even better, memorize the easy-to-remember keyboard shortcut [Ctrl][H] (Win) or ⌘[H] (Mac) to hide edges. Show edges again by clicking View on the Menu bar, then clicking Show Edges. With this in mind, memorize the quick key for hiding and showing guides, which is [Ctrl][;] (Win) or ⌘[;] (Mac). With these two sets of quick keys in your skills set, you can quickly and effectively hide and show what you want to see and what you don't want to see on the artboard at any given time.

Resizing an Object

Once you create an object, Illustrator offers you a number of options for resizing that object. At any time, you can show an object's bounding box. The **bounding box** is a rectangle whose size matches the width and height of the selected object. When the bounding box is visible, it shows **selection handles**, small white squares that you can drag to resize the object. The Free Transform tool works almost identically to the bounding box for resizing an object. The **Transform panel** shows you specific height and width values for an object, along with other information. You can also enter specific information into the Transform panel and apply that information to the selected object. ▨▨▨▨ Jon informs you that his designers do not know how to resize objects. He asks you to demonstrate three methods for resizing objects.

STEPS

1. **Click** Window **on the Menu bar, click** Transform **to display the Transform panel, click the** Selection tool ▨ **on the Tools panel, then click the** rectangle **to select it**

   The W and H text boxes on the Transform panel show the width and height of the rectangle to be 5" and 3" respectively, exactly the values you entered in the Rectangle dialog box.

2. **Click the** square **to select it**

   The W and H values on the Transform panel are identical because the object is a perfect square.

3. **On the Transform panel, double-click the** W **text box, type** 1, **press** [Tab] **to automatically select the** H **text box, type** 1, **then press** [Enter] **(Win) or** [return] **(Mac) to apply the new values to the square**

   As shown in Figure B-4, the selected square is resized, and the Transform panel reflects the new width and height information.

4. **Click the** rectangle **to select it, click** View **on the Menu bar, then click** Show Bounding Box

   As shown in Figure B-5, eight handles appear at the edges of the selected object.

5. **Drag the** middle handle **on the right edge to resize the width of the rectangle to any other size**

6. **Drag the same handle to the left so that the rectangle is taller than it is wide, then click the** Selection tool ▨ **anywhere on the artboard to deselect the rectangle**

7. **Click** View **on the Menu bar, click** Hide Bounding Box, **then click the** 1-inch square **to select it**

   Only the standard selection edges are visible because the bounding box is no longer visible.

8. **Click the** Free Transform tool ▨ **on the Tools panel, then drag any of the handles on the square to change it to a rectangle that is wider than it is tall**

9. **Click** ▨, **cut one of the two rectangles, click** View **on the Menu bar, point to** Guides, **then click** Show Guides

   The artboard is 8" × 8" and the guides divide the artboard into four 4" × 4" squares.

10. **Use the Transform panel to resize the remaining rectangle to 4" × 4" square, drag the 4" × 4" square to the upper-left quadrant of the artboard, as shown in Figure B-6, then save your work**

FIGURE B-4: Using the Transform panel to resize the square

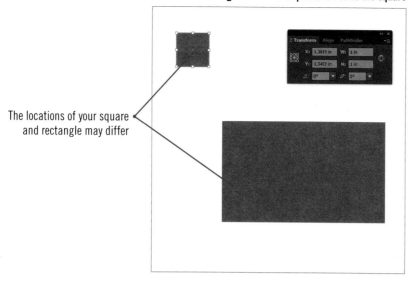

The locations of your square and rectangle may differ

FIGURE B-5: Handles visible on an object with bounding box showing

Handles that appear when the bounding box is showing

FIGURE B-6: Repositioning the 4" × 4" square

Duplicating an Object

Much of your work in Adobe Illustrator will involve duplicating objects—so much that duplicating objects can be seen as part of the drawing process. As with most other functions in Illustrator, you have many different options for duplicating objects. The most essential methods involve copying and pasting an object or "dragging and dropping" a copy of an object. Another great option is using the Move dialog box, which allows you not only to move an object a specific distance, but to move a copy of an object a specific distance. ▓▓▓▓▓ Jon asks you to create a simple illustration showing basic operations for objects in Illustrator. He asks that you start with a layout that involves the duplication of a square to create a background element.

STEPS

1. **Click View on the Menu bar, click Fit Artboard in Window, verify that the red square is selected, click Edit on the Menu bar, then click Copy**
   The Copy command copies the selected object to a temporary storage location, called the **clipboard**.

2. **Click Edit on the Menu bar, then click Paste**
   As shown in Figure B-7, the copy is pasted in the center of the artboard; the center point of the square is aligned at the intersection of the guides. The Paste command pastes the contents of the clipboard to the center of the visible window.

3. **Click Edit on the Menu bar, click Undo Paste, click Edit again, then click Paste in Front**
   A copy of the rectangle is pasted exactly above the original. The Paste in Front command pastes the contents of the clipboard in front of a selected object.

4. **Position the Selection tool ▧ over the square**
   The selection arrow changes to a black move pointer. The move pointer allows you to move the object.

QUICK TIP
If you make a mistake, undo your last step, then try Step 5 again. Make sure that you press [Shift] after you click the anchor point. If you press [Shift] too soon, you will deselect the copied square.

5. **Click the upper-left anchor point, press and hold [Shift], then, without releasing the mouse button, drag to the right until the upper-left anchor point is on top of the upper-right anchor point of the original object, then release the mouse button**
   When two anchor points are aligned, the black arrow changes to white. Pressing [Shift] forces an object to move along its horizontal or vertical axis.

6. **Click CMYK Blue on the Swatches panel to change the fill color of the new square**
   There are now two squares on the artboard, the red square you created originally, and the blue square, which is a copy of the red square.

7. **Press and hold [Shift][Alt] (Win) or [shift][option] (Mac), then drag the blue square straight down to create a third square, as shown in Figure B-8**
   Pressing [Alt] creates a copy of the selected object as you drag. This method of duplication is called "dragging and dropping" a copy. The double arrow icon you see when dragging indicates a copy is being made.

8. **Click the C=0 M=50 Y=100 K=0 (orange) swatch on the Swatches panel to change the fill color of the new object, click Object on the Menu bar, point to Transform, then click Move**
   The Move dialog box opens, offering you the ability to specify the distance you want to move the object on both the horizontal and vertical axes.

9. **Type -4 in the Horizontal text box, press [Tab], type 0 in the Vertical text box, press [Tab], then compare your dialog box to Figure B-9**
   The Move dialog box indicates that the object—or a copy of the object—will move four inches to the left on the horizontal axis and will not move at all on the vertical axis. For important information about the Move dialog box, read the information about *Using the Move dialog box* on page 40.

10. **Click Copy, change the fill on the new square to CMYK Cyan, then save your work**

FIGURE B-7: The copy of the square pasted at the center of the artboard

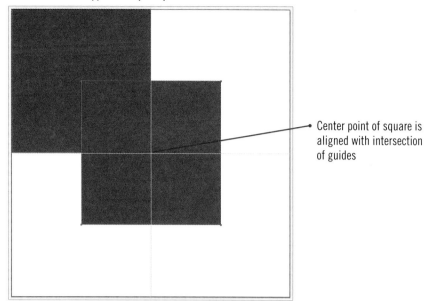

Center point of square is aligned with intersection of guides

FIGURE B-8: "Dragging and dropping" the second copy

FIGURE B-9: Move dialog box

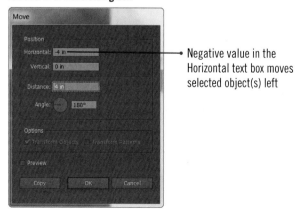

Negative value in the Horizontal text box moves selected object(s) left

Transforming and Coloring an Object

The term **transform** is used often in Adobe Illustrator to refer to tools and operations that modify objects. Moving, scaling, rotating, reflecting, and shearing are all examples of transformations. Use the Scale tool to enlarge and reduce an object. Use the Rotate tool to do just that: rotate it. In addition to transforming objects, you can also change an object by applying color to it. A **fill** is the color that you apply to the interior of an object. A **stroke** is the color that you apply to the outline of an object. Use the Stroke panel to change the **weight** (thickness) of the stroke, in addition to a number of other interesting effects that can be applied to the stroke. 🎨🖌 You are now ready to build upon your "four-square" illustration by showing the designers how to use the Scale and Rotate tools and apply fills and strokes.

STEPS

1. **Select the red square, then double-click the Scale tool 🔲 on the Tools panel**
   Double-clicking any of the transform tools opens the tool's dialog box, allowing you to enter specific values for the transformation.

2. **Type 50 in the Uniform text box, then click OK**

3. **Click Edit on the Menu bar, then click Undo Scale**

4. **Double-click 🔲 again, type 50 in the Scale text box, then click Copy**
   By default, when you transform by double-clicking a tool and entering a value, the transformation is executed using the object's center point as the point of origin for the transformation. In other words, the object is scaled from its center.

5. **Fill the new square with CMYK Magenta**

6. **Double-click the Rotate tool 🔄, type 45 in the Angle text box, then click OK**
   The object is rotated 45° counterclockwise from its center point.

7. **Click the Stroke button 🔲 on the Tools panel so that it is in front of the Fill button, as shown in Figure B-10, click the Swatches panel icon 🔳 to open the Swatches panel, then click the CMYK Yellow swatch on the Swatches panel**
   A yellow stroke is applied to the outline of the object.

8. **Click the Stroke panel icon 🔳 to open the Stroke panel, click the Stroke panel menu button 🔳, click Show Options to expand the panel, then increase the value in the Weight text box to 18 pt**

9. **Click the Align Stroke to Inside button 🔳 on the Stroke panel**
   Your screen should resemble Figure B-11. By default, a stroke is applied equally inside and outside of the object. For example, the 18-point stroke was first applied with 9 points inside the object's path and 9 points outside the object's path. The change you made in Step 9 resulted in the entire stroke being aligned completely inside the object's path.

Stroke button is in
front of Fill button

FIGURE B-11: Applying a stroke to the rotated object

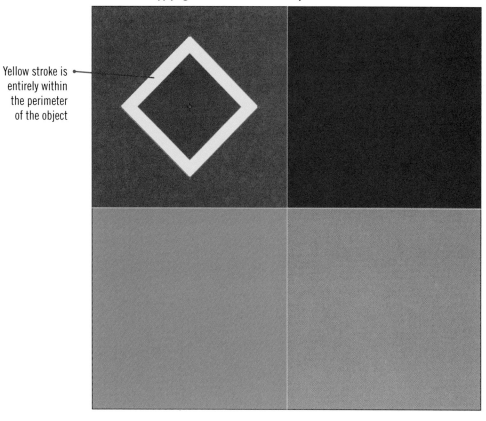

Yellow stroke is
entirely within
the perimeter
of the object

Using the Transform Again Command

The Transform Again command, found on the Object menu, is one of the most powerful commands related to the transform tools. Whenever you transform an object, executing the Transform Again command repeats the transformation. For example, if you scale a square 50%, the Transform Again command will scale the square 50% again. The power of the command comes in combination with copying transformations. For example, start with a square and create a copy rotated at 20°. You will have two copies, the second slightly rotated. If you apply the Transform Again command repeatedly, you can make a chain of rotated squares. Applying Transform Again is a great way to create complex geometric shapes from basic objects. ▩▩▩ Jon likes your transform exercise and asks that you create an example of how the Transform Again command is used in conjunction with other transformations to create complex graphics.

STEPS

1. **Click and hold the Rectangle tool ▣ on the Tools panel to expose the hidden tools, choose the Ellipse tool ⬭, then click anywhere on the artboard**
   The Ellipse dialog box opens, offering you the ability to enter specific values for the width and height for the ellipse you are about to create.

2. **Type 3 in the Width text box, type .5 in the Height text box, then click OK**
   The ellipse is created with the current fill and stroke colors.

3. **Change the fill color to [None], change the stroke color to CMYK Blue, then reduce the weight of the stroke to 3 pt**

QUICK TIP
The best way to access the Transform Again command is to press [Ctrl][D] (Win) or ⌘[D] (Mac). See Table B-1 on the next page for other useful quick keys.

4. **Verify that the Align Stroke to Center button ⬓ is selected on the Stroke panel, click the Selection tool ▸, then position the ellipse as shown in Figure B-12**

5. **Double-click the Rotate tool ⟳ on the Tools panel, type 22.5 in the Angle text box, then click Copy**

6. **Click Object on the Menu bar, point to Transform, then click Transform Again**

7. **Repeat the previous step five times so that your artboard resembles Figure B-13**

QUICK TIP
The Select commands are very useful for quickly selecting multiple objects.

8. **With the last ellipse you created still selected, click Select on the Menu bar, point to Same, then click Stroke Color**
   All the ellipses are selected because they all have the same stroke color.

9. **Click Object on the Menu bar, click Group, then save your work**
   The ellipses are combined as one object. See *Grouping objects* below for more information about grouping.

Grouping objects

When multiple objects are grouped, Illustrator regards them as a single object. The most notable result of grouping objects is that, when you click on any grouped object with the Selection tool, all of the objects in the group will be selected. For complex illustrations composed of dozens or even hundreds of objects, grouping becomes a much-needed solution for making selections quickly and effectively.

FIGURE B-12: Positioning the stroked ellipse

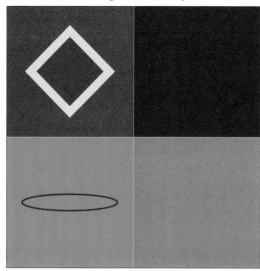

FIGURE B-13: Seven ellipses created from one original

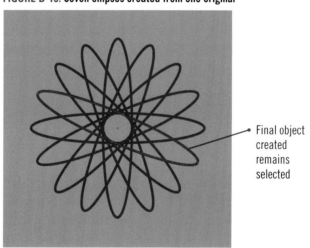

Final object
created
remains
selected

TABLE B-1: Helpful quick keys

command	result	quick key (Win)	quick key (Mac)
Cut	Selected object(s) are removed and copied to the clipboard	[Ctrl][X]	⌘[X]
Copy	Selected object(s) are not removed but are copied to the clipboard	[Ctrl][C]	⌘[C]
Paste	Objects on the clipboard are added to the artboard	[Ctrl][V]	⌘[V]
Hide/Show Guides	Hides/shows guides	[Ctrl][;]	⌘[;]
Hide/Show Edges	Hides/shows selection edges on selected objects	[Ctrl][H]	⌘[H]
Hide/Show Bounding Box	Hides/shows bounding box on selected objects	[Shift][Ctrl][B]	[Shift]⌘[B]
Undo	Undoes the last step	[Ctrl][Z]	⌘[Z]
Redo	The last step is redone	[Shift][Ctrl][Z]	[Shift]⌘[Z]

Specifying a Point of Origin

The previous lesson was a great example of the point of origin for a transformation. When you rotated the ellipse, it rotated at its center point. By default, all transformations will be executed from an object's center point. The **point of origin** is the point from which a transformation is executed. However, you can specify a different point from which you want to execute the transformation. ▓▓▓ Jon asks you to repeat the same transformation with the ellipse, but from a different point of origin, to create an entirely different illustration.

1. **Hide the guides, click the Selection tool ▧ on the Tools panel, click one of the background squares, press and hold [Shift], then select the other three background squares**

   Pressing [Shift] while selecting objects allows you to select more than one object at a time.

Make a note of the quick key, [Ctrl][2] (Win) or ⌘[2] (Mac), for locking objects.

2. **Click Object on the Menu bar, point to Lock, then click Selection**

   When objects are locked, they are visible but cannot be selected. Locking objects protects them from being moved accidentally and makes it easier to select other objects on the artboard.

3. **Switch the view to Outline mode, click the Ellipse tool ⬭ on the Tools panel, click the artboard, type .25 in the Width text box, type 1.75 in the Height text box, then click OK**

4. **Position the ellipse in the upper-right square so that its bottom anchor point is aligned with the center point of the square, as shown in Figure B-14**

5. **Switch the view to Preview mode, then change the fill color to [None], the stroke color to CMYK Yellow, and the weight of the stroke to 2 pt**

6. **Click the Rotate tool ⟳, then, in one motion, click and drag anywhere on the page**

   As you drag, the ellipse is rotated from its center point. There are four options for transforming objects. Table B-2 on the next page describes these options, using the Rotate tool as an example.

7. **Undo the rotation, click the left anchor point of the ellipse, release the mouse button, then drag the mouse pointer**

   As you drag, the object is rotated from the point you clicked. Clicking the anchor point specifies the point of origin for the rotation.

8. **Undo the rotation, press and hold [Alt] (Win) or [option] (Mac), then click the bottom anchor point of the ellipse**

   The Rotate dialog box opens.

9. **Type 22.5 in the Angle text box, then click Copy**

   A rotated copy is created, using the bottom anchor point as the point of origin for the rotation.

10. **Apply the Transform Again command 14 times, deselect, then compare your artboard to Figure B-15**

FIGURE B-14: Positioning the ellipse

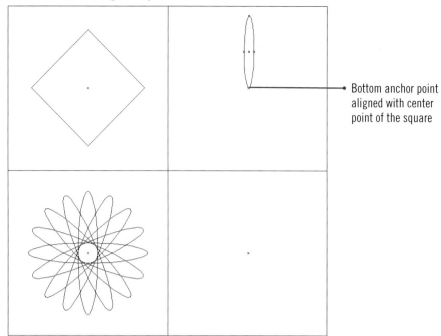

Bottom anchor point
aligned with center
point of the square

FIGURE B-15: Ellipse rotated from specified point of origin

TABLE B-2: Options for transforming objects using Rotate as an example

action	result
Click and drag in one motion	Object will rotate at its center point.
Click the artboard then drag	Object will rotate using the point you clicked as the point of origin.
Double-click the Rotate tool	Rotate dialog box will open. Object will rotate from its center point, using the value you enter in the dialog box. Use this method for precise transformations.
Press and hold [Alt] (Win) or [option] (Mac), then click the point of origin on the artboard	Rotate dialog box will open. Object will rotate using the point you clicked as the point of origin and the value you enter in the dialog box. Use this method for precise transformations.

Using the Star and Reflect Tools

The Reflect tool is another transform tool, like the Scale and Rotate tools. Use the Reflect tool to "flip" an object over an imaginary axis. The best way to understand the Reflect tool is to imagine positioning a mirror perpendicular to a sheet of paper with a word written on it. The angle at which you position the mirror in relation to the word is the reflection axis. The reflection of the word in the mirror is the end result of what the Reflect tool does. For example, text reflected across a horizontal axis would appear upside down and inverted. Text reflected across a vertical axis would appear to be inverted and running backwards. You can use the Reflect tool on any object, not just text. The Star tool offers a number of options for creating stars for illustrations, and you can use the Reflect tool on the star object to vary the position of the star on the artboard. Because your client is a toy company, illustrations you create for them will likely involve a number of stars and "bursts." Jon asks that you demonstrate how to use the Star tool and how to use the Reflect tool to transform a star object.

STEPS

1. **Select the Star tool on the Tools panel, then click anywhere on the artboard**

   The Star tool is behind the current shape tool on the Tools panel. The Star dialog box opens.

2. **Type 1 in the Radius 1 text box, type 5 in the Radius 2 text box, type 5 in the Points text box, then click OK**

   The **radius** is a straight line extending from the center of a circle to its outer edge. A star has two radii; the first is from the center of the star to the inner point, and the second is from the center of the star to the outer point. See Figure B-16 for an example. You will now scale the star to make it smaller.

3. **Double-click the Scale tool on the Tools panel, type 20 in the Scale text box, then click OK**

   The star is scaled 20%.

4. **Fill the star with CMYK Yellow, then remove the stroke**

5. **Click the Selection tool on the Tools panel, then move the star so that it is centered at the intersection of the four rectangles**

6. **Click and hold the Rotate tool on the Tools panel, then choose the Reflect tool**

7. **Double-click, click the Horizontal option button, then click OK**

   As shown in Figure B-17, the star "flips" over an imaginary horizontal axis.

8. **Use the arrow keys to position the star at the center of the artboard, if necessary**

   By default, arrow keys move a selected item in one point ($\frac{1}{72}$ of an inch) increments, known as the keyboard increment. Press and hold [Shift] when pressing an arrow key, and the selected object will move in 10-point increments.

9. **Save your work**

Using the Move dialog box

The Move dialog box moves objects—that's pretty straightforward. There is, however, one component of using the Move dialog box that you'll need to get accustomed to: positive and negative values. In Illustrator, any move to the right or down requires a positive value. Any move left or up requires a negative value. For example, if you have an object in the center of the artboard and you want to move a copy of it to the upper-left corner, you'd need to enter a negative value in both the Horizontal and Vertical text boxes.

FIGURE B-16: Identifying a star's radii

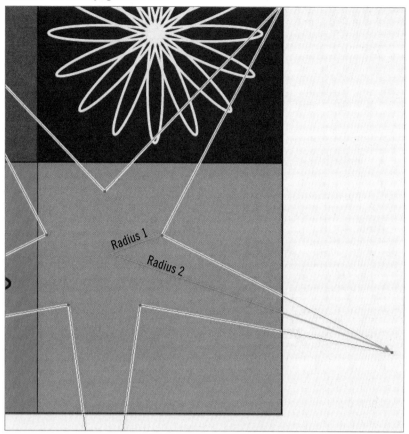

FIGURE B-17: Positioning the star

Using the Polygon Tool

The Polygon tool is an essential tool that you can use to quickly create basic shapes. Because the Polygon dialog box offers you the option of choosing the number of sides for the polygon, you can quickly create triangles, pentagons, octagons, and so on. ▓▓▓▓ Jon asks you to create an exercise showing how to create other basic shapes, like triangles, using the Polygon tool.

STEPS

QUICK TIP
The Polygon tool is beneath the current shape tool on the Tools panel.

1. **Click the Polygon tool ▣ on the Tools panel**

2. **Click anywhere on the orange square**
   The Polygon dialog box opens.

3. **Type 1.5 in the Radius text box, type 3 in the Sides text box, then click OK**

4. **Fill the triangle with CMYK Yellow, if necessary**

5. **Change the stroke color to CMYK Blue and the stroke weight to 22 pt**

6. **Verify that the Align Stroke to Center button ▣ is selected on the Stroke panel**

7. **Position the triangle so that it is centered within the orange square, then deselect all**
   Your completed project should resemble Figure B-18.

8. **Save your work, close basic shapes_AI-B.ai, then exit Illustrator**

Setting unit preferences

Picas and points were once the standard units of measure for all layouts. A pica is measured at $1/6$ of an inch. Each pica is composed of 12 points, so a point is $1/72$ of an inch. Many designers prefer to work in inches for page measurements. However, type and stroke weights are almost universally measured in points. Whatever your preference, you can choose how you want to work in the Units section of the Preferences dialog box, which can be found on the Edit (Win) or Illustrator (Mac) menu. Units for this textbook are set as inches for General measurements and points for both Typography and Strokes.

Illustrator CS6

Practice

Concepts Review

Label the elements of the Illustrator screen shown in Figure B-19.

FIGURE B-19

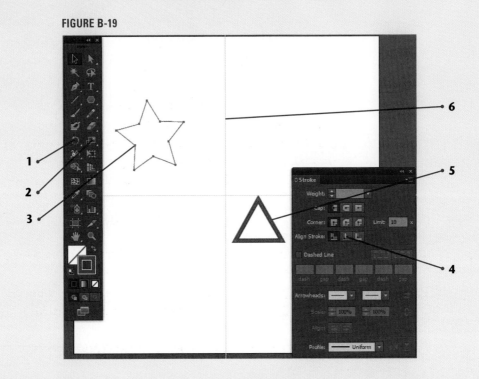

Match each term with the statement that best describes it.

7. **Bounding box**
8. **Move dialog box**
9. **Free Transform tool**
10. **Transform**
11. **Fill**
12. **Point of origin**

    a. Point from which a transformation is executed
    b. Color applied to the interior of an object
    c. Offers the option to copy an object
    d. A tool that acts like the bounding box
    e. Rectangle with selection handles
    f. To modify an object

Select the best answer from the list of choices.

13. To drag and drop a copy of an object, press and hold _____.
    a. [Alt] (Win) or [option] (Mac)
    b. [Shift]
    c. [Enter] (Win) or [return] (Mac)
    d. [Ctrl] (Win) or ⌘ (Mac)

14. Scale and Rotate are examples of _____ tools.
    a. move
    b. object
    c. stroke
    d. transform

15. A star shape has two _____.
    a. dimensions
    b. sides
    c. radii
    d. positions

Skills Review

1. **Create an object.**
   a. Open the file AI B-2.ai from the drive and folder where you store your Data Files, save it as **shape review_AI-B**, click Window on the Menu bar, point to Workspace, then click Reset Essentials.
   b. Click the Fill button on the Tools panel so that it is in front of the Stroke button, open the Swatches panel, if necessary, then click the C=50 M=100 Y=0 K=0 swatch. (*Hint*: Look for a dark purple swatch.)
   c. Select the Rectangle tool on the Tools panel, position the insertion point anywhere on the artboard, then drag and release to create a rectangle of any size.
   d. Click Edit on the Menu bar, click Cut to remove the rectangle from the artboard, press and hold [Shift], then draw a new square of any size, using the [Shift] key.
   e. Press [Ctrl][X] (Win) or ⌘[X] (Mac) to cut the object, note that the Rectangle tool is still active on the Tools panel, then click once anywhere on the artboard.
   f. Type 5 in the Width text box, press [Tab], type **3** in the Height text box, then click OK.
   g. Create a perfect square of any size that is smaller than the rectangle anywhere on the artboard, then save your work.

2. **Resize an object.**
   a. Use a command on the Window menu to open the Transform panel, click the Selection tool on the Tools panel, then click the 5" × 3" rectangle to select it.
   b. Make a note of the width and height of the rectangle on the Transform panel.
   c. Click the square to select it, then make a note of the width and height of the square on the Transform panel.
   d. On the Transform panel, double-click the W text box, type **2**, press [Tab] to automatically select the H text box, type **2**, then press [Enter] (Win) or [return] (Mac) to apply the new values to the square.
   e. Click the 5" × 3" rectangle to select it, click View on the Menu bar, then click Show Bounding Box.
   f. Drag the upper-right handle to resize the width and height of the rectangle to any other size.
   g. Drag the same handle to the left until the rectangle is taller than it is wide.
   h. Click View on the Menu bar, click Hide Bounding Box, click the Selection tool on the Tools panel, then click the 2" × 2" square to select it.
   i. Click the Free Transform tool on the Tools panel, then drag any of the handles on the 2" × 2" square to change it to a rectangle that is wider than it is tall.
   j. Click the Selection tool on the Tools panel, cut the rectangle that you just resized in Step i, click View on the Menu bar, point to Guides, then click Show Guides, if necessary.
   k. Use the Transform panel to resize the remaining rectangle to 4" × 4", drag the object so that it aligns with the upper-left quadrant, then save your work.

3. **Duplicate an object.**
   a. Click View on the Menu bar, click Fit Artboard in Window, verify that the square is selected, click Edit on the Menu bar, then click Copy.
   b. Click Edit on the Menu bar, then click Paste.
   c. Click Edit on the Menu bar, click Undo Paste, click Edit again, then click Paste in Front.

Skills Review (continued)

    d. Position the Selection tool over the square.

    e. Click the upper-left anchor point, press and hold [Shift], then, without releasing the mouse button, drag to the right until the upper-left anchor point is on top of the upper-right anchor point of the original object, release the mouse button, then release [Shift]. (*Hint*: If you make a mistake, undo your last step, then try Step e again. Make sure that you press [Shift] after you click the anchor point. If you press [Shift] too soon, you will deselect the copied square.)

    f. Verify that the Fill button is selected on the Tools panel, click CMYK Green on the Swatches panel.

    g. Click the green square, press and hold [Alt][Shift] (Win) or [option][Shift] (Mac), then drag straight down to create a third square.

    h. Click the C=85 M=50 Y=0 K=0 swatch on the Swatches panel to change the fill color of the new object, click Object on the Menu bar, point to Transform, then click Move. (*Hint*: Look for a blue swatch.)

    i. Type -**4** in the Horizontal text box, press [Tab], type **0** in the Vertical text box, then click Copy.

    j. Change the fill on the new square to C=0 M=50 Y=100 K=0, then save your work. (*Hint*: Look for an orange swatch.)

4. Transform and color an object.

    a. Select the purple square, then double-click the Scale tool on the Tools panel.

    b. Type **35** in the Uniform text box, then click OK.

    c. Click Edit on the Menu bar, then click Undo Scale.

    d. Double-click the Scale tool again, type **35** in the Uniform text box, then click Copy.

    e. Fill the new square with CMYK Yellow.

    f. Double-click the Rotate tool, type **16** in the Angle text box, then click OK.

    g. Click the Stroke button on the Tools panel so that it is in front of the Fill button.

    h. Click the Black swatch on the Swatches panel.

    i. Open the Stroke panel, then increase the value in the Weight text box to 10 pt.

    j. Click the Align Stroke to Outside button on the Stroke panel, then save your work.

5. Use the Transform Again command.

    a. Click and hold the Rectangle tool on the Tools panel, choose the Ellipse tool, then click anywhere on the artboard.

    b. Type **1** in the Width text box, type **2** in the Height text box, then click OK.

    c. Change the fill color to [None], the stroke color to CMYK Yellow, and the weight of the stroke to 2 pt.

    d. Select the Align Stroke to Center button on the Stroke panel, if necessary, click the Selection tool, then position the ellipse in the approximate center of the green square.

    e. Double-click the Rotate tool, type **15** in the Angle text box, then click Copy.

    f. Click Object on the Menu bar, point to Transform, then click Transform Again.

    g. Repeat Step f nine times to create a unique design.

    h. With the last ellipse you created still selected, click Select on the Menu bar, point to Same, then click Stroke Color.

    i. Click Object on the Menu bar, then click Group.

    j. Save your work.

6. Specify a point of origin.

    a. Hide the guides, click the Selection tool, click one of the background squares, press and hold [Shift], then select the three remaining background squares on the artboard.

    b. Click Object on the Menu bar, point to Lock, then click Selection.

    c. Switch the view to Outline mode, select the Ellipse tool on the Tools panel, click the artboard, type **.75** in the Width text box, type **1.85** in the Height text box, then click OK.

    d. Click the Selection tool, then position the ellipse so that its center anchor point is aligned with the center point of the orange square (lower left).

    e. Switch the view to Preview mode, then change the fill color to None, the stroke color to CMYK Blue, and the weight of the stroke to 2 pt.

    f. Click the Rotate tool, then, in one motion, click and drag anywhere on the page.

    g. Undo the move, click the left anchor point of the ellipse, release the mouse pointer, then drag the mouse pointer.

Skills Review (continued)

h. Undo the move, press and hold [Alt] (Win) or [option] (Mac), then click the center anchor point of the ellipse.

i. Type **30** in the Angle text box, then click Copy.

j. Apply the Transform Again command on the Object menu four times, select all ellipses, group the ellipses, deselect, then save your work.

7. Use the Star and Reflect tools.

a. Select the Star tool on the Tools panel, then click anywhere on the artboard. (*Hint*: Click and hold the Ellipse tool to expose the Star tool.)

b. Type **.75** in the Radius 1 text box, type **2** in the Radius 2 text box, type **8** in the Points text box, then click OK.

c. Double-click the Scale tool, type **50** in the Uniform text box, then click OK.

d. Fill the star with White, then remove the stroke.

e. Use the Selection tool to move the star so that it is centered at the intersection of the four rectangles.

f. Use the arrow keys to position the star at the center of the artboard, if necessary.

g. Save your work.

FIGURE B-20

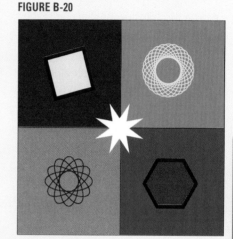

8. Use the Polygon tool.

a. Select the Polygon tool on the Tools panel. (*Hint*: Click and hold the Star tool to expose the Polygon tool.)

b. Click anywhere on the blue square.

c. Type **1** in the Radius text box, type **6** in the Sides text box if necessary, then click OK.

d. Fill the hexagon with CMYK Magenta.

e. Change the stroke color to Black and the stroke weight to 10 pt.

f. Use the Selection tool to center the hexagon in the blue square, then click the artboard to deselect the hexagon.

g. Save your work, compare your screen to Figure B-20, then close shape review_AI-B.ai.

Independent Challenge 1

EyeCare Vision Labs has asked your design firm to create a new logo for them. After researching the company, you learn that they are a biotech firm whose mission is to develop cures for genetic blindness and vision problems. You decide to use the idea of an iris to create the logo.

a. Create a new document that is 8" × 8" and with Print as the document profile.

b. Save the document as **eyecare vision design_AI-B**.

c. Use the Ellipse tool to create an ellipse that is 1" × 3", and position it at the horizontal center of the artboard.

d. Fill the ellipse with [None], and add a one-point CMYK Blue stroke.

e. Create a copy of the ellipse rotated at 15°.

FIGURE B-21

f. Apply the Transform Again command ten times.

g. Select all and group the ellipses.

h. Create a copy of the group rotated at 5°.

i. Apply a CMYK Green stroke to the new group, then transform again.

j. Apply a CMYK Cyan stroke to the new group.

k. Select all, then rotate a copy of the ellipses 2.5°.

l. Create a perfect circle that is 1" × 1", fill the circle with black, then remove the stroke from the circle.

m. Position the black circle at the center of the ellipses.

n. Deselect all, then save your work.

o. Compare your screen to Figure B-21, then close eyecare vision design_AI-B.ai.

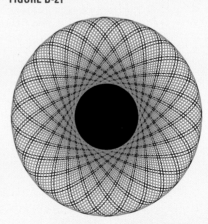

Independent Challenge 2

You work for a design firm, and you are creating a logo for a local shop that sells vintage game boards. You decide to create an 8" × 8" checkerboard, which you will later incorporate into your logo.

a. Create a new 8" × 8" document, then save it as **checkerboard_AI-B**.

b. Use the Rectangle tool to create a 1" square anywhere on the artboard, fill it with C=100 M=90 Y=0 K=0 and no stroke, then position it so that it snaps to the upper-left corner of the artboard.

c. Open the Move dialog box.

d. Type **1** in the Horizontal text box, type **0** in the Vertical text box, then click Copy.

e. Select the new square (if necessary), change its fill color to C=0 M=35 Y=85 K=0, then select both squares.

f. Open the Move dialog box again, type **2** in the Horizontal text box, type **0** in the Vertical text box, then click Copy.

FIGURE B-22

g. Use the Transform Again command two times.

h. Select all, open the Move dialog box, type **0** in the Horizontal text box, **1** in the Vertical text box, then click Copy.

i. Double-click the Rotate tool, type **180** in the Angle text box, then click OK.

j. Select all, open the Move dialog box, type **0** in the Horizontal text box, type **2** in the Vertical text box, then click Copy.

k. Use the Transform Again command two times.

l. Select all, then use a command on the Object menu to group the selection.

m. Deselect all, save your work, then compare your screen to Figure B-22.

n. Close checkerboard_AI-B.ai.

Independent Challenge 3

You teach a continuing education class in Adobe Illustrator CS6 at a local university. The class has been recently introduced to the Move dialog box. You create a fun and challenging exercise for your students in order to test their knowledge.

a. Open the file AI B-3.ai from the location where you store your Data Files, then save it as **on the move_AI-B**. (*Hint*: This document's size is 3" × 3", and a 1" × 1" square is centered on the artboard.)

b. Select the square, then open and use the Move dialog box to copy the center square to the upper-right corner of the artboard.

c. Use the Move dialog box to copy either of the two squares to the upper-left corner of the artboard.

d. Use the Move dialog box to copy the top two squares to the two lower corners of the artboard.

e. Fill each square with a different color, and then deselect all.

f. Save your work, compare your screen to the sample shown in Figure B-23, then close on the move_AI-B.ai.

FIGURE B-23

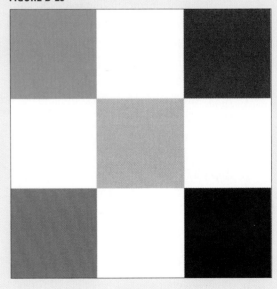

Real Life Independent Challenge

Your friend has created a business card to pass out to potential customers. She needs some help in creating simple graphics to enhance the card. You help her by creating a design using the shape tools, transform tools, and the Swatches panel.

a. Open AI B-4.ai from the location where you store your Data Files, then save it as **business card_AI-B**.

b. Using any combination of shape tools, transform tools, and colors on the Swatches panel, create a simple illustration to complement the card. Figure B-24 shows one example.

c. Save your work, then close business card_AI-B.ai.

FIGURE B-24

Visual Workshop

Create a new 8.5" × 11" document, then save it as **shape stack_AI-B**. Using Figure B-25 as a guide, create the artwork shown in the figure. (*Hint*: The dimensions of the yellow square are approximately 5.75" × 5.75".) Save your work, then close shape stack _AI-B.ai.

FIGURE B-25

Going Beyond the Basics

Files You Will Need:

To view a list of files needed for this unit, see the Data Files Grid in the back of the book.

In Illustrator, you have many kinds of options, tools, and commands to modify basic objects in order to create complex shapes. In this chapter, you'll learn essential techniques for modifying objects, including the use of the Direct Selection tool as well as the Transform Each and the Offset Path commands. You'll also get an introduction to the Pathfinder panel with the Unite feature, which combines multiple objects into a single object. You will also learn about effects and the Appearance panel. MegaPixel has been hired by their toy manufacturing client to design a number of game boxes that will involve creating graphics from basic shapes. Jon asks you to create a series of training exercises that demonstrate options and techniques for modifying basic Illustrator objects.

OBJECTIVES

Use the Transform Each command

Select within groups and make guides

Modify objects with the Direct Selection tool

Work with the stacking order

Create interlocking objects

Use the Unite shape mode

Add visual complexity with the stacking order

Apply effects

Using the Transform Each Command

The Transform Each command offers you the option to transform multiple objects simultaneously but individually, unlike the transform tools that transform multiple objects as one. The Transform Each command can be a very powerful option for making a complex pattern from a simple illustration. ▚▚▚▚ Jon tells you that he's noticed that many designers, even those who use Illustrator regularly, are unfamiliar with the Transform Each command. He asks you to demonstrate the power of the Transform Each command. This will be useful to the designers when they work on game package designs.

STEPS

1. Open the file AI C-1.ai from the location where you store your Data Files, then save it as transform each_AI-C

QUICK TIP
The shortcut key for Select All is [Ctrl][A] (Win) or ⌘[A] (Mac).

2. Click Select on the Menu bar, click All to select all of the objects, click Edit on the Menu bar, click Copy, click Edit again, then click Paste in Front

   A copy of the checkerboard is pasted directly in front of the original checkerboard. The copied checkerboard is selected.

3. Double-click the Rotate tool 🔄 on the Tools panel, type 90 in the Angle text box, then click OK

   The entire front checkerboard is rotated 90° counterclockwise. This means that behind every pink square is a purple square, and behind every purple square is a pink square.

4. Click Object on the Menu bar, point to Transform, then click Transform Each

   The Transform Each dialog box opens.

5. In the Scale section, type 70 in the Horizontal text box, press [Tab], type 70 in the Vertical text box, verify that the Horizontal and Vertical values in the Move section are both 0 in, then notice the center reference point in the Transform Each dialog box, as shown in Figure C-1

   In the Transform Each dialog box, one of nine reference points can be selected to indicate which point the selected object will transform from.

6. Click OK

   Each of the 64 squares is scaled 70%, as shown in Figure C-2. Each individual square is transformed using its own center point as the point of origin for the transformation. In other words, 64 individual transformations take place.

QUICK TIP
The Transform Each dialog box does not reset itself. Be sure to check the values in the dialog box before clicking OK.

7. Open the Transform Each dialog box, in the Scale section, type 100 in both the Horizontal and Vertical text boxes, then type 15 in the Angle text box in the Rotate section

8. Click OK, deselect all then compare your result to Figure C-3

9. Save your work, then close transform each_AI-C.ai

FIGURE C-1: Transform Each dialog box

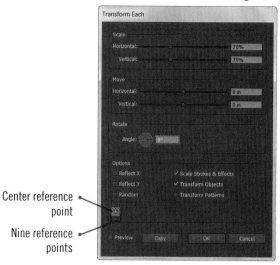

Center reference point

Nine reference points

FIGURE C-2: Squares are scaled 70%

FIGURE C-3: Pattern created with the Transform Each command

Understanding the reference point

The nine reference points in the Transform Each dialog box and on the Transform panel represent the nine points of a selected object. These reference points offer you additional options for making transformations. Simply click one of nine points in the Transform Each dialog box or the Transform panel to set the point of origin for the transformation. By default, the center reference point is selected.

Selecting Within Groups and Making Guides

Many times, when creating an illustration with multiple objects, you'll group the objects. When grouped, multiple objects are all selected when you click any member of the group with the Selection tool. This makes it much easier to work with multiple objects. Sometimes, though, you'll want to select individual objects within a group. To do so, use the Direct Selection tool. In Unit A, you learned how to make horizontal and vertical ruler guides. You can also use the Make Guides command to convert Illustrator objects into guides. These types of guides are called **object guides**. One of the designers asks you to explain what the Direct Selection tool is used for. You explain that the Direct Selection tool plays a number of important roles in Illustrator, and decide to first show how you can use it to select one part of a grouped object and create object guides.

STEPS

1. **Open the file AI C-2.ai, save it as** direct selections_AI-C, **then click the** Selection tool **on the Tools panel**

2. **Click the** yellow square **in the upper-left corner of the artboard**

   Both the yellow square and the purple rectangle behind it are selected because they are grouped.

3. **Click anywhere on the artboard to deselect all, then click the** Direct Selection tool **on the Tools panel**

4. **Click the** yellow square

   Only the square is selected because the Direct Selection tool selects individual objects within a group.

5. **Click the** purple rectangle **behind the yellow square to select it**

   > **QUICK TIP**
   > By default, all guides appear in front of objects on the artboard.

6. **Click** View **on the Menu bar, point to** Guides, **click** Make Guides

   As shown in Figure C-4, the purple rectangle is converted to an object guide. Its edge changes to the default guide color, and it no longer has a fill. Notice also that even though the original object was behind the yellow square, the entire guide is now visible in front of the square.

   > **QUICK TIP**
   > Only Illustrator objects can be converted to object guides. Bitmap images cannot.

7. **Click the** orange starburst **in the upper-right corner to select it, then press [Ctrl][5] (Win) or ⌘[5] (Mac)**

   [Ctrl][5] (Win) or ⌘[5] (Mac) is the quick key for Make Guides. The starburst is now an object guide, as shown in Figure C-5.

8. **Save your work**

Working with guides

Some designers work with guides as a standard part of their working method. Others use them only now and then. In either case, it's a good idea to memorize the quick keys for the Guide commands and to familiarize yourself with preferences available to you for guides. Click the View menu, point to Guides, then note the quick keys for Hide, Lock, Make, and Release Guides. Click Edit (Win) or Illustrator (Mac) on the Menu bar, point to Preferences, then click Guides & Grid to open the Preferences dialog box with the Guides & Grid settings. Use this dialog box to change the color of guides or to change the style of guides, such as changing them from lines to dots.

FIGURE C-4: Converting the rectangle to an object guide

Object guide
created from
rectangle

FIGURE C-5: Viewing two object guides

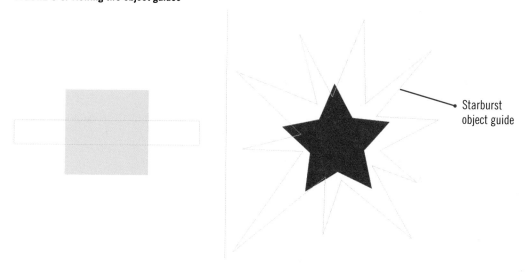

Starburst
object guide

Modifying Objects with the Direct Selection Tool

The Direct Selection tool performs two essential functions in Illustrator. It selects individual objects within a group, and it selects individual components of a single vector object. In this lesson, you'll use the Direct Selection tool to select individual paths and anchor points on vector objects. You'll see that this is an essential method for modifying basic objects to create unique and original shapes. ▬▬▬▬▬ Now you're ready to demonstrate the other important role that the Direct Selection tool plays: modifying objects.

STEPS

1. **Deselect all objects on the artboard, then click the top path of the yellow square with the Direct Selection tool** ▶
   The four anchor points appear white or hollow. Hollow anchor points can be selected individually. The important point you must realize is that the top path that you clicked is the only path selected, even though the three other paths have the same appearance.

2. **Click and drag the top path of the square so that it is aligned with the top edge of the guide, as shown in Figure C-6**

QUICK TIP
Press and hold
[Shift] when drag-
ging to constrain the
movement on the
horizontal or vertical
axis, and release
[Shift] before you
begin again.

3. **Repeat Step 2 to align the three other paths to the corresponding edges of the object guide**

4. **Click any path of the red star to make the hollow anchor points appear**
   The object is a five-pointed star and is drawn using ten anchor points. The object guide behind it is a ten-pointed starburst.

5. **Click Object on the Menu bar, point to Path, then click Add Anchor Points**
   Additional anchor points are added between the existing anchor points, but this does not change the shape of the object. The star is now drawn with 20 anchor points. The anchor points are no longer hollow, because when you apply the Add Anchor Points command, the entire object becomes selected.

6. **Click anywhere on the artboard to deselect the star, then click any edge of the star**
   The anchor points appear hollow.

7. **Using Figure C-7 as a guide, click and drag the lower-right anchor point of the star and align it with the corresponding point on the starburst object guide**

8. **Repeat Step 7 to align all of the remaining points of the star with the corresponding points on the starburst guide, then deselect**
   Your screen should resemble Figure C-8.

9. **Save your work**

Adding anchor points

Remember one of the essential components of this exercise was adding anchor points. At any time, you can apply the Add Anchor Points command to an object, and it won't change the shape of the object. You can even apply the command multiple times.

Additional anchor points offer you more control and more options for modifying an object. The command should become an essential component of your skill set, one that you remember that you have on hand at any time you need it to modify an object.

FIGURE C-6: Repositioning and resizing the 4" × 4" square

FIGURE C-7: Moving a single anchor point

FIGURE C-8: Recreating the starburst

Working with the Stacking Order

The **stacking order** refers to the order of how objects are arranged in front of and behind other objects on the artboard. Every time you create an object, it is created in front of the existing objects. (Note that this discussion does not include any role of layers and the Layers panel.) You can manipulate the stacking order with the Arrange commands on the Object menu. See Table C-1 on the next page for descriptions of each Arrange command. You can also use the Draw Behind drawing mode to create an object behind a selected object or at the bottom of the stacking order. You instruct your students how to manipulate an object's position within the stacking order using four objects. Then, you add a fifth object using the Draw Behind drawing mode.

STEPS

1. **Note the four objects in the bottom-left quadrant of the artboard**

   The blue oval is at the back, the purple rectangle is in front of the blue oval, the curvy yellow line is in front of the purple rectangle, and the red rectangle is at the front.

2. **Click the Selection tool on the Tools panel, click the red rectangle, click Object on the Menu bar, point to Arrange, then click Send to Back**

   As shown in Figure C-9, the red rectangle moves to the back of the stacking order.

3. **Select the yellow line, click Object on the Menu bar, point to Arrange, then click Send Backward**

   The line moves one level back in the stacking order. When discussing the stacking order, it's smart to use the term *level* instead of *layer*. Layers in Illustrator are different from the stacking order.

4. **Select the blue oval, click Object on the Menu bar, point to Arrange, then click Bring Forward**

   As shown in Figure C-10, the blue oval moves one level forward in the stacking order.

5. **Click the double arrow at the top of the Tools panel to view the Tools panel as two columns, if necessary**

6. **Select the purple rectangle, then click the Draw Behind button on the Tools panel**

   There are three drawing modes: Draw Normal, Draw Behind, and Draw Inside.

7. **Click the Ellipse tool on the Tools panel, then draw a circle that is a little bigger than a quarter at the center of the blue oval**

   The circle is created behind the purple rectangle. In the Draw Behind mode newly created objects are positioned one level behind any selected object on the artboard. If no object is selected, the new object will be positioned at the back of the stacking order.

8. **Click the Eyedropper tool , click the red rectangle, then compare your artboard to Figure C-11**

   The Eyedropper tool samples the fill and stroke color from the red rectangle and applies it to the selected object.

9. **Click the Draw Normal button , then save your work**

FIGURE C-9: Red rectangle sent to the back of the stacking order

FIGURE C-10: Moving the blue oval forward in the stacking order

FIGURE C-11: The new red circle behind the purple rectangle

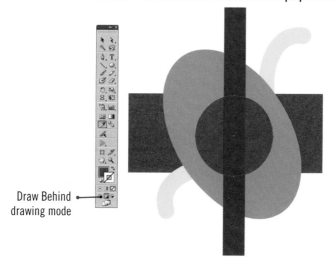

Draw Behind
drawing mode

TABLE C-1: Arrange commands

command	result	quick key (Win)	quick key (Mac)
Bring Forward	Brings a selected object forward one position in the stacking order	[Ctrl][right bracket]	⌘[right bracket]
Bring to Front	Brings a selected object to the very front of the stacking order—in front of all other objects	[Shift][Ctrl][right bracket]	[Shift]⌘[right bracket]
Send Backward	Sends a selected object backward one position	[Ctrl][left bracket]	⌘[left bracket]
Send to Back	Sends a selected object to the very back of the stacking order—behind all other objects	[Shift][Ctrl][left bracket]	[Shift]⌘[left bracket}

Creating Interlocking Objects

When you click a path with the Direct Selection tool, you are only selecting part of a path, known as a **line segment**. Line segments fall within each set of two anchor points. One of the many fun aspects of Adobe Illustrator is realizing that many effects are illusions. For example, being able to copy and paste paths is a technique that is very useful for creating the illusion of interlocking objects. Creating interlocking objects involves an important technique in Illustrator: using the Paste In Front command. Jon asks that you create an exercise that shows a technique for creating the effect of interlocking objects.

STEPS

1. **Click the** Direct Selection tool **on the Tools panel, then click the** right side of the orange path, **as shown in Figure C-12**

   The objects are stacked in this order because the green object was created first, then the purple, then the orange, then the blue. By default, when you create a new object, its position in the stacking order is in front of the already existing objects on the artboard.

2. **Copy the path, click** Edit **on the Menu bar, then click** Paste in Front

   A copy of the stroked path is pasted directly in front of the original.

3. **Click** Object **on the Menu bar, point to** Arrange, **click** Bring to Front, **then compare your artwork to Figure C-13**

   With the orange path in front of the blue path, the illusion of interlocking the two objects is achieved. The Bring to Front command brings any selected object(s) to the very front of the stacking order. Thus, the single orange path is now the front object on the artboard.

4. **Click the** top of the green path, **as shown in Figure C-14, then copy the path**

5. **Click the** left side of the purple object, **as shown in Figure C-15, click** Edit **on the Menu bar, then click** Paste in Front

   A green copy is *positioned* exactly in front of the original green path in the stacking order, but it is *stacked* in front of the purple path.

   QUICK TIP
   The orange path remains the front object in the stacking order.

6. **Using Figure C-16 as a guide, press [Ctrl] (Win) or ⌘ (Mac) and click to select the two anchor points shown**

7. **Click** Object **on the Menu bar, point to** Arrange, **then click** Send to Back

   The selected anchor points and their two associated paths are sent to the back of the stacking order.

   QUICK TIP
   When you select a single anchor point, the anchor point and the two paths attached to it are all selected.

8. **Deselect, compare your result to Figure C-17, save your work, then close direct selections_AI-C.ai**

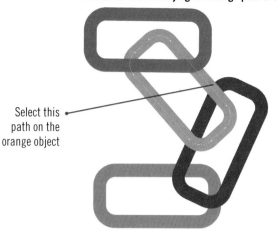

FIGURE C-12: Identifying the orange path to select

Select this path on the orange object

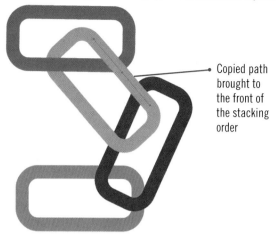

FIGURE C-13: A copy of the orange path is in front of all objects

Copied path brought to the front of the stacking order

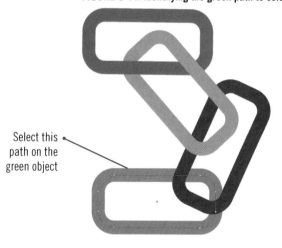

FIGURE C-14: Identifying the green path to select

Select this path on the green object

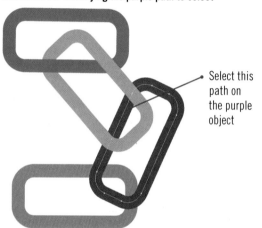

FIGURE C-15: Identifying the purple path to select

Select this path on the purple object

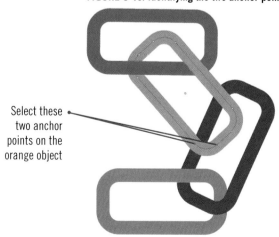

FIGURE C-16: Identifying the two anchor points to select

Select these two anchor points on the orange object

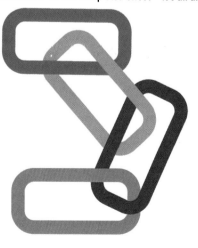

FIGURE C-17: The completed effect—it's all an illusion

Using the Unite Shape Mode

The Pathfinder panel is one of the coolest features in Illustrator. It contains pre-programmed actions that perform basic functions on selected objects, allowing you to create new shapes from overlapping objects. The buttons in the top row of the Pathfinder panel are called **shape modes**, and the buttons in the bottom row are called **pathfinders**. In this lesson, you'll experiment with the Unite shape mode. The Unite shape mode unites multiple paths as a single object. For example, let's say you had two circles that overlapped each other slightly. If you apply the Unite shape mode, the two circles will be united as a single closed path. Jon asks that you create a lesson demonstrating complex artwork created with the Offset Path command, and then incorporate the Unite shape mode to patch holes often created when offsetting letterforms.

STEPS

1. **Open the file AI C-3.ai, then save it as** just chillin_AI-C

2. **Select all, then copy the object**

   The text on this page is not editable text; it is a collection of closed paths created by converting text to outlines.

3. **Click Edit on the Menu bar, click Paste in Front, click Object on the Menu bar, point to Hide, then click Selection**

   The copy is hidden. When an object is hidden, it exists and will be saved with the file, but it can't be seen or selected.

4. **Select all, click Object on the Menu bar, point to Path, click Offset Path, type .25 in in the Offset text box, then click OK**

   A copy of the selection is offset .25" from the original.

5. **Open the Swatches panel, verify that the Fill button is selected on the Tools panel, then fill the selection with CMYK Yellow**

   The new offset path is created as a separate selection from the original path and is behind the original in the stacking order. Much of the new offset path overlaps, and the original is completely within the boundary of the offset path.

6. **Select all, click Window on the Menu bar, click Pathfinder, click the Unite button on the Pathfinder panel, then deselect**

   As shown in Figure C-18, all of the objects on the artboard are united into one filled object. The resulting object retained the color fill of the front object in the selection.

7. **Select all, fill with CMYK Yellow, copy, paste in front, then hide the selection**

   You now have two hidden paths.

8. **Select all, click Object on the Menu bar, point to Path, click Offset Path, verify that 0.25 in (inches) appears in the Offset text box, then click OK**

9. **Select all, then click on the Pathfinder panel**

   Your result should resemble Figure C-19. Note that the way the various paths are overlapping is creating odd negative spaces, or holes where paths didn't overlap.

10. **Click the Rectangle tool on the Tools panel, draw a small rectangle to cover each of the three holes, then select all so that your screen resembles Figure C-20**

11. **Click on the Pathfinder panel, fill the object with CMYK Red, then save your work**

FIGURE C-18: Uniting all the paths

FIGURE C-19: Odd "holes" remain where paths didn't overlap

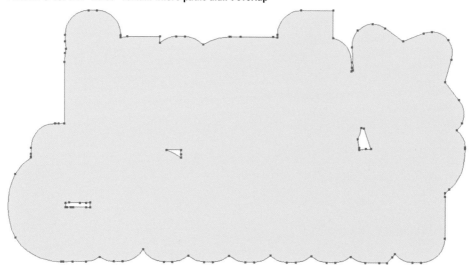

FIGURE C-20: Drawing rectangles over holes

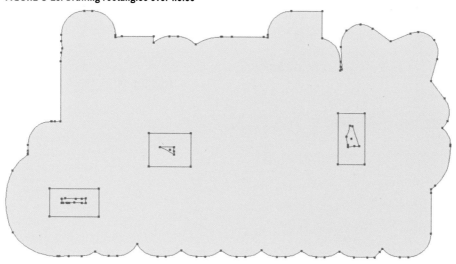

Adding Visual Complexity with the Stacking Order

Whenever you create complex illustrations, the stacking order comes into play simply because you'll need to manage which objects are in front of or behind other objects. You'll also find that you can use the stacking order to add visual complexity to an illustration. By pasting new objects in front of or behind existing objects, you can add a sense of dimension, layering, and depth to the illustration. Jon likes the illustration you're building and asks that you paste in a few more objects within the stacking order to add additional depth to the illustration and a shadow behind the front artwork.

STEPS

QUICK TIP
The keyboard shortcut for Show All is [Alt][Ctrl][3] (Win) or [option]⌘[3] (Mac).

1. **Click Object on the Menu bar, then click Show All**
   The two hidden paths are revealed, and their selection marks are visible. In terms of the stacking order, they are behind the red object on the artboard.

2. **Click Object on the Menu bar, point to Arrange, then click Bring to Front**
   Your screen should resemble Figure C-21.

3. **Deselect all, click the Selection tool ▸ on the Tools panel, press and hold [Shift], click each magenta object, change the fill color of the magenta objects to White, then deselect all**

4. **Click the Color panel icon 🎨, click the Color panel menu button ☰, click Show Options to expand the panel and show the text boxes, then change the yellow object to C=10 M=100 Y=50 K=0 (raspberry), change the back red object to C=85 M=50 Y=0 K=0 (royal blue), then deselect**

5. **Select all the pink objects, copy them, click Edit on the Menu bar, then click Paste in Back**

6. **Fill the selection with C=100 M=100 Y=25 K=25 (dark blue), press and hold [Shift], press ➡ one time, press ⬆ one time, then deselect**
   Your screen should resemble Figure C-22.

7. **Select all of the white objects, copy them, then paste them in back**

8. **Fill the selection with Black, press ⬅ eight times, then press ⬇ eight times**

9. **Click Edit on the Menu bar, click Copy, click Edit again, then click Paste in Front**

10. **Fill the selection with CMYK Cyan, press ➡ four times, then press ⬆ four times**

11. **Deselect then compare your result to Figure C-23, then save your work**

Using the Offset Path command

The Offset Path command works by making a copy of a path and moving it a specific distance from the original path. It is a great way to make **concentric circles**, which are circles that have a common center. When offsetting a path, a negative input value creates a smaller path inside the original, while a positive input value creates a larger path outside the original. The Offset Path command does not work like a transform tool; therefore, the Transform Again command does not apply when creating offset paths. Figure C-24 shows an example of concentric circles created using the Offset Path command. The circles were created by applying a – .5 inch offset to the original circle.

FIGURE C-24: Concentric and evenly spaced circles

FIGURE C-21: Bringing the paths to the front

FIGURE C-22: Pasted path with dark blue fill

Moved with arrow keys

FIGURE C-23: Final illustration

Understanding shape modes

The Pathfinder panel contains operations called shape modes and operations called pathfinders. What's the difference? When applied, the pathfinders always produce a final result—one that can't be modified. The shape modes, however, produce a final result or a result that can be manipulated. If you overlap two circles then click the Unite shape mode, one united object will be created as a final result of the operation. However, if you [Alt]-click (Win) or [option]-click (Mac) the Unite shape mode, the result can be manipulated. The two circles will still be united, but each will remain selectable and able to be manipulated independently from the other.

Applying Effects

Effects are operations that you can apply to an object to alter its appearance without actually altering the object itself. You can apply effects that distort, transform, warp, outline, and offset a path—among others—without changing the original size, anchor points, and shape of the object. When you apply an effect to an object, the effect is listed on the Appearance panel, where it can be hidden or shown, reordered with other effects, and deleted. The term **appearance** refers to what an object looks like when an effect has been applied to it. Working with effects offers you the ability to edit your artwork at any time, because each effect can be quickly modified or removed without disturbing other effects that may be applied. Pucker & Bloat is an interesting and often practical distortion effect that either constricts (Pucker) or expands (Bloat) an object. You'll also find the Convert to Shape effects interesting: make a circle into a square, or vice versa. Once you have applied effects, you have the option to expand the appearance using the Expand command. Think of the Expand command as creating individual, selectable objects. A new project calls for some fairly dramatic shapes, and Jon asks you to prepare an exercise showing some of the Distort & Transform effects and the Convert to Shape effects.

STEPS

1. Open the file AI C-4.ai from the location where you store your Data Files, save it as pucker & bloat_AI-C, click Window on the Menu bar, then click Appearance

2. Click the Selection tool ▶, then select the red square

3. Click the Effect menu, point to Distort & Transform in the Illustrator Effects section of the menu, then click Pucker & Bloat

4. Type 85 in the text box, click OK, then compare your result to Figure C-25

   The Bloat effect is applied, and Pucker & Bloat is listed on the Appearance panel. In the Pucker & Bloat dialog box, a positive value produces a Bloat effect; a negative value produces a Pucker effect.

5. Select the blue circle, click the Object on the Menu bar, point to Path, then click Add Anchor Points

QUICK TIP
The last effect applied is always listed at the top of the Effect menu.

6. Click the Effect menu, click Pucker & Bloat in the top section of the menu to open the dialog box, drag the slider to -85, then click OK

   The negative value creates a Pucker effect.

7. Select the yellow square, click the Effect menu, point to Convert to Shape, then click Ellipse

   The Shape Options dialog box opens, offering you options for converting the shape. The Absolute option allows you to enter a specific width and height for the ellipse you are creating. The Relative option allows you to specify size dimensions to the ellipse relative to the original selected shape.

8. Click the Relative option button, type 0 in the Extra Width and Extra Height text boxes, click OK, then compare your result to Figure C-26

   The appearance of the square changes to a circle; Ellipse is listed on the Appearance panel.

9. Select all, click the Object menu, then click Expand Appearance

   The appearances are applied to the objects, and the objects become selectable as their new shapes.

10. Save your work, close pucker & bloat_AI-C.ai, then exit Illustrator

---

Using the Expand command

The Expand Appearance command on the Object menu is another example of how the term "expand" is used in Illustrator as something of a synonym for "make it selectable." With an effect, only the original object is selectable: the effect is just an appearance. But when you expand the appearance, the appearance is rendered as selectable Illustrator objects. With this in mind, you can use appearances as a means to an end: rather than draw certain shapes by hand, you can create them with appearances, then expanad the appearances to access them as selectable objects.

FIGURE C-25: Viewing the Bloat effect

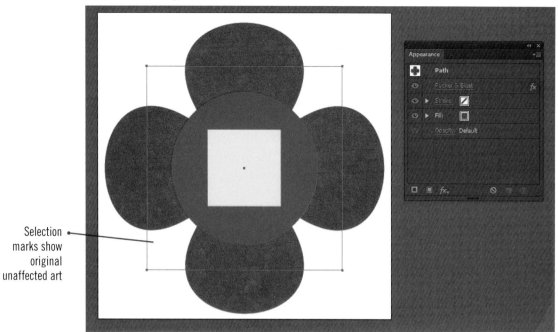

Selection marks show original unaffected art

FIGURE C-26: Viewing the square with the appearance of a circle

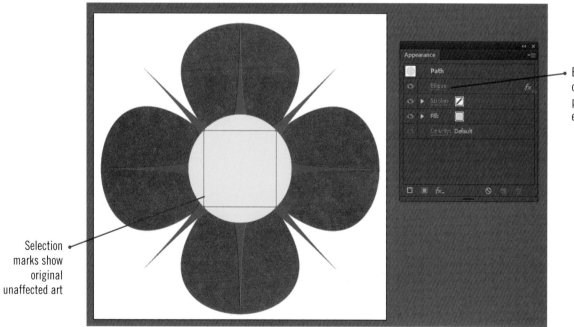

Ellipse listed on Appearance panel as an effect

Selection marks show original unaffected art

Scaling paths vs. offsetting paths

The Scale tool will not give you the same result as the Offset Path command when creating concentric circles. If you use the Scale tool to try and create concentric circles, each successive circle is a *percentage* of a different size original circle. Percentages are relative, not absolute, so the space between each circle and the original from which it was scaled keeps getting smaller, because the original keeps getting smaller. Each time you repeat the transformation, the distance between the new circle and its original will be reduced by half. With the Offset Path command, the offset is an absolute. So if you make five copies offset at .25", each copy will be offset .25" from its original.

Practice

Concepts Review

Label the elements of the Illustrator screen shown in Figure C-27.

FIGURE C-27

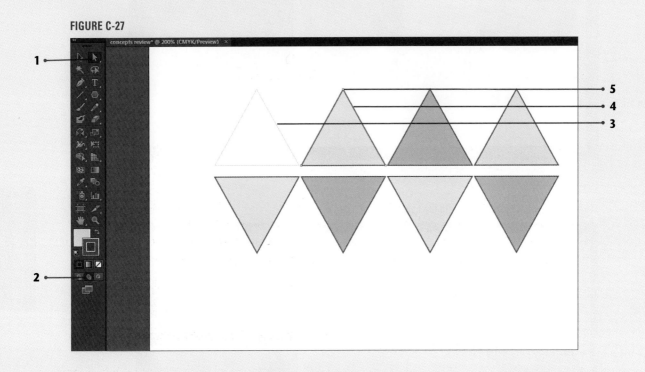

Match each term with the statement that best describes it.

6. **Object guides**
7. **Paths**
8. **Draw Behind**
9. **Expand**
10. **Pathfinder panel**
11. **Stacking order**

a. Allows you to create new shapes
b. Make into individual selectable objects
c. Placed between anchor points
d. Made from vector graphics
e. How objects are arranged on the artboard
f. A drawing mode

Select the best answer from the list of choices.

12. The Paste in Front command pastes the copied object _____.

    a. directly in front of the selected object
    c. as the top object on the artboard

    b. in the exact center of the artboard
    d. directly in front of the top object on the artboard

13. When you click a path with the _____ tool, you are only selecting part of a path, known as a line segment.

    a. Selection
    c. Path

    b. Direct Selection
    d. Anchor

14. The top row of buttons on the Pathfinder panel are known as _____.

    a. compound shapes
    c. path modes

    b. shape modes
    d. pathfinders

15. The _____ command works with objects that have effects applied to them.

    a. Unite
    c. Expand

    b. Pathfinder
    d. Transform Again

Skills Review

1. Use the Transform Each command.

    a. Start Illustrator, open the file AI C-5.ai, then save it as **triangles_AI-C**.

    b. Select all, copy the objects, then use a command on the Edit menu to paste it in front.

    c. Double-click the Rotate tool on the Tools panel, type **180** in the Angle text box, then click OK.

    d. Use a command on the Object, Transform menu to open the Transform Each dialog box.

    e. Type **60** in both the Horizontal and Vertical text boxes in the Scale section, verify that the Horizontal and Vertical values in the Move section are set to 0, type **10** in the Angle text box in the Rotate section, then click OK.

    f. Save and close triangles_AI-C.ai.

2. Select within groups and make guides.

    a. Open the file AI C-6.ai, then save it as **selection review_AI-C**.

    b. Use the Selection tool to select the yellow square in the upper-left corner of the artboard, then notice that the yellow square and the blue octagon are grouped.

    c. Deselect the objects, use the Direct Selection tool to select just the yellow square, then click just the blue octagon.

    d. Use a command on the View, Guides menu to make the blue octagon into an object guide.

    e. Save your work.

3. Modify objects with the Direct Selection tool.

    a. Deselect all objects, then use the Direct Selection tool to select the top path of the yellow square. (*Hint*: The anchor points should be hollow.)

    b. Use a command on the Object, Path menu to add anchor points.

    c. Deselect the object.

    d. Click the upper-left anchor point on the path and drag it to the upper-left point on the octagon object guide.

    e. Repeat Step d to drag the upper-middle anchor point to the upper-right point on the octagon object guide, as shown in Figure C-28.

    f. Drag each of the remaining six anchor points to the corresponding six points of the octagon object guide.

    g. Save your work.

FIGURE C-28

Skills Review (continued)

4. Work with the stacking order.

FIGURE C-29

   a. Note the four objects in the upper-right quadrant of the artboard.

   b. Click the Selection tool, select the orange rectangle, click Object on the Menu bar, point to Arrange, then click Send to Back.

   c. Select the pink rectangle, click Object on the Menu bar, point to Arrange, then click Send Backward.

   d. Select the green oval, then apply the Bring Forward command.

   e. Select the red rectangle, then click the Draw Behind button on the Tools panel. (*Hint*: Change the Tools panel to double-rows to see the Draw Mode buttons.)

   f. Click the Ellipse tool, then draw a circle that is a little bigger than a quarter at the center of the green oval.

   g. Click the Eyedropper tool, click the orange rectangle.

   h. Click the Draw Normal button, deselect all, compare your result to Figure C-29, then save your work.

5. Create interlocking objects.

   a. Click the Direct Selection tool, then, in the lower half of the artboard, click the blue circle at approximately four o'clock.

   b. Copy the path, then paste it in front.

   c. Use a command on the Object, Arrange menu to bring it to the front.

FIGURE C-30

   d. Click the black path at approximately nine o'clock to select the section of the path, click Edit, then click Cut.

   e. Select any edge on the yellow path, click Edit, then click Paste in Back.

   f. Using the same steps, link the rings as shown in Figure C-30.

   g. Save your work, then close selection review_AI-C.ai.

6. Use the Unite shape mode.

   a. Open the file AI C-7.ai, save it as **wow_AI-C**, select all, then copy the object. (*Hint*: The object on this page is not editable text; it is a collection of closed paths created by converting text to outlines.)

   b. Paste it in front, then hide the selection.

   c. Select all, open the Offset Path dialog box, type **.25 in** in the Offset text box, then click OK.

   d. Verify that the Fill button is selected on the Tools panel, fill the selection with CMYK Yellow.

   e. Select all, show the Pathfinder panel, then click the Unite button.

   f. Select all, fill the path with CMYK Yellow, copy the path, paste it in front, then hide the selection. (*Hint*: You now have two hidden paths.)

   g. Select all, open the Offset Path dialog box, type **.25 in** in the Offset text box, then click OK.

   h. Select all, click the Unite button on the Pathfinder panel, then fill the path with CMYK Red.

   i. Save your work.

7. Add visual complexity with the stacking order.

   a. Click Object on the Menu bar, then click Show All. (*Hint*: The two hidden paths are revealed, and their selection marks are visible.)

   b. Click Object on the Menu bar, point to Arrange, then click Bring to Front.

   c. Deselect the paths, change the yellow element to white and the red element to orange, then deselect.

   d. Select the white element, copy it, then paste it in back.

   e. Fill the selection with light blue, press and hold [Shift], press ➔ one time, then press ⬆ one time.

   f. Select the white element, copy it, then paste it in back.

Skills Review (continued)

FIGURE C-31

g. Fill the selection with Black, press ◄ eight times, then press ▼ eight times.

h. Deselect all, compare your screen to Figure C-31, then save and close wow_AI-C.ai.

8. Apply effects.

a. Open the file AI C-8.ai from the location where you store your Data Files, save it as **distort skills_AI-C**, click the Selection tool if necessary, then select the green square.

b. Click the Effect menu, point to Distort & Transform, then click Pucker & Bloat.

c. Type **100** in the text box, then click OK.

d. Select the blue circle, click Object on the Menu bar, point to Path, then click Add Anchor Points.

e. Click the Effect menu, click Pucker & Bloat in the top section of the menu to open the dialog box, drag the slider to -85, then click OK.

f. Select the yellow diamond, click the Effect menu, point to Convert to Shape, then click Rounded Rectangle.

g. Click the Absolute option button, type **1** in the Width and Height text boxes, then click OK.

h. Select all, click Object on the Menu bar, then click Expand Appearance.

i. Save your work, then close distort skills_AI-C.ai.

Independent Challenge 1

It's the last day of an art course you are taking. The instructor challenges you to create a comb by using only the shape tools. The completed comb must be one object, and this must be achieved without grouping any individual pieces of the comb. You realize that the instructor wants you to unite the comb pieces into one object.

a. Start Illustrator, create a new document that is 8" × 8", then save it as **comb_AI-C**.

b. Use the Rounded Rectangle tool to create a rounded rectangle that is .5" × 5" then position it on the left side of the artboard.

c. Fill the rounded rectangle with C=85 M=50 Y=0 K=0 (royal blue), then remove any stroke, if necessary.

d. Create a rectangle that is .75" × .0395".

FIGURE C-32

e. Position the rectangle at the top of the rounded rectangle so that it is slightly overlapping the rounded rectangle's right edge, then drag and drop a copy of it below, leaving only a small amount of white space. (*Hint*: Press and hold [Shift][Alt] (Win) or [Shift][option] (Mac) to drag and drop a copy on the same vertical axis. Think of how close the teeth of a comb are together.)

f. Use the Transform Again command repeatedly until you have enough teeth to fill the comb.

g. Select all, show the Pathfinder panel, then click the Unite shape mode button.

h. Deselect the objects, then save your work.

Advanced Challenge Exercise

- Click Edit (Win) or Illustrator (Mac) on the Menu bar, point to Preferences, then click Guides & Grid.
- Click the Color list arrow in the Guides section, then click Light Red.
- Click the Style list arrow in the Guides section, then click Dots.
- Click Cancel to close the Preferences dialog box and change the guides back to their default settings.

i. Compare your screen to Figure C-32, then close comb_AI-C.ai.

Independent Challenge 2

Your neighbors are organizing a night of card playing. You're in charge of creating a flyer with details about the evening. You decide to incorporate the four suit images into the flyer and start off by drawing the spade.

a. Open the file AI C-9.ai from the location where you store your Data Files, then save it as **spade_AI-C**.

b. Click and drag the square so that it overlaps the two circles, as shown in Figure C-33.

c. Deselect, click the Direct Selection tool, then drag the top point of the square so that it is within the boundary of the two circles, not outside of them.

d. Select all three objects, then apply the Unite shape mode.

e. Rotate the heart object 180°.

f. Fill the heart object with black, remove the stroke, then hide the heart object.

g. Create a square that is 1.5" × 1.5" with no fill color and a 1-pt Black stroke.

h. Create a circle that is 1.75" in width and height.

i. Duplicate the circle, then position the two circles over the square as shown in Figure C-34.

j. Select the three shapes, then apply the Minus Front shape mode on the Pathfinder panel.

k. Fill the new stem object with Black and no stroke.

l. Show the hidden heart object, then overlap the stem object so that the two resemble a spade from a deck of playing cards.

m. Apply the Unite shape mode to create the shape shown in Figure C-35.

Advanced Challenge Exercise

- Verify that the spade is selected.
- Click Window on the Menu bar, then click Transform to show the Transform panel.
- Click the upper-right reference point on the Transform panel.
- Type **15** in the Rotate text box on the Transform panel, then press [Enter] (Win) or [return] (Mac) to rotate the spade from its upper-right reference point.

n. Save your work, then close spade_AI-C.ai.

FIGURE C-33

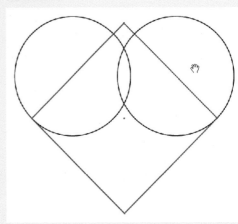

FIGURE C-34

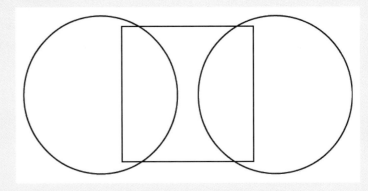

FIGURE C-35

Independent Challenge 3

You teach Adobe Illustrator CS6 to a group of continuing education students.
You have a few students who are more advanced than the rest of the group. You decide to create a challenging exercise for them for this evening's class in case they finish the Independent Challenge 2 assignment early. The challenge: Create the illusion that one object intersects perfectly with another.

a. Open AI C-10.ai, then save it as **intersect_AI-C**.

b. Select both objects, then click the Intersect button on the Pathfinder panel. (*Hint*: Only the intersection of the two objects remains.)

Independent Challenge 3 (continued)

FIGURE C-36

c. Click Edit on the Menu bar, click Undo Intersect, then deselect all.

d. Select only the black spade object, copy it, click Edit, then click Paste in Front.

e. Press and hold [Shift], then click the red object to add it to the selection.

f. Click the Intersect button on the Pathfinder panel.

g. Deselect, then compare your screen to Figure C-36.

h. Save your work, then close intersect_AI-C.ai.

Real Life Independent Challenge

Your friend has a simple business card that you designed for her a while ago. She has run out of copies and asks you to order some more. While looking at the card on the artboard, you see room for improvement, so you ask if it would be OK to make some changes to the card by modifying some of the artwork. Your friend agrees, confident that anything you come up with will be great.

a. Start Illustrator, open the file AI C-11.ai from the location where you store your Data Files, then save it as **card redesign_AI-C**.

b. Use a command on the Path submenu from the Object menu to add anchor points.

c. Copy paths, then using the Paste in Front and Paste in Back commands on the Edit menu, change the four ovals on the logo so that they are interlocking. (*Hint*: You'll need to use the transform tools to arrange the overlapping ovals.)

d. Change any fill and stroke colors that you wish to.

e. Remove any objects and add any new design elements that you wish to.

f. Save and close card redesign_AI-C.ai.

Visual Workshop

Create a new 6" × 6" document, then save it as **club_AI-C** in the location where you store your Data Files. Using Figure C-37 as a guide, create the club shown in Figure C-37 by overlapping three circles and using the Pathfinder panel. Create the stem by overlapping two circles and a square and using the Pathfinder panel. Save your work, compare your screen to Figure C-37, then close club_AI-C.ai.

FIGURE C-37

Creating Blends and Complex Artwork

Files You Will Need:

To view a list of files needed for this unit, see the Data Files Grid in the back of the book.

Once you become comfortable creating and selecting objects, Illustrator offers you a number of smart and effective options for manipulating and modifying those objects to create new designs and artwork. Pathfinders offer you preset operations to create new objects from overlapping objects. Use compound paths whenever you want to knock out a hole in an object. With the Blend tool, you create multiple "in-between" objects as the blend transitions from one object to another. When you mask an object, you use a given shape to define the perimeter of another object. And the Stroke panel offers you all kinds of options for making simple and complex dashed strokes to apply to lines. In this unit, you'll learn how to work with all of these features to make new and interesting Illustrator artwork.  MegaPixel's toy manufacturing client is looking for an increase in the complexity of the designs you are submitting. Jon asks you to create training exercises that cover how to create complex artwork using more advanced Illustrator features.

OBJECTIVES

Use the Divide pathfinder

Create compound paths

Create complex patterns with compound paths

Blend objects

Create a clockwise blend

Create a clipping mask

Use the Draw Inside drawing mode

Apply arrowheads and dashes to strokes

Design complex layered strokes

Using the Divide Pathfinder

Divide is one of the most powerful and useful pathfinders for creating visually complex artwork in Illustrator. Simply put, the Divide pathfinder cuts objects where they overlap. For example, if you overlap two circles and then apply the Divide pathfinder, the result will be three objects: the overlapping area and the two areas that don't overlap. You can also overlap an object with just a line, then use the Divide pathfinder to slice the object where the line overlaps the object. ▓▓▓ The project at hand calls for an illustration of a star. Jon asks you to show the design team how to use the Divide pathfinder to create a more complex star with more dimension than a simple flat star.

STEPS

1. Open AI D-1.ai from the location where you store your Data Files, save it as divided star_AI-D, click the Selection tool 🢒, then select the vertical line

2. Double-click the Rotate tool 🔄, type 72 in the Angle text box, then click Copy

   This star has five points; a complete circle has 360° (360 ÷ 5 = 72).

QUICK TIP

To access the Transform Again command click the Object menu, point to Transform, then click Transform Again or use the quick keys [Ctrl][D] (Win) or ⌘[D] (Mac).

3. Apply the Transform Again command three times, click the Selection tool 🢒, press and hold [Shift], then select the five lines

4. Use the arrow keys to move the selected lines to the location shown in Figure D-1 so that each of the five star points is bisected by the lines

   Because the lines were rotated at 72°, the five lines will align with each of the star points when positioned correctly.

5. Click Window on the Menu bar, click Pathfinder, press [Ctrl][A] (Win) or ⌘[A] (Mac) to select all the objects on the artboard, then click the Divide button 🔳 on the Pathfinder panel

   The star is sliced, or divided, into 10 separate objects where the lines overlapped the star.

6. Click the Direct Selection tool 🢒, deselect all, then select the left side of the top point of the star, as shown in Figure D-2

   Note that when an object is divided, the resulting components are automatically grouped. To select an individual component, you can either use the Direct Selection tool or ungroup the components.

7. Press and hold [Shift], select every other object in a clockwise direction, so that five objects are selected, then fill the objects with CMYK Cyan on the Swatches panel

8. Click Select on the Menu bar, click Inverse, fill the selection with CMYK Blue, then click the artboard to deselect

   Your screen should resemble Figure D-3.

9. Save your work, then close divided star_AI-D.ai

More about the Divide pathfinder

You'll use the Divide pathfinder many times to add dimension and complexity to objects, as you did with the star in this lesson. One of the great things about the Divide pathfinder is that it works effectively with multiple objects and complex artwork. No matter how many overlapping objects you have, the Divide pathfinder can quickly and easily divide them into smaller components that you can then manipulate. When straight or curved open paths are used to divide artwork, the paths themselves no longer remain after the artwork is divided. In this lesson, even though the paths exceeded the perimeter of the star, once divided, only the pieces of the star remained—the paths were gone.

FIGURE D-1: Positioning the five lines with the points on the star

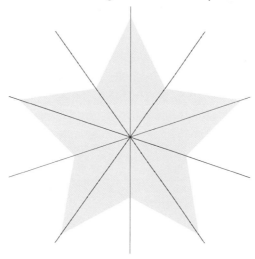

FIGURE D-2: Selecting a piece of the divided star

Left side of top
point of star

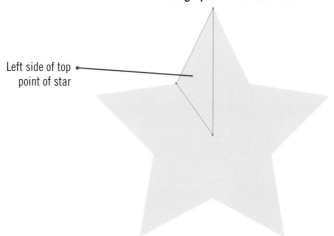

FIGURE D-3: Finished artwork

Creating Compound Paths

A **compound path** occurs when a single object is composed of two or more paths. The letter T, for example, is drawn with a single closed path. The letter O, on the other hand, is created with two paths: the outer edge and the inner edge. Compound paths do not necessarily overlap, but the best example of a compound path is when one path cuts a hole in another path. Using the letter O as an example, the inner, smaller circle cuts a hole in the outer larger circle, like a donut. ▰▰▰▰ Jon mentions to you that the client is asking for increasingly complex artwork and asks that you design a lesson demonstrating the basic concepts of working with compound paths.

STEPS

1. **Open AI D-2.ai from the location where you store your Data Files, save it as** simple compound paths_AI-D, **click the Selection tool 🖰, then click the letter** C
   The letter C was created with a single closed path.

2. **Drag the** orange triangle **to create a letter** A, **as shown in Figure D-4**
   The letter A is created with two paths: the outer path and the triangle within the outer path that creates the inner edge.

QUICK TIP
Use the quick keys [Ctrl][8] (Win) or ⌘[8] (Mac) to make compound paths quickly.

3. **Select both components of the** letter A, **click** Object **on the Menu bar, point to** Compound Path, **then click** Make
   The triangle becomes a hole in the outer shape. The fish pattern is visible through the hole. For compound paths, use the terms positive and negative. When compounded, the triangle creates a *negative* space in the outer *positive* object. It's also important to note that Illustrator identifies a compound path as a single object.

4. **Position the two orange objects to create the letter** B, **select the three components of the** letter B, **click** Object **on the Menu bar, point to** Compound Path, **then click** Make

5. **Deselect, then compare your screen to Figure D-5**
   As shown in the figure, the two orange objects create two negative spaces in the outer object

6. **Select the** blue circle **and the** orange star **on the artboard, create a compound path, then deselect all**

7. **Click the** Direct Selection tool 🖰, **click the top point of the star, press [Shift], then select the remaining** nine points **of the star**

TROUBLE
If you do not click directly on the edge of the star before moving it, you may drag just one path. Undo your last step and try again, if necessary.

8. **Click the** edge of the star, **drag the star to the right so that it is halfway outside of the circle, deselect, then compare your artwork to Figure D-6**
   Figure D-6 illustrates an important concept about compound paths. When two paths are compounded, a negative space will be created only where they overlap. In this case, the area where the star doesn't overlap the circle becomes positive and takes on the same fill color of the compounded object.

9. **Save your work, then close simple compound paths_AI-D.ai**

Working with compound paths

A good way to think of compound paths is in terms of practical and artistic perspectives. From the practical perspective, use compound paths whenever you need to create a hole in an object. In this lesson, you focused more on the practical, and the letters *A* and *B* are good examples of how compound paths are commonly used for all kinds of graphics. Note that when you compounded the letter *B*, it was not necessary to first group the two orange objects;

when compounded, Illustrator used both objects to create negative spaces in the back shape. Finally, when you compound two objects, the area where they overlap becomes negative space. However, as you saw with the star, if the objects only partially overlap, the area where they don't overlap will remain positive. This can lead to some interesting graphics, made by experimenting with negative and positive space and compound paths.

FIGURE D-4: Positioning the orange triangle

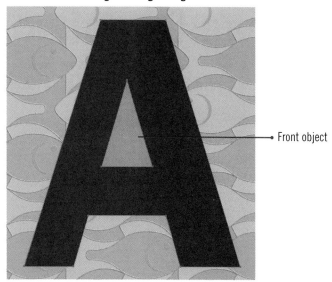

Front object

FIGURE D-5: Creating a compound path with three objects

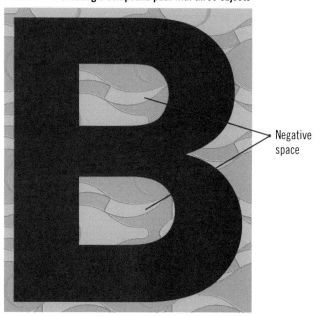

Negative space

FIGURE D-6: Overlapping half of the star

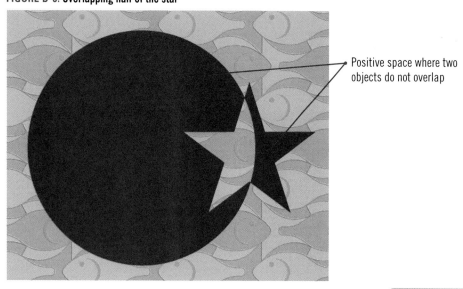

Positive space where two objects do not overlap

Creating Complex Patterns with Compound Paths

When you overlap multiple objects and then compound them, the positive and negative spaces create interesting geometrical patterns. Because the relationship of the compound paths is maintained, you can move individual objects within the compounded paths to create additional complex patterns. These types of patterns can be very useful if you're designing repetitive patterns like you might see for fabric, wallpaper, or wrapping paper. Jon tells you that the client is asking for complex patterns as a background for their packaging. He asks that you design a lesson demonstrating the complex graphics you can make with compound paths.

STEPS

1. Open AI D-3.ai from the location where you store your Data Files, save it as complex compound paths_AI-D, then select all

   The pink square in the background won't be selected because it is locked. The six selected objects are five circles positioned over a larger circle.

2. Click Object on the Menu bar, point to Compound Path, then click Make

3. Deselect, click the Direct Selection tool ▶, then click the edge of the large red circle

4. Click the center point of the large red circle so that only the large circle is selected, double-click the Scale tool ▦, type 50 in the Uniform text box, then click OK so that your screen resembles Figure D-7

5. Click Select on the Menu bar, then click Inverse

6. Click Object on the Menu bar, point to Transform, then click Transform Each

7. Type 225 in the Horizontal and Vertical text boxes in the Scale section, click OK, then deselect all

   Your screen should resemble Figure D-8.

8. Verify that the Direct Selection tool is selected, click the edge of the center circle, click its center point so that only the circle is selected, double-click ▦, type 120 in the Uniform text box, then click Copy

   The new circle creates more complex positive and negative relationships between the objects.

9. Scale the new circle (which is still selected) 120%, then note the change to the artwork

10. Apply the Transform Again command, deselect, save your work, then compare your screen to Figure D-9

11. Close complex compound paths_AI-D.ai

Design Matters

Experimenting

Never underestimate the role that experimentation plays in graphic design, especially in Illustrator, which has so many different options for manipulating paths and objects. Very seldom is a finished piece exactly what a designer envisions when starting. Instead, designers have a goal in mind when they begin, and it's often experimentation that leads to the final result. With that in mind, go back to the beginning of this lesson and experiment with different transformations at different values than those listed in the steps. Experiment, and see what kinds of interesting complex compound path effects you can come up with.

FIGURE D-7: A simple pattern created with compound paths

One of the five
negative spaces

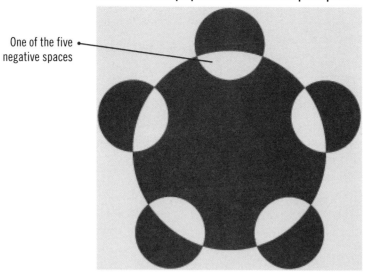

FIGURE D-8: A more interesting pattern

FIGURE D-9: Final artwork

Creating Blends and Complex Artwork

Blending Objects

A **blend** is a series of intermediate objects between two objects. Every blend begins with a starting object and an ending object. The Blend tool offers options for choosing the number of intermediate objects between the starting and ending objects. Both closed paths (such as a square) and open paths (such as a line) can be used in blends. Blends are most commonly used to create interesting shape patterns, color blends, or both. They are also a great way to add dimension to an object. ⬛⬛⬛ Jon asks you to design an introductory exercise about blends, demonstrating all the basic concepts involved with working with blends.

STEPS

1. Open AI D-4.ai from the location where you store your Data Files, save it as blend tutorial_AI-D, then double-click the Blend tool 🔲 to open the Blend Options dialog box

2. Click the Spacing list arrow, click Specified Steps, type 7 in the text box, then click OK

   Specified steps represent the number of in-between objects that will be created in the blend.

3. Click the upper-left corner of the green square, then click the upper-left corner of the yellow square

   Seven squares are added between the two originals. The horizontal line between the two original objects is called the **spine** of the blend.

4. Deselect all, click the Direct Selection tool 🔲, then click and drag the original small yellow square left so that it is half the distance from the original green square

   As shown in Figure D-10, the blend is redrawn. Anything you do to the original objects—move them, scale them, rotate them, and so forth—will redraw the blend.

5. Deselect all, click the Selection tool 🔲, select the blue and orange components of the flower, click Object on the Menu bar, click Group, click the Eyedropper tool 🔲, then click the red circle

   The Eyedropper tool samples the color attributes of the circle—red fill with no stroke—and applies them to both selected objects in the flower. Because the flower is created with two objects, it needed to be grouped to be used in a blend.

6. Double-click 🔲, change the number of specified steps to 5, click OK, click the top of the red circle, then click the top of the red flower

7. Click View on the Menu bar, then click Outline

   As shown in Figure D-11, only the two original objects and the spine are visible. Objects in a blend are "virtual"; they can't be selected individually unless you expand the blend. To expand the blend means to remove the spine and convert each intermediate object into an object that can be selected.

8. Return to Preview mode, click Object on the Menu bar, point to Blend, then click Expand

   As shown in Figure D-12, the blend is expanded. The spine disappears, and each intermediate object can be selected.

9. Double-click 🔲, change the number of specified steps to 256, click OK, blend the four stars, then deselect

   Your screen should resemble Figure D-13.

10. Save your work, then close blend tutorial_AI-D.ai

FIGURE D-10: Redrawing the seven-step blend

Moved object

FIGURE D-11: Original objects and spine

FIGURE D-12: Expanding the blend

FIGURE D-13: Blending four stars

Creating a Clockwise Blend

In addition to creating blends between objects, you can also create blends between simple paths: straight paths or curved paths. This offers you a great deal of flexibility and a great number of options for creating interesting color effects. One of those effects is a clockwise blend, in which colors blend like the hands of a clock sweeping around a center point. There is not a specific tool in Illustrator that will create this effect; it can only be made with blends between paths. 🎨 A new job calls for color effects, and Jon asks that you create a clockwise blend training exercise using six colors.

1. **Open AI D-5.ai from the location where you store your Data Files, save it as** clockwise blend_AI-D, **click the** Selection tool ▶, **then select the** stroked path **on the artboard**

2. **Click the** Rotate tool ⟳, **press and hold** [Alt] (Win) or [option] (Mac), **then click the** bottom anchor point **of the path**

   The Rotate dialog box opens. Given that we want six colors in this clockwise blend, we determine the angle using the following equation: 360° in a circle divided by 6 colors = 60° per color.

3. **Type** 60 **in the Angle text box, click** Copy, **then apply the** Transform Again **command four times**

4. **Using Figure D-14 as a guide, change the stroke color of the six lines using the swatches in the fourth row of the Swatches panel so that your screen resembles the figure**

5. **Double-click the** Blend tool ▣, **change the number of specified steps to** 256, **click** OK, **click the top of the** red path, **then click the top of the** pink path

   256 paths are created between the red path and the pink path, as shown in Figure D-15.

6. **Click the top of the** yellow path **to create the second blend**

7. **Using the same method, create the clockwise blend using the remaining lines**

8. **Deselect all, save your work, then compare your screen to Figure D-16**

Specifying blend options

The three blending options are defined as follows:

- **Smooth Color:** If you're blending two objects that have different colors, Illustrator will insert as many steps as necessary for the color transition between the two objects to be smooth. This is an especially good option to use if you're blending across a far distance—like across a two-page spread in a layout.

- **Specified Steps:** The number of steps you specify equals the number of objects that will be inserted between the beginning and ending objects of the blend. The objects are always distributed evenly between the two ends.

- **Specified Distance:** The number you enter defines the distance of each successive object in the blend. For example, if you enter a specified distance of .5", each object in the blend will be .5" from the previous object. Illustrator inserts as many objects as necessary at that offset value to complete the transition from start to finish.

FIGURE D-14: Applying stroke colors

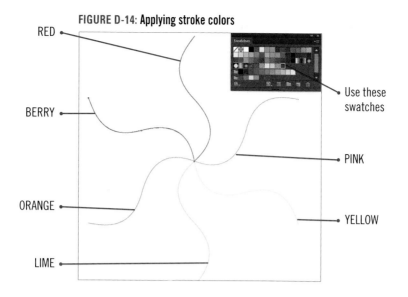

RED

BERRY

ORANGE

LIME

Use these swatches

PINK

YELLOW

FIGURE D-15: Creating the first blend

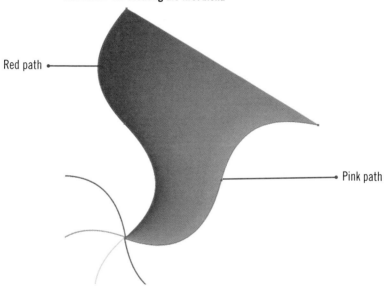

Red path

Pink path

FIGURE D-16: Completed clockwise blend

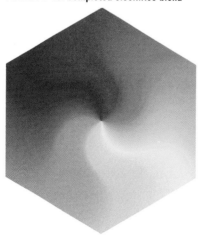

Creating Blends and Complex Artwork

Creating a Clipping Mask

A **clipping mask** is any object that you use to "clip" other objects so that only the parts of the objects that are clipped are visible and the parts that are not clipped are not visible. For example, let's say you had a few square objects on the artboard and you used a circle as a clipping mask. By definition, the circle clipping mask would only show the parts of the squares where the circle overlaps them. Any part of the squares outside of the circle would not be visible. In Illustrator jargon, they would be "masked," or "clipped," by the circle. In a group of selected objects, the top object is always the clipping mask. Since there can only be one top object, it stands to reason that an object being used as a clipping mask must be a single object. Jon asks you to demonstrate how to clip the clockwise blend into other objects.

STEPS

1. **Click the Selection tool** 🔲**, select the pink starburst, then drag it and position it over the clockwise blend**

   The starburst is behind the blend in the stacking order. Since a clipping mask must be in front of the objects it will mask, you will need to bring the starburst in front of the blend.

2. **Click Object on the Menu bar, point to Arrange, click Bring to Front, then select both the starburst and the blend**

3. **Click Object on the Menu bar, point to Clipping Mask, then click Make**

   As shown in Figure D-17, the starburst defines the perimeter of visibility of the blend. Any part of the blend that is inside the starburst is clipped, or masked.

4. **Click Object on the Menu bar, point to Clipping Mask, click Release, deselect all, select the starburst shape, then press [Delete]**

   When you release a clipping mask, the mask loses its original fill and stroke colors.

   > **TROUBLE**
   > Since the starburst shape now has no fill or stroke and is difficult to select, switch to Outline mode, delete the starburst, and then switch back to Preview mode.

5. **Select the five green circles, make them into a compound path, position them over the clockwise blend, bring the circles to the front, select both the compound path and the clockwise blend, apply the Make Clipping Mask command, then deselect**

   See Figure D-18. As a compound path, all five circles compose a single path, allowing them to be used as a clipping mask.

   > **QUICK TIP**
   > The Select/Object/ Clipping Masks command sequence is the easiest way to select clipping masks.

6. **Click Select on the Menu bar, point to Object, click Clipping Masks, then drag the clipping mask over different areas of the blend**

   As you move the clipping mask, different areas of the clockwise blend become visible within the mask.

7. **Deselect, then click any of the circles**

   When you click a masked object with the Selection tool, everything is selected—the clipping mask itself and all the masked objects.

8. **Release the clipping mask, switch to Outline mode, delete the five circles, switch back to Preview mode, position the red compound path over the clockwise blend, bring it to the front, select both the clockwise blend and the red compound path, then apply the Make Clipping Mask command**

9. **Deselect, click Select on the Menu bar, point to Object, click Clipping Masks, then apply a 1.5-pt black stroke to it**

   Your screen should resemble Figure D-19.

10. **Save your work, then close clockwise blend_AI-D.ai**

FIGURE D-17: Masking the blend with the starburst

FIGURE D-18: Masking the blend with five compounded circles

FIGURE D-19: Applying a stroke to the clipping mask

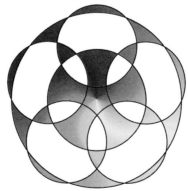

Clipping masks and the stacking order

The stacking order plays a big role in clipping masks, because whenever you select a group of objects and apply the clipping mask command, the top object is used as the clipping mask. Illustrator identifies the clipping mask and all the objects clipped into it as a **clipping set**. Illustrator also remembers the stacking order within the clipping set. This means that you can bring clipped objects forward or move them backward within the clipping mask. Also, if you create a new object, it will be created outside of the clipping mask. However, if you cut (or copy) the new object, select a masked object, then click Paste in Front or Paste in Back, the new object will be pasted into the mask.

Using the Draw Inside Drawing Mode

The Draw Inside drawing mode does just what its name implies: it allows you to create one object inside (within the perimeter) of another object. Drawing one object inside another is essentially the same thing as creating a clipping mask. When you draw an object inside another, the two objects behave the same way any two objects behave in a clipping set. The relationship can also be undone with the Release Clipping Mask command. The big difference between using the Draw Inside drawing mode and making a clipping mask is that the draw inside option can involve only two objects. Now that you've taught clipping masks, Jon asks you to demonstrate the Draw Inside drawing mode as a comparison to clipping masks.

STEPS

1. **Open AI D-6.ai, save it as** draw inside_AI-D**, click the** Selection tool **, then select the** blue square **at the top of the document**

   The Fill and Stroke buttons on the Tools panel display the selected object's fill and stroke: blue fill and no stroke.

2. **Click the** Draw Inside button **on the Tools panel, then click the** Ellipse tool

   Because you must have an object selected to use the Draw Inside drawing mode, the object you draw will have the same fill and stroke color as the object you're drawing into. You can apply different colors after you draw inside.

3. **Draw an ellipse—approximately the same size as the pink ellipse already on the artboard— that overlaps the blue square**

4. **With the ellipse still selected, change its fill color to yellow**

   Figure D-20 shows one example of how the ellipse is drawn within the blue square. Dotted lines around the four corners of the blue square indicate that it is functioning as a mask for the ellipse. So long as you stay in Draw Inside drawing mode, any object you create will be drawn inside the blue square.

5. **Click the** Draw Normal button **on the Tools panel, click** **, select the word** MASK**, click the** Type menu**, then click** Create Outlines

6. **With the outlines still selected, click the** Object menu**, point to** Compound Path**, click** Make**, then fill them with any green swatch on the Swatches panel**

   Defined as a compound path, the letter outlines are now a single object and can be drawn into.

7. **Select the** pink ellipse**, click the** Edit menu**, click** Cut**, select the** MASK **outlines, then click the** Draw Inside button

   Dotted lines appear around the MASK outlines, indicating they can be drawn into.

8. **Click the** Edit menu**, click** Paste**, then verify that the ellipse overlaps the** MASK **outlines as shown in Figure D-21**

9. **Save your work, then close** draw inside_AI-D.ai

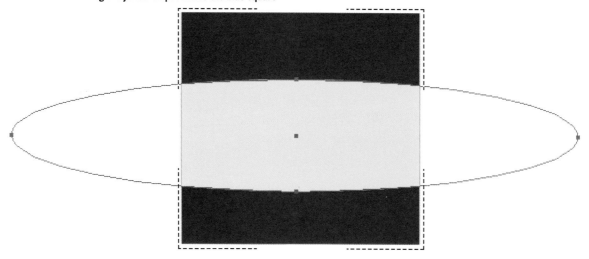

Illustrator CS6

Applying Arrowheads and Dashes to Strokes

Strokes can be used as important design concepts in illustrations, and the Stroke panel offers controls to create complex dashed strokes. When you create a dashed stroke, end caps determine the appearance at the ends of the path. The Stroke panel offers three end caps to choose from: a Butt Cap (the default) is a blunt cap that ends at the anchor points; a Round Cap creates an oval at the ends of the path, and a Projecting Cap extends the stroke past the anchor points to a distance that is equal to one-half the point size of the stroke itself. In addition to caps, the Stroke panel offers many different arrowheads that you can apply to the endpoints of a path. Once you apply the arrowhead that you want, you can use the Scale option on the Stroke panel to specify the size of the arrowhead that you think looks best. Jon asks you to review the three end caps available on the Stroke panel, and then to create a dashed stroke.

STEPS

1. Open AI D-7.ai from the location where you store your Data Files, then save it as arrows_AI-D

2. Click the Selection tool, open the Stroke panel, click the Stroke panel menu button, click Show Options, then select the top stroked path on the artboard

3. On the Stroke panel, click the first Arrowheads list arrow, click Arrow 1, click the second Arrowheads list arrow, then click Arrow 19

   Your stroke should resemble Figure D-22.

4. Select the bottom stroked path, then click the Dashed Line check box on the Stroke panel to activate it

   The dash text boxes on the Stroke panel define the length of the dashes; the gap text boxes define the width of the gaps between the dashes.

5. Select the existing value in the first dash text box, type 2, press [Tab], type 4 in the first gap text box, press [Tab], type 6, press [Tab], type 8, press [Tab], type 10, press [Tab], type 12, then press [Tab]

6. Click the Round Cap button on the Stroke panel

7. Type 0 in the first dash text box, type 8 in the first gap text box, delete the contents of the remaining four text boxes, deselect, then compare your result to Figure D-23

   The Round Cap creates a dotted stroke. For any weight stroke, a 0-dash with a Round Cap will create a dotted stroke—so long as the gap is wide enough to show the entire dot.

8. Increase the weight of the stroke to 24 pt, then increase the gap value to 48

9. Save your work, then close arrows_AI-D.ai

About dashed strokes

On the Stroke panel, the dash and gap values are repeating. In other words, if you enter just one dash value and one gap value, those values will be repeated across the length of the stroke. If you enter three dash values and three gap values, the set of three dashes and three gaps will be repeated across the length of the stroke. If you envision a dashed stroke moving from left to right, you can think of the dash and gap values as being *horizontal* measurements. The *vertical* height of each dash is determined by the weight of the stroke.

Creating Blends and Complex Artwork

FIGURE D-22: Stroke with arrowheads

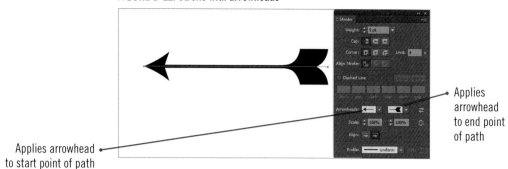

Applies arrowhead
to start point of path

Applies
arrowhead
to end point
of path

FIGURE D-23: Dotted stroke with round caps

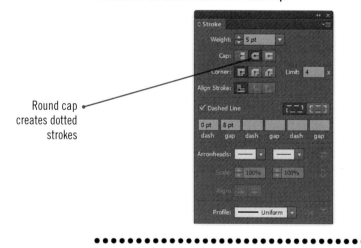

Round cap
creates dotted
strokes

Designing Complex Layered Strokes

Layered strokes produce some of the best illusions in Illustrator. You can create a number of different dashed effects with a single dashed stroke. However, it's when you position dashed and non-dashed strokes on top of one another that you can create some really cool and eye-popping effects. Complex layered strokes are very useful for borders on artwork and for repeating patterns. You're designing a number of borders on artwork for a client, and Jon asks you to create two borders using layered strokes.

STEPS

1. Open AI D-8.ai from the location where you store your Data Files, then save it as complex dashed strokes_AI-D

2. Select the red stroked path, on the Stroke panel, change the Weight to 20 pt, copy, paste in front, then change the stroke color to White

3. Increase the stroke weight to 21 pt, click the Round Cap button on the Stroke panel, click the Dashed Line check box on the Stroke panel, set the dash value to 0, set the gap value to 22, then press [Tab]

4. Copy the white stroke, paste in front, change the stroke color to CMYK Red, reduce the weight to 14 pt, then deselect the path
   Your artwork should resemble Figure D-24.

5. Click the black path, change its weight to 24 pt, copy the path, paste in front, then change the stroke color to White

6. Click the Dashed Line check box, type 4 in the dash text box, type 12 in the gap text box, then reduce the stroke weight to 20 pt

7. Copy the path, paste in front, then change the stroke color to Black

8. Click the Dashed Line check box to remove the check mark, reduce the stroke weight to 12 pt, then deselect
   Your artwork should resemble Figure D-25.

9. Save your work, then close complex dashed strokes_AI-D.ai

Creating Blends and Complex Artwork

FIGURE D-24: "Bull's-eye" stroke with three layered strokes

FIGURE D-25: "Film strip" stroke with three layered strokes

Practice

Concepts Review

Label the elements of the Illustrator screen shown in Figure D-26.

FIGURE D-26

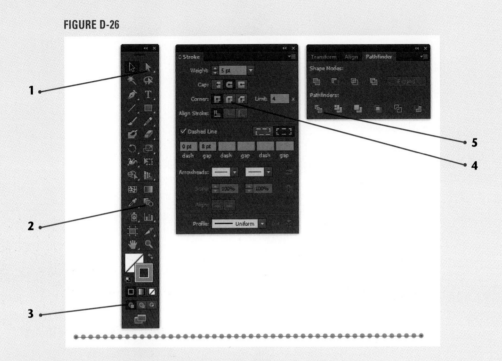

Match each term with the statement that best describes it.

6. Spine
7. Clipping mask
8. End cap
9. Compound path
10. Divide pathfinder
11. Expand

a. Cuts objects where they overlap
b. Converts blend steps into selectable objects
c. Line between two original blend objects
d. Determines appearance of the end of a path
e. Single object composed of two or more paths
f. Shows only those objects within its boundaries

Select the best answer from the list of choices:

12. After the Divide pathfinder is applied, the resulting objects are _____.

   a. ungrouped   **c.** grouped

   b. compound paths   **d.** offset paths

13. Objects do not need to be selected in order to be _____.

   a. compounded   **c.** grouped

   b. sliced   **d.** blended

14. A clipping mask must be a(n) _____ object.

   a. expanded   **c.** divided

   b. single   **d.** layered

15. End caps determine the appearance of the ends of a(n) _____.

   a. path   **c.** object

   b. compound shape   **d.** blend

Skills Review

1. Use the Divide pathfinder.

   a. Open the file AI D-9.ai from the location where you store your Data Files, then save it as **kaleidoscope_AI-D**.

   b. Click the Selection tool, then click the black circle on the artboard.

   c. Click the Rotate tool, press and hold [Alt] (Win) or [option] (Mac), then click the black x on the artboard.

FIGURE D-27

   d. Type **30** in the Angle text box, then click Copy.

   e. Apply the Transform Again command 10 times.

   f. Click the Selection tool, then select all of the circles.

   g. Open the Pathfinder panel if necessary, then click the Divide button.

   h. Deselect all objects, click the Direct Selection tool, then click one of the shapes along the outside edge, as shown in Figure D-27.

   i. Press and hold [Shift], then select the remaining identical shapes along the outer edge.

   j. Click the Fill button on the Tools panel, open the Swatches panel, then click C=90 M=30 Y=95 K=30 (dark green) on the Swatches panel.

FIGURE D-28

   k. Click one of the black objects between the two green objects, press and hold [Shift], then select the remaining identical shapes.

   l. Click C=50 M=0 Y=100 K=0 (lime green) on the Swatches panel, deselect, then compare your screen to Figure D-28.

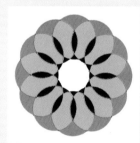

   m. Using the same technique, complete filling the individual pieces of the artwork, using CMYK Yellow and CMYK Red, so that your screen looks like Figure D-29, then save and close the document. (*Hint*: Make the stroke of the yellow segments 1 pt, CMYK Red.)

   n. Save and close kaleidoscope_AI-D.ai.

2. Create compound paths.

   a. Open the file AI D-10.ai from the location where you store your Data Files, then save it as **purple paths_AI-D**.

FIGURE D-29

   b. Use the Selection tool to drag the first black shape over the *P* letterform.

   c. Select both components of the letter *P*, click Object on the Menu bar, point to Compound Path, then click Make.

   d. Repeat Steps b & c for the second *P* letterform.

   e. Select the two stars on the artboard, create a compound path, then deselect all.

Skills Review (continued)

f. Click the Direct Selection tool, click the edge of the smaller star shape that has been knocked out, press and hold [Shift], then select the anchor points of the inner star.

g. Press and hold [Shift], then press ➝ 10 times.

h. Click the artboard to deselect all, compare your screen to Figure D-30, then save your work.

FIGURE D-30

i. Close purple paths_AI-D.ai.

3. **Create complex patterns with compound paths.**

a. Open the file AI D-11.ai from the location where you store your Data Files, save it as **complex circle_AI-D**, then press and hold [Ctrl][A] (Win) or ⌘[A] (Mac) to select all the objects on the artboard.

b. Click Object on the Menu bar, point to Compound Path, then click Make.

c. Deselect, click the Direct Selection tool, then click the edge of the large green circle.

d. Click the center point of the large green circle to select only the circle, double-click the Scale tool, type **120** in the Uniform text box, then click OK.

e. Keeping the circle selected, double-click the Scale tool, type **50** in the Uniform text box, then click Copy.

f. Click Select on the Menu bar, then click Inverse.

g. Click Object on the Menu bar, point to Transform, then click Transform Each.

h. Type **120** in the Horizontal and Vertical text boxes in the Scale section, click OK, click the Selection tool, then deselect all.

i. Click the Direct Selection tool, click the edge of the center circle, click its center point to select the entire circle, double-click the Scale tool, type **120** in the Uniform text box, then click OK.

j. Apply the Transform Again command, deselect, then compare your screen to Figure D-31.

FIGURE D-31

k. Save your work, then close complex circle_AI-D.ai.

4. **Blend objects.**

a. Open the file AI D-12.ai from the location where you store your Data Files, save it as **blend review_AI-D**, then double-click the Blend tool to open the Blend Options dialog box.

b. Click the Spacing list arrow, click Specified Steps, type **256** in the text box, then click OK.

c. Click the top of the top petal of the green flower, then click the top edge of the yellow circle.

d. Double-click the Blend tool, change the number of specified steps to 5, then click OK.

e. Click Object on the Menu bar, point to Blend, click Expand, then deselect.

f. Double-click the Blend tool, change the number of specified steps to 256, then blend the four circles by clicking the top of the white circle, the top of the yellow circle, the top edge of the orange circle, and then the top edge of the red circle.

g. Click the Selection tool, then click the artboard to deselect all.

h. Save your work, then close blend review_AI-D.ai.

Skills Review (continued)

5. **Create a clockwise blend.**

   a. Open the file AI D-13.ai from the location where you store your Data Files, save it as **jagged blend_AI-D**, click the Selection tool, then click the stroked path on the artboard.

   b. Click the Rotate tool, press and hold [Alt] (Win) or [option] (Mac), then click the bottom anchor point of the path.

   c. Type **60** in the Angle text box, click Copy, then apply the Transform Again command four times.

   d. Show the Swatches panel, then using Figure D-32 as a guide, apply the following stroke colors to the five new paths in a clockwise direction, keeping the original path as CMYK Red: Line 2: C=0 M=50 Y=100 K=0 (orange); Line 3: CMYK Yellow; Line 4: CMYK Green; Line 5: CMYK Cyan; and Line 6: CMYK Blue.

   e. Double-click the Blend tool, change the number of specified steps to 256, click OK to close the dialog box, click the top of the red path, then click the top of the orange path.

   f. Click the top of the yellow path.

   g. Using the same method, create the clockwise blend using the remaining four pairs of lines.

   h. Click the Selection tool, click the artboard to deselect all, then compare your screen to Figure D-33.

   i. Save your work.

6. **Create a clipping mask.**

   a. Use the Selection tool to select the green triangle, then drag it and position it over the clockwise blend so that it is centered within the blend.

   b. Select both the triangle and the blend.

   c. Click Object on the Menu bar, point to Clipping Mask, then click Make.

   d. Click the artboard to deselect all.

   e. Click Select on the Menu bar, point to Object, then click Clipping Masks.

   f. Show the Stroke panel if necessary, then apply a 4-pt Black stroke to the clipping mask.

   g. Save your work, then close jagged blend_AI-D.ai.

7. **Use the Draw Inside drawing mode.**

   a. Open AI D-14.ai, save it as **draw inside skills_AI-D**, click the Selection tool, then select the pink circle.

   b. Click the Draw Inside button on the Tools panel, then click the Ellipse tool.

   c. Draw a circle that overlaps the right side of the pink circle.

   d. Draw three more circles that overlap the top, bottom and left of the pink circle.

   e. Fill the circles with colors of your choice, then deselect.

   f. Click the Draw Normal button on the Tools panel, then compare your results to Figure D-34.

   g. Save your work, then close draw inside skills_AI-D.ai.

FIGURE D-32

FIGURE D-33

FIGURE D-34

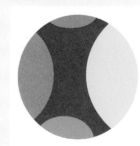

Skills Review (continued)

8. **Apply arrowheads and dashes to strokes.**

   a. Open the file AI D-15.ai from the location where you store your Data Files, then save it as **caps review_AI-D**.

   b. Use the Selection tool to select the top blue path, then click the Round Cap button on the Stroke panel.

   c. Click the Projecting Cap button on the Stroke panel, then click the Round Cap button on the Stroke panel.

   d. Click the bottom blue path, then click the Dashed Line check box on the Stroke panel to activate it.

   e. Select the existing contents in the first dash text box, type **3**, press [Tab], type **5**, press [Tab], type **10**, press [Tab], type **2**, then delete the contents of any of the remaining text boxes, if necessary.

   f. Click the Round Cap button on the Stroke panel.

   g. Type **0** in the first dash text box, type **6** in the first gap text box, then delete the contents of the remaining four text boxes.

   h. Select the top blue path, click the Dashed Line check box, change the first dash value to 25, then delete the contents of any of the remaining text boxes, if necessary.

   i. On the Stroke panel, click the first Arrowheads list arrow then click Arrow 5.

   j. Click the second Arrowheads list arrow, then click Arrow 5.

   k. Reduce the Scale value on both arrowheads to 40%, then verify that the Preserves exact dash and gap lengths button is selected on the Stroke panel.

   l. Save your work, then close caps review_AI-D.ai.

9. **Design complex layered strokes.**

   a. Open the file AI D-16.ai from the location where you store your Data Files, then save it as **complex stroke review_AI-D**.

   b. Use the Selection tool to select the black path, copy the path, then paste it in front.

   c. Change the weight of the copied path to 34 pt, then change the stroke color of the path to CMYK Yellow.

   d. Click the Dashed Line check box on the Stroke panel to activate it.

   e. Set the first dash text box to 6 pt, press [Tab], set the first gap text box to 2 pt, then delete the contents of any of the remaining text boxes, if necessary.

   f. Copy the yellow path, paste in front, then change the stroke color to C=25 M=40 Y=65 K=0. (*Hint*: Look for a light brown swatch.)

   g. Decrease the stroke weight to 14 pt.

   h. Deselect the brown stroke, then compare your screen to Figure D-35.

   i. Save your work, then close complex stroke review_AI-D.ai.

FIGURE D-35

Independent Challenge 1

You are working on a brochure about the importance of regular eye examinations. You decide to create a fun border for the brochure using an eyeball graphic and layered stroked paths.

a. Open the file AI D-17.ai from the location where you store your Data Files, then save it as **eyeball stroke_AI-D**.

b. Click the black path on the artboard, make sure the Stroke panel is open, click the Dashed Line check box to select it, type **0** in the first dash text box, press [Tab], type **48**, press [Tab], type **0**, press [Tab], type **60**, then click the Round Cap button.

c. Copy the path, then paste it in front.

d. Change the stroke color of the new path to White.

e. Change the weight to 36 pt on the Stroke panel.

f. Copy the white path, then paste it in front.

g. Change the color of the path to Black and the weight of the path to 16 pt.

h. Press ➡ six times, then press ⬇ eight times.

i. Deselect all, compare your screen to Figure D-36, then save your work.

Advanced Challenge Exercise

- Select the Black 16 pt. stroke.
- Change the weight of the stroke to 8 pt.
- Click the Projecting Cap button on the Stroke panel.
- Change the color of the stroke to CMYK Cyan.

FIGURE D-36

j. Close eyeball stroke_AI-D.ai.

Independent Challenge 2

You teach Adobe Illustrator CS6 at a local university. This week's lesson is about clipping masks. You create an exercise for your students and then test it out using the Clipping Mask command.

a. Open the file AI D-18.ai from the location where you store your Data Files, then save it as **mask_AI-D**.

b. Use the Selection tool to drag the colorful pieces of artwork except the word *MASK* over each other so that they overlap in any arrangement that you like. (*Hint*: The word MASK will be the clipping mask that clips the arrangement of art. Figure D-37 shows a sample. You can change the stacking order of the objects as you like.)

c. Drag the word *MASK* over the arrangement of artwork.

d. Click Object on the Menu bar, point to Arrange, then click Bring to Front, if necessary.

e. Select all, click Object on the Menu bar, point to Clipping Mask, then click Make.

FIGURE D-37

f. Click the artboard to deselect all.

g. Click Select on the Menu bar, point to Object, then click Clipping Masks.

h. Show the Swatches panel, verify that the Fill button is in front of the Stroke button on the Tools panel, then click CMYK Blue to fill the clipping mask with CMYK Blue.

i. Click the Stroke button on the Tools panel, then click Black on the Swatches panel.

j. Show the Stroke panel, change the stroke weight to 2 pt, deselect the mask, then save your work.

Independent Challenge 2 (continued)

Advanced Challenge Exercise

- Click Select on the Menu bar, point to Object, then click Clipping Masks.
- Using the arrow keys, change the appearance of the mask by moving the mask up, down, left, and right so that the mask covers different areas of the artwork.
- Change the fill color of the mask to Black.
- Change the stroke color of the mask to Red.

k. Compare your screen to the sample shown in Figure D-37, then close mask_AI-D.ai.

Independent Challenge 3

You are working on a package design for toy train tracks using Illustrator. After some thought, you realize that you can create the look of train tracks using layered stroked paths.

a. Open AI D-19.ai from the location where you store your Data Files, then save it as
train tracks_AI-D.

b. Select the black path on the artboard, then change the stroke weight to 36 pt.

c. Change the path to a dashed line, then change the first dash value to 6 pt and the first gap value to 12 pt.

FIGURE D-38

d. Copy the path, then paste it in front.

e. Verify that the stroke color is black, change the stroke weight to 21 pt, then remove the check mark in the Dashed Line check box to create a solid path.

f. Copy the path, then paste in front.

g. Change the stroke color to white and the stroke weight to 18 pt.

h. Copy the path, then paste in front.

i. Change the stroke color to black and the stroke weight to 15 pt.

j. Copy the path, then paste in front.

k. Change the stroke color to white and the stroke weight to 12 pt.

l. Copy the path, then paste in front.

m. Change the stroke color to black, select the Dashed Line check box, then verify that the first dash and gap values are 6 pt and 12 pt.

n. Deselect all, save your work, then compare your screen to Figure D-38.

o. Close train tracks_AI-D.ai.

Real Life Independent Challenge

Your friend owns a landscape company and has a basic business card. She likes the card but wants to add some floral images to it without changing its overall appearance. You offer to help her achieve this goal by using the Clipping Mask command.

a. Open the file AI D-20.ai from the location where you store your Data Files, then save it as **landscape card_AI-D**.

b. Use the Selection tool to select the white background rectangle.

c. Copy the rectangle, then paste in front.

d. Fill the copied rectangle with the Water Lilies Color pattern swatch on the Swatches panel.

e. Select the four gray ovals on the card, then create a compound path.

f. With the compound path still selected, press and hold [Shift], click the rectangle filled with the pattern, then create a clipping mask.

g. Click Object on the Menu bar, point to Arrange, then click Send to Back.

h. Select the white rectangle, click Object on the Menu bar, point to Arrange, then click Send to Back.

i. Click Select on the Menu bar, point to Object, then click Clipping Masks.

j. Apply a 1-pt CMYK Green stroke to the clipping mask.

k. Save and close landscape card_AI-D.ai.

Visual Workshop

Open the file AI D-21.ai from the location where you store your Data Files, then save it as **stroke challenge_AI-D**. Using Figure D-39 as a guide, create the layered stroke design shown in the figure by overlapping three stroked paths. The weight of the largest stroked path is 50 pt, the middle is 25 pt, and the smallest is 10 pt. Save your work, compare your screen to Figure D-39, then close stroke challenge_AI-D.ai.

FIGURE D-39

Working with Text and Gradients

Files You Will Need:

To view a list of files needed for this unit, see the Data Files Grid in the back of the book.

Text is everywhere. With pretty much any software application you work with, you have the option of working with text: creating, formatting, and editing it. What's different about text in Illustrator is that you have all of Illustrator's tools and techniques at your disposal to create dramatic and exciting typographical effects. With Illustrator, you can place text on a curvy path or a circle. You can distort text and warp text. Of all the applications, Illustrator offers the most options for designing dazzling text. Like text, gradients often play an important role in Illustrator artwork. Illustrator allows you to create both linear and radial gradients that you can apply as fills and strokes to objects. From a design perspective, gradients add dimension and complexity to the illustrations you create. Your team has been hired to create a logo for a TV show called Atlas, which travels the globe in search of interesting travel destinations. Jon asks you to prepare exercises demonstrating the use of gradients and dramatic typography for dimension and complexity.

OBJECTIVES

Create a gradient

Create and format text

Use the Gradient tool

Create a drop shadow for text

Place a bitmap image

Apply a radial gradient

Make an object transparent

Create text on a path

Creating a Gradient

A **gradient** is a type of fill that provides a transition between colors. You design gradients using the Gradient panel. Here, you can specify whether you want a **linear gradient**, in which color gradates in one straight direction, or a **radial gradient**, in which color radiates outward from a central point. On the Gradient panel, gradients are composed of two or more **color stops**—the colors that are blended. As you manipulate the gradient on the Gradient panel, the **gradient slider** shows you a preview of what the gradient will look like. Between any two color stops you will find a **midpoint slider**. The midpoint slider determines where the two colors are blended with 50% of each color. In a blue-to-yellow gradient, for example, the color at the midpoint would be green. ▰▰▰▰ Jon asks you to first demonstrate how to specify a radial gradient on the Gradient panel.

STEPS

1. **Open AI E-1.ai from the location where you store your Data Files, save it as** atlas_AI-E, **click the** workspace switcher **on the Menu bar, then click** Reset Essentials **to refresh the Essentials workspace**

2. **Click the** Selection tool ▨, **click the** blue circle, **click the** Fill button ☐ **on the Tools panel, click the** Swatches panel button ▦, **then click the** Linear Gradient swatch **on the Swatches panel, as shown in Figure E-1**

   The circle is filled with the Linear Gradient swatch.

3. **Click the** Gradient panel button ▨ **to display the Gradient panel, click the** Type list arrow **on the Gradient panel, click** Radial, **then click the** white color stop, **as shown in Figure E-2**

   You select a color stop in order to change its color.

QUICK TIP

When a color stop is selected, the triangle at the top of the color stop is highlighted.

4. **Press and hold** [Alt] (Win) or [option] (Mac), **click** Black **on the Swatches panel, click the** right color stop, **press and hold** [Alt] (Win) or [option] (Mac), **then click** CMYK Blue **on the Swatches panel**

   Pressing [Alt] (Win) or [option] (Mac) applies the selected swatch to the color stop instead of the entire object. Now you are ready to add a third color stop.

5. **Position the mouse pointer just below the middle of the gradient slider on the Gradient panel so that you see a small white arrow with a + (plus sign) beside it, then click to add a new color stop**

   The plus sign next to the pointer indicates a new color stop will be added when you click. The Location text box on the Gradient panel identifies where on the gradient slider you clicked, from 0% on the left to 100% on the right.

QUICK TIP

You can double-click a color stop to open and use the Color panel or the Swatches panel to change the color of the color stop.

6. **Press and hold** [Alt] (Win) or [option] (Mac), **then click** CMYK Cyan **on the Swatches panel**

   Your Gradient panel should resemble Figure E-3. Your artwork will differ depending on the location that you added the third stop.

7. **Double-click the** Location text box **on the Gradient panel, type** 84, **then press** [Enter] (Win) or [return] (Mac)

   The CMYK Cyan color stop is repositioned on the gradient slider at the 84% mark and remains selected. Now you're going to move the midpoint slider between the first two color stops to change how the first color stop gradates to the second color stop.

8. **Drag the** midpoint slider (diamond) **between the first and second color stops on the gradient slider to the right until the Location text box reads approximately 86%; deselect, then compare your screen to Figure E-4**

   The black component of the gradient is increased dramatically.

9. **Click the** Swatches panel menu button ▤, **click** New Swatch, **type** Blue Radial **in the Swatch Name text box, click** OK, **then save your work**

FIGURE E-1: Identifying the Linear Gradient swatch

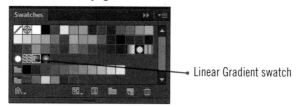

Linear Gradient swatch

FIGURE E-2: Elements of the Gradient panel

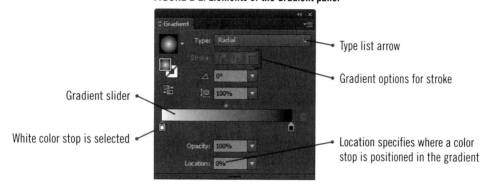

Type list arrow

Gradient options for stroke

Gradient slider

White color stop is selected

Location specifies where a color stop is positioned in the gradient

FIGURE E-3: Viewing three color stops

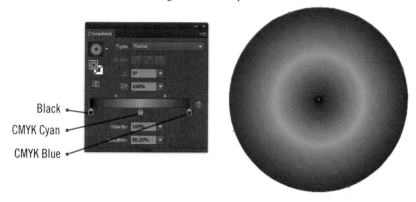

Black

CMYK Cyan

CMYK Blue

FIGURE E-4: Moving a midpoint slider

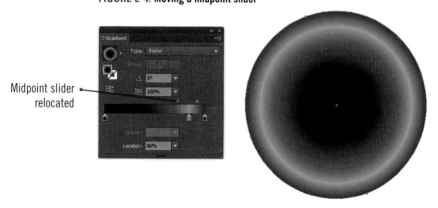

Midpoint slider relocated

About gradients with transparency

In addition to changing the fill color of a color stop on a gradient, you can also change the opacity of a color stop. The default Fading Sky gradient on the Swatches panel is an example of this. The gradient starts with 100% blue and fades to 0% blue. To change the opacity of a color stop, click the color stop on the gradient ramp, then change the Opacity setting on the Gradient panel.

Creating and Formatting Text

In Illustrator, text is a click away. Simply click the Type tool on the artboard, then start typing. Once created, text functions pretty much like any other Illustrator object: you can select it, move it, fill and stroke it, and you can transform it with any of the transform tools. Use the Character panel to specify the font and the font size, as well as other options such as kerning. **Kerning** is the process of adjusting the space between pairs of characters to improve the overall visual appearance of text. Kerning becomes more of an issue with large-sized display text, like headlines. With large text, kerning is necessary when the spacing between letters appears inconsistent—the larger font size makes the inconsistency more noticeable. Inattention to kerning often stands out. ▨▨▧ Jon asks you to create the type for the Atlas logo and kern two pairs of characters to improve their appearance.

STEPS

1. **Click the** View menu, **click** Fit Artboard in Window, **click the** Type tool ▣, **then click on the left side of the artboard**
   A blinking cursor appears.

2. **Type** ATLAS **in capital letters, then click the** Selection tool ▣
   When you click the Selection tool, the text becomes selected.

3. **Click the** Window menu, **point to** Type, **then click** Character **to view the Character panel**

4. **On the Character panel, click the** panel menu button ▣, **then click** Show Options **to view all of the options on the Character panel**
   As shown in Figure E-5, the Character panel has settings for font family, font style, font size, tracking, kerning, leading, horizontal and vertical scale, character rotation, and baseline shift. There are also buttons for applying special formatting such as all caps, small caps, superscript, subscript, underline, and strikethrough. At the bottom of the panel are two menus, one for language and one for choosing an anti-aliasing setting.

QUICK TIP
You can also change the height of text by changing the Vertical Scale value on the Character panel.

5. **Set the font to** Times New Roman Regular, **then set the font size to** 146
   The spacing between the letters appears a bit inconsistent. There's too much space on both sides of the second letter *A*. You need to kern the letter pairs.

6. **Click** ▣, **then click between the letter** *L* **and the letter** *A*
   The text cursor appears flashing between the two letters.

7. **On the Character panel, select the value in the** Kerning text box ▣, **type** –40, **then press** [Enter] (Win) **or** [return] (Mac)
   The two letters move closer together.

8. **Click between the letter** *A* **and the letter** *S*, **change the Kerning value to** –40 **on the Character panel, then press** [Enter] (Win) **or** [return] (Mac)

9. **Deselect, compare your screen to Figure E-6, then save your work**

Kerning vs. tracking

Kerning refers to manipulating space between two characters. Tracking affects the overall spacing of words, like what you'd find in a sentence or in a paragraph. When you have large amounts of type, you can use tracking as an overall control of the space between the words—whether to save space or to increase space to fill a specific area of your layout. Remember it this way: kerning is used for very precise changes to letters, and tracking is used for global changes to large amounts of text.

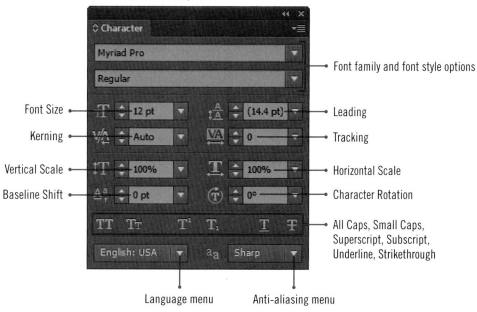

Font family and font style options

Font Size
Kerning
Vertical Scale
Baseline Shift

Leading
Tracking
Horizontal Scale
Character Rotation

All Caps, Small Caps,
Superscript, Subscript,
Underline, Strikethrough

Language menu

Anti-aliasing menu

Illustrator CS6

FIGURE E-6: Two kerned pairs of letters

Space reduced

Using the Gradient Tool

Once you fill or stroke an object with a gradient, you can use the Gradient tool to define the *length* and *angle* of the gradient within the option. The Gradient tool works by clicking and dragging it. Where you start to click and drag is where the gradient begins, and where you stop dragging to is where the gradient ends. You can click and drag in any direction, and you can click and drag at any length. You can drag a short gradient completely within the object, or you can drag a long gradient that exceeds the perimeter of the object. ▰▰▱▱ Jon asks you to fill the ATLAS text with a linear gradient and then use the Gradient tool to manipulate the gradient fill.

STEPS

QUICK TIP
When you convert text to outlines, the resulting objects are grouped.

1. **Click the Selection tool ▶, then select the ATLAS text, click the Type menu, then click Create Outlines**

   The text is converted into Illustrator objects. The text is no longer editable as text. Now that the text has been converted into objects, you can fill it with a gradient.

2. **Click the Blue Radial gradient swatch on the Swatches panel**

   The Blue Radial gradient is applied to each of the letter objects.

3. **On the Gradient panel, click the Type list arrow, click Linear, then change the location of the middle color stop to 60%**

   The gradient fill is converted to a linear gradient and the location of the middle color is 60%.

4. **On the Gradient panel, click anywhere between the first and middle color stops to add a new color stop, set its location to 50%, then set its color to White**

   Your screen should resemble Figure E-7. The linear gradient fills each letter object from left to right.

5. **Click the first color stop on the gradient slider, press and hold [Alt] (Win) or [option] (Mac), then click the C=0 M=0 Y=0 K=10 (light gray) swatch on the Swatches panel**

6. **Using the same method, apply the same color to the last color stop on the gradient slider**

QUICK TIP
If you ungroup a grouped object, then click the Gradient tool, a gradient annotator will appear on each object, allowing you to manipulate each gradient fill independently.

7. **Click the Gradient tool ▦, press and hold [Shift], then click and drag from the left of the first letter *A* to the right of the letter *S***

   As shown in Figure E-8, the linear gradient gradates across the five selected objects. The bar that appears as you drag the Gradient tool is called the **gradient annotator**. It appears as you drag the Gradient tool to show the length and direction of the gradient.

8. **Press and hold [Shift], drag the Gradient tool from the top of the letter *T* to the bottom of the letter *T*, then deselect all**

   As shown in Figure E-9, the gradient now gradates from the top to the bottom of the objects.

9. **Click the Swatches panel menu button ▦, click New Swatch, type Blue Linear in the Swatch Name text box, then click OK**

   It's important to note that none of the changes made to the gradient on the Gradient panel affected the original Blue Radial swatch on the Swatches panel.

Using the Gradient tool

Where you click, drag, and release the Gradient tool determines the length and the angle of the gradient. What's interesting is that the Gradient tool manipulates the gradient independently of the object or objects that contain the gradient. For example, you can create a small gradient in a large object, or you can create a gradient that starts and ends outside of the object. As you saw in this lesson, you can also apply a single gradient across multiple selected objects already filled with the gradient. The more you play with the Gradient tool, the more you'll discover cool and interesting gradient effects that can be achieved.

FIGURE E-7: Viewing the linear gradient in the letter objects

FIGURE E-8: Using the Gradient tool

FIGURE E-9: Gradient flowing from top to bottom

Start

End

Creating a Drop Shadow for Text

Drop shadows are classic effects used to enhance type. We say classic because drop shadows were used in graphic design long before the advent of computer graphics. Quite literally, they go back centuries. The basic concept of a drop shadow is to offset a copy of text, usually black, behind the main text. The term offset means that the two are not aligned—the shadow is visible in a slightly different location. This creates the effect of a shadow, but also as important, the blackness behind the main text makes the main text stand out more from any background. In this lesson, you'll learn two techniques for creating drop shadows. ▓▓▓▓ Jon asks you to experiment with adding a drop shadow behind the ATLAS text to give it more dimension and make it stand out.

STEPS

1. **Click the Selection tool ▸, select the ATLAS text, copy the text, click the Edit menu, then click Paste in Back**

   The copy is pasted beneath the ATLAS text and remains selected.

2. **Fill the selection with Black, press ↓ five times, press ← five times, deselect, then compare your result to Figure E-10**

   This is a simple drop shadow. However, note that because this text is so large, the "jump" between the gradient text and the black shadow text is very apparent and visually a bit jarring.

3. **Select the ATLAS text filled with the gradient, click the Edit menu, click Paste in Front, click the Object menu, point to Hide, then click Selection**

   A copy of the gradient text is hidden for later use.

4. **Select the original ATLAS text, fill it with Black, then select both the black ATLAS text and the black drop shadow text**

   You will blend the two sets of black text to create a more gradual drop shadow.

5. **Double-click the Blend tool ▦ to open the Blend Options dialog box, click the Spacing list arrow, click Specified Steps, type 256, then click OK**

6. **Click the Object menu, point to Blend, then click Make**

   The original ATLAS text and the drop shadow are blended using 256 steps.

7. **Click the Object menu, click Show All, click ▸, deselect, click the ATLAS text, apply a .75 pt Black stroke to the selection, then deselect**

   Figure E-11 shows the artwork with the selection edges hidden. Note how smooth the black drop shadow now appears. Note that when you applied the Show All command, a red circle that was hidden when you opened the file has become visible.

8. **Select all of the text, click the Object menu, then click Group**

9. **Position the group as shown in Figure E-12, then save your work**

ATLAS

Illustrator CS6

Placing a Bitmap Image

Digital photographic images often play important visual roles in illustrations. Because Illustrator and Photoshop are sister applications, you'll find that it's easy to bring images from Photoshop into Illustrator using the Place command. Once the image is in Illustrator, you can treat it in many ways like an Illustrator object: transform it, move it, apply a stroke to it, and so on. You can even use Illustrator objects as clipping masks for placed imagery. ▰▰▰▰ Jon asks you to demonstrate how to place a bitmap image into Illustrator. You place an image that represents travel on a grand scale.

STEPS

1. **Select the** grouped text, **hide it, select the** red circle, **then copy it**

2. **Click the** Edit menu, **click** Paste in Front, **then hide the copy**

3. **Click the** File menu, **click** Place, **navigate to the location where you store your Data Files, click** Globe.tif, **click** Place, **then drag the globe image to the left side of the circles, as shown in Figure E-13**

4. **Click the** Edit menu, **click** Cut **to cut the image, select the** red circle, **click the** Edit menu, **then click** Paste in Back

   The image is now behind the red circle in the stacking order, which means you can position the red circle over the globe image and use it as a clipping mask to mask the image.

5. **Position the red circle over the globe image, as shown in Figure E-14**

6. **Select both the** globe image **and the** red circle, **click the** Object menu, **point to** Clipping Mask, **then click** Make

   The globe image is clipped by the red circle.

7. **Click the** View menu, **click** Outline, **then drag the center point of the clipped image to the right until it is aligned with the center point of the blue circle**

8. **Click the** View menu, **click** Preview, **deselect, compare your screen to Figure E-15, then save your work**

   You now have two hidden objects: the text group and the copy of the red circle.

Bitmap graphics vs. vector graphics

Digital images are called **bitmap** graphics because they are created with **pixels**—small squares of color that create the image, like tiles in a mosaic. This is in contrast to Illustrator's **vector graphics**, which are created with paths and fills. The key point to understand about vector graphics is that they are created based on mathematics; thus, they can be enlarged or reduced dramatically with no effect whatsoever on quality. This is not the case with bitmap graphics: whenever you scale pixels, it has an effect on the quality of the image. That effect is a negative effect, especially when you dramatically enlarge a bitmap graphic; the pixels start to show. Thus, whenever you incorporate bitmap graphics into your Illustrator artwork, it's a smart idea to do any manipulation to the image in Photoshop, then place it in Illustrator at the size you want to use it. Photoshop is much more adept at editing bitmap graphics.

Working with Text and Gradients

FIGURE E-13: Viewing the placed image

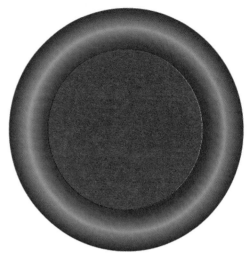

FIGURE E-14: Positioning the red circle

FIGURE E-15: Positioning the clipped image

Applying a Radial Gradient

Radial gradients are like concentric circles; the colors in radial gradients *radiate* outward from a small circle in the center and then get increasingly larger. When you use the Gradient tool with radial gradients, where you click represents the center of the radial gradient, and how far you drag from that center represents the length that the gradient will gradate outwardly from the center. With radial gradients, the Gradient tool presents a circular dotted line to show you the size at which the radial gradient will appear in the object. ▰▰ Jon tells you that the globe image looks good, but that it's competing with the headline. He suggests you solve the problem with color and says you should start by covering the globe with a radial gradient, which you can later make semi-transparent.

STEPS

1. **Click the Object menu, click Show All, then click the artboard to deselect all**

2. **Verify that the Fill button ▢ is selected on the Tools panel or the Swatches panel, select the red circle, then click the Radial Gradient swatch on the Swatches panel, as shown in Figure E-16**

3. **On the Gradient panel, click the right (black) color stop, press and hold [Alt] (Win) or [option] (Mac), then click the CMYK Cyan swatch on the Swatches panel**

   The gradient changes from black to cyan. Now you can specify how you want the radial gradient to fill the circle.

4. **Click the Gradient tool ▦**

   Because the circle is already filled with a gradient, the gradient annotator bar becomes visible. You could use the gradient annotator to modify the existing gradient fill, but instead you are going to redraw the gradient entirely.

5. **Position your cursor as shown in Figure E-17**

6. **Using Figure E-18 as a guide, click and drag towards the center of the circle, releasing where shown in the figure**

   Where you click is where the gradient starts, and where you release is where the gradient ends. The dotted circle indicates the circumference of the radial gradient as you drag.

7. **Deselect, then compare your result to Figure E-19**

   The gradient starts with white and radiates out to cyan. Outside of the gradient area, the remainder of the circle is solid cyan.

8. **Click the Swatches panel menu button ▦, click New Swatch, type Blue Sphere in the Swatch Name text box, then click OK**

9. **Save your work**

FIGURE E-16: Identifying the Radial Gradient swatch

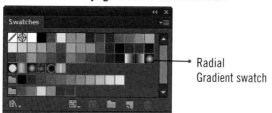

Radial Gradient swatch

FIGURE E-17: Positioning the Gradient tool

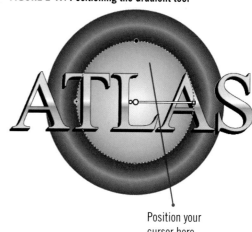

Position your cursor here

FIGURE E-18: Redrawing the radial gradient fill

Stop dragging here and release the mouse pointer

FIGURE E-19: Viewing the radial gradient

Start   End

About the gradient annotator

Whenever you select an object with a gradient fill and then click the Gradient tool, the gradient annotator appears on the object itself. The annotator shows you the length and angle of the gradient. The large circle on one end indicates the start of the gradient, and the small square at the other end indicates the end of the gradient. You can think of the gradient annotator as an option for editing the gradient fill locally. If you float the cursor over the gradient annotator, color stops appear on the annotator, as shown in Figure E-20. You can click and drag the color stops to modify the way the gradient fills the object. You can also click and drag the gradient annotator itself to move the gradient to another location on the object or to rotate the gradient, thus changing the angle of how it fills the object. Any changes you make on the gradient annotator will be updated on the Gradient panel, and vice versa.

FIGURE E-20: The gradient annotator

Making an Object Transparent

Opacity is derived from the word opaque. When an object is opaque, you cannot see through it. In Illustrator, the term **opacity** refers to how opaque the fill or stroke of an object is. You specify an object's opacity on the **Transparency panel**. When an Illustrator object has 100% opacity, you can't see through it. If an object has 0% opacity, it is completely transparent and therefore can't be seen. With any opacity value in the middle—let's say 50% opacity, for example—the result is semi-transparent, and that can create some interesting visual effects in Illustrator artwork. Jon suggests that you make the new gradient semi-transparent, which will appear to add color to the globe and integrate it more into the logo illustration.

STEPS

1. **Click the Window menu, then click Transparency**

   The Transparency panel opens. When you select an object or objects on the artboard, they appear in the preview section of the Transparency panel.

2. **Click the Selection tool, then click the blue circle with the radial gradient fill**

   A preview of the blue circle appears as a thumbnail view on the Transparency panel, as shown in Figure E-21.

3. **On the Transparency panel, click the Opacity list arrow, then click 0%**

   The blue circle becomes invisible.

4. **Change the Opacity to 50%, deselect the blue circle, then compare your screen to Figure E-22**

   The blue circle colorizes the globe, bringing it into the same color palette as other parts of the illustration. Also, the blue circle reduces the brightness and contrast of the globe. Therefore, the globe no longer competes with the ATLAS text for attention. As a result, the simple blue semi-transparent circle is a unifying element and does great work in integrating the globe into the illustration.

5. **Save your work**

About blending modes

The Transparency panel also includes a menu of blending modes. Blending modes are preset mathematical algorithms that create different color effects when different color objects overlap. You simply select one or more objects, then choose a blending mode from the Transparency panel. Most of what you do with blending modes is experimentation. After a while, you'll become familiar with the various modes and the effects they produce.

FIGURE E-21: Transparency panel

Preview of selected object

Opacity value

FIGURE E-22: Viewing the semi-transparent circle and its effect

Creating Text on a Path

You use the Type on a Path tool to position type on curved paths, straight paths, and on objects, such as a circle. If you select type on a path with the Selection tool, both the text and the path on which the text has been set are selected. When the Type on a Path tool is selected, a center bracket appears on the path that can be dragged to move the text along the path or to position it on the other side of the path. Once you've placed type on a path, you use the Character panel to format the text just like any other text element in Illustrator. A baseline shift is one formatting option that becomes very useful when working with type on a path. A **baseline shift** specifies how far above or below the path the text is positioned. A positive value positions the text above the path, a negative value below the path. ▄▄▄▄ To finish the illustration, Jon asks that you add text to the outer blue gradient that circles around the center globe.

STEPS

1. Click the Selection tool ▶, then click the blue circle filled with the Blue Sphere gradient

2. Press [Ctrl][Shift][M] (Win) or [Shift]⌘[M] (Mac) to open the Move dialog box, type –5.5 in the Horizontal text box, type 0 in the Vertical text box, then click Copy

   You will use the copy of the circle as the path for the text. You wouldn't want to place text on the original blue sphere circle because an object loses its fill color when it serves as a path for text.

3. Click and hold the Type tool **T**, select the Type on a Path tool ◥, then click the path of the copied blue circle at approximately the 11 o'clock position

   The circle's fill disappears, and a blinking cursor appears on the path.

   QUICK TIP

   If you do not have Arial Black, use a similar font.

4. Set the font to Arial (Win) or Arial Black (Mac), set the font style to Black (Win), set the font size to 36 pt, then type EVENT TV

   QUICK TIP

   The center bracket is sensitive and can produce some unexpected results when you drag it. Use the Undo command if you need to start over.

5. Click ▶, then click and drag the center bracket slowly to center the text over the top of the circle, as shown in Figure E-23

   You can use the center bracket to move the text around the outside of the circle. If you drag the center bracket toward the center of the circle, you can drag the text around the inside of the circle.

6. Open the Move dialog box, type 5.5 in the Horizontal text box, type 0 in the Vertical text box, then click OK

   Now you're ready to move the text up so that it is centered between the globe and the edge of the blue outer circle.

7. Click the Character panel menu button ▤, click Show Options to expand the panel, then type 14 in the Set the baseline shift text box

   The baseline of the text is repositioned 14 points outside of the circle.

8. Verify that the circle is still selected, set the fill color for the type to C=0 M=0 Y=0 K=5 (very light gray), then apply a 1-pt black stroke

9. Double-click the Rotate tool ↻, type 180 in the Angle text box, then click Copy

10. Select all, double-click ↻, type 20 in the Angle text box, click OK, deselect all, then compare your screen to Figure E-24

11. Save your work, then close atlas_AI-E.ai

FIGURE E-23: Using the center bracket to position the text

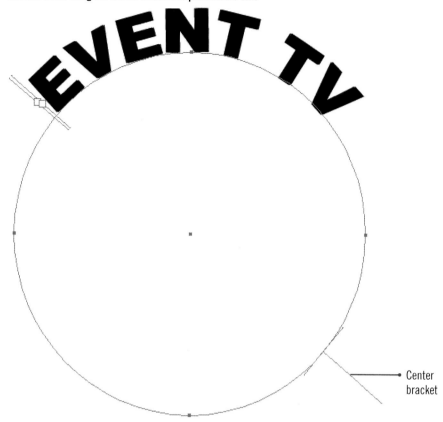

Center bracket

FIGURE E-24: Viewing the final illustration

Practice

Concepts Review

Label the elements of the Illustrator screen shown in Figure E-25.

FIGURE E-25

Match each term with the statement that best describes it.

6. **Kerning**
7. **Baseline shift**
8. **Radial gradient**
9. **Opacity**
10. **Gradient annotator**
11. **Gradient slider**

a. Represents the gradient fill on the Gradient panel
b. The amount of transparency applied to an object
c. Changes the space between two characters
d. Appears on an object filled with a gradient and shows how the gradient was built
e. Colors radiate from center
f. How far above or below the path the text is positioned

Select the best answer from the list of choices.

12. To insert bitmap images into Illustrator, use the _____ command.

   a. Import

   b. Insert

   c. Place

   d. Picture

13. The basic concept of a(n) _____ is to offset a black copy of text behind the main text.

   a. drop shadow

   b. gradient

   c. outline

   d. linear gradient

14. An object with 50% opacity applied is _____.

   a. opaque

   b. semi-transparent

   c. completely invisible

   d. blended

15. The midpoint of two colors is represented by a _____.

   a. triangle

   b. bar

   c. diamond

   d. square

Skills Review

1. Create a gradient.

   a. Open AI E-2.ai from the location where you store your Data Files, then save it as **green_AI-E**.

   b. Click the Selection tool, click the orange circle, then click the Linear Gradient swatch on the Swatches panel.

   c. Display the Gradient panel, click the Type list arrow, click Radial, then click the first color stop.

   d. Press and hold [Alt] (Win) or [option] (Mac), click Black on the Swatches panel, click the second color stop, press and hold [Alt] (Win) or [option] (Mac), then click C=90 M=30 Y=95 K=30 (dark green) on the Swatches panel.

   e. Position the mouse pointer just below the gradient slider on the Gradient panel so that you see a + (plus sign) next to the small white arrow, then click to add a new color stop.

   f. Press and hold [Alt] (Win) or [option] (Mac), then click C=50 M=0 Y=100 K=0 (lime green) on the Swatches panel.

   g. Double-click the Location text box on the Gradient panel, type **86**, then press [Enter] (Win) or [return] (Mac).

   h. Drag the midpoint slider between the first and second color stops on the gradient slider to the right until the Location text box reads approximately 55.

   i. Click the Swatches panel menu button, click New Swatch, type **Green Radial** in the Swatch Name text box, then click OK.

   j. Save your work.

2. Create and format text.

   a. Click the View menu, click Fit Artboard in Window, click the Type tool, then click on the left side of the artboard.

   b. Type **GREEN** in capital letters, then click the Selection tool.

   c. Click the Window menu, point to Type, then click Character to show the Character panel.

   d. Set the font to Times New Roman Regular.

   e. Set the font size to 146.

   f. Click the Type tool, then click between the letter *G* and the letter *R*.

   g. On the Character panel, select the value in the Kerning text box, type **–25**, then press [Enter] (Win) or [return] (Mac).

   h. Click between the first letter *E* and the second letter *E*, then change the kerning value to **–25** on the Character panel.

   i. Click between the second letter *E* and the letter *N*, then change the kerning value to **–25** on the Character panel.

   j. Save your work.

3. Use the Gradient tool.

   a. Click the Selection tool, verify that the GREEN text is selected, click the Type menu, then click Create Outlines.

   b. Click the Green Radial gradient swatch on the Swatches panel.

   c. On the Gradient panel, click the Type list arrow, click Linear, then change the location of the middle color stop to 60%.

   d. Click the first color stop on the gradient slider, press and hold [Alt] (Win) or [option] (Mac), then click the C=0 M=0 Y=0 K=10 (light gray) swatch on the Swatches panel.

Skills Review (continued)

 e. Click the last color stop on the gradient slider, press and hold [Alt] (Win) or [option] (Mac), then click White on the Swatches panel.

 f. Click the Gradient tool, press and hold [Shift], then click and drag from the left of the letter "G" to the right of the letter "N."

 g. Press and hold [Shift], drag the Gradient tool from the top of the letter *R* to the bottom of the letter *R*, click the Selection tool, then deselect all.

 h. Click the Swatches panel menu button, click New Swatch, type **Green Linear** in the Swatch Name text box, then click OK.

4. Create a drop shadow for text.

 a. Click the Selection tool, select the GREEN text, copy the text, click the Edit menu, then click Paste in Back.

 b. Fill the selection with Black, press ▼ five times, press ◄ five times, then deselect.

 c. Select the GREEN text filled with the gradient, click the Edit menu, click Paste in Front, click the Object menu, point to Hide, then click Selection.

FIGURE E-26

 d. Select the original GREEN text, fill it with Black, then select both the black GREEN text and the black drop shadow text.

 e. Double-click the Blend tool to open the Blend Options dialog box, click the Spacing list arrow, click Specified Steps, type **256**, then click OK.

 f. Click the Object menu, point to Blend, then click Make.

 g. Click the Object menu, click Show All, click the Selection tool, then deselect all.

 h. Select the GREEN text filled with the gradient, then apply a .75-pt black stroke to it.

 i. Click and drag the Selection tool around all the text to select it all, click the Object menu, then click Group.

FIGURE E-27

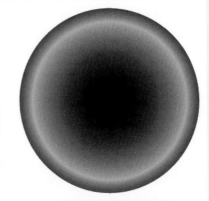

 j. Position the group as shown in Figure E-26, then save your work.

5. Place a bitmap image.

 a. Select the grouped text, hide it, select the red circle, then copy it.

 b. Click the Edit menu, click Paste in Front, then hide the copy.

 c. Click the File menu, click Place, navigate to the location where you store your Data Files, click Silver Globe.psd, then click Place.

FIGURE E-28

 d. Drag the globe image to the left side of the circles.

 e. Click the Edit menu, click Cut, select the red circle, click the Edit menu, then click Paste in Back.

 f. Position the red circle over the globe image, as shown in Figure E-27.

 g. Select both the silver globe image and the red circle, click the Object menu, point to Clipping Mask, then click Make.

 h. Click and drag the clipped image so that it is positioned on top of the artwork, as shown in Figure E-28.

 i. Save your work.

Skills Review (continued)

6. **Apply a radial gradient.**

   a. Click the Object menu, click Show All, then click the artboard to deselect all.

   b. Select the red circle, then click the Radial Gradient swatch on the Swatches panel.

   c. On the Gradient panel, click the right (black) color stop, press and hold [Alt] (Win) or [option] (Mac), then click the C=75 M=0 Y=100 K=0 (medium green) swatch on the Swatches panel.

   d. Click the Swatches panel menu button, click New Swatch, type **Green Sphere** in the Swatch Name text box, then click OK.

   e. Save your work.

7. **Make an object transparent.**

   a. Click the Window menu, then click Transparency to show the Transparency panel, if necessary.

   b. Click the Selection tool, then click the green inner circle, if necessary.

   c. On the Transparency panel, click the Opacity list arrow, then click 0%.

   d. Change the Opacity to 25%, then save your work.

8. **Create text on a path.**

   a. Verify that the small inner circle filled with the Green Sphere gradient is still selected.

   b. Press [Ctrl][Shift][M] (Win) or [Shift]⌘[M] (Mac) to open the Move dialog box, type **−5.5** in the Horizontal text box, type **0** in the Vertical text box, then click Copy.

   c. Click and hold the Type tool, select the Type on a Path tool, then click the path of the copied circle at approximately the 11 o'clock position.

   d. On the Character panel, set the font to Arial Black, set the font size to 30 pt. (*Hint*: Choose a similar font if you do not have Arial Black.)

   e. Type **A NEW EARTH**, then click the Selection tool.

   f. Click and drag the center bracket slowly to center the text over the top of the circle, if necessary, as shown in Figure E-29.

   g. Open the Move dialog box, type **5.5** in the Horizontal text box, type **0** in the Vertical text box, then click OK.

   h. Click the Character panel menu button, click Show Options to expand the panel if necessary, then type **16** in the Set the baseline shift text box.

   i. Verify that the circle is still selected, set the fill color for the type to C=0 M=0 Y=0 K=5 (very light gray), then apply a 1-pt black stroke.

   j. Double-click the Rotate tool, type **180** in the Angle text box, then click Copy.

   k. Select all, double-click the Rotate tool, type **20** in the Angle text box, click OK, deselect all, then compare your screen to Figure E-30.

   l. Save your work, then close green_AI-E.ai.

FIGURE E-29

FIGURE E-30

Independent Challenge 1

Your town's local high school swim team has made it to the finals to compete for the national title. You create a sign for your storefront window showing your support.

a. Open the file AI E-3.ai from the location where you store your Data Files, then save it as **tigers_AI-E**.

b. Convert the text to outlines, then click the Linear Gradient swatch on the Swatches panel.

c. Change the first color stop to Burnt Sienna. (*Hint*: Press and hold [Alt] (Win) or [option] (Mac) when choosing the new color.)

d. Create a new color stop between the first and second color stops, then change its color to Mustard.

e. Change the location of the middle color stop to 70%.

f. Save the gradient as a new gradient swatch named **Desert Sun**.

g. Click the Gradient tool, then drag from the top of the letter *T* to the bottom of the letter *T*.

h. Click the Rectangle tool, then create a rectangle that surrounds the text and fill it with the Desert Sun gradient.

i. Click the Gradient tool, then drag the Gradient tool from the bottom of the rectangle to the top of the rectangle.

j. Click the Object menu, point to Arrange, then click Send to Back.

FIGURE E-31

k. Apply a 1-pt black stroke to **GO TIGERS!**.

l. Deselect, save your work, then compare your screen to Figure E-31.

Advanced Challenge Exercise

- Click the Selection tool, then click the background rectangle.
- Fill the rectangle with Black.
- Select the GO TIGERS! text, then click the Swap Fill and Stroke button on the Tools panel so that the Desert Sun gradient is applied to the stroke and the text is filled with Black.
- Click the Stroke panel icon to open the Stroke panel, then change the width of the stroke to 4 pt.

m. Close tigers_AI-E.ai.

Independent Challenge 2

Your boss has asked you to teach your co-workers how to create different gradient fills using one gradient. You create a linear gradient and then demonstrate how to change its appearance using the gradient annotator.

a. Open the file AI E-4.ai from the location where you store your Data Files, then save it as **gradient lesson_AI-E**.

b. Click the Selection tool, then select the square on the artboard.

c. Click the Gradient tool and notice the gradient annotator that appears on the gradient fill.

d. Position the mouse pointer over the gradient annotator until the color stops appear on the gradient ramp.

e. Position the mouse pointer directly outside of the diamond shape on the right side of the gradient annotator until you see the rotate icon, then drag slowly counter-clockwise.

f. Release the mouse pointer, then view the new Angle value on the Gradient panel.

g. Drag the Gradient tool pointer from the left edge of the artboard to the right side of the artboard, then drag the Gradient tool pointer from the upper-left corner of the square to the lower-right corner of the square.

h. Drag the Gradient tool pointer from the top edge of the artboard to the bottom edge of the artboard, then drag the Gradient tool pointer horizontally about one inch in length in the center of the square.

i. Press and hold [Shift], drag the circle icon on the left side of the gradient annotator to the left edge of the square, then drag the diamond icon on the gradient annotator to the right edge of the square so that the original gradient fill is restored.

Independent Challenge 2 (continued)

Advanced Challenge Exercise

- Click the square filled with the gradient to select it.
- Click the Gradient tool.
- Delete the two white color stops from the gradient annotator by dragging them off of the gradient annotator.
- On the Gradient panel, drag the middle color stop to the left so that its location is at 15%.
- Add a new color stop to the right of the middle color stop, then change its color to CYMK Yellow.

FIGURE E-32

j. Save your work, compare your screen to Figure E-32, then close gradient lesson_AI-E.ai.

Independent Challenge 3

You work at a television station where you design posters and advertisements for the station's website. Your boss asks you to come up with a design for a new documentary about ice fishing named *On Thin Ice*. You rely on your knowledge of gradients and drop shadows to make an interesting title.

a. Create a new 6" × 6" document, then save it as **thin ice_AI-E**.

b. Type **ON THIN ICE**, using 48-pt font size and a bold font of your choice. (*Hint*: The font used in Figure E-33 is Arial Black.)

c. On the Character panel, change the Vertical Scale to 50% or another value that makes the text appear shorter.

d. Convert the text to outlines.

e. On the Swatches panel, click the Fading Sky swatch.

f. Change the first color stop to white.

g. Change the last color stop to black, then change the Opacity value of the last color stop to 100%.

h. Drag the Gradient tool from the exact bottom to the exact top of the letters.

i. Copy the letters, then paste them in front.

j. Fill the copied letters in front with White.

k. Using your arrow keys, move the white letters two points to the left and three points up.

l. Switch to the Selection tool to deselect, save your work, then compare your text with Figure E-33.

m. Close thin ice_AI-E.ai.

FIGURE E-33

Real Life Independent Challenge

Think of a possible part-time job you would like. Design a business card for yourself using your name, title, telephone number, e-mail address, and any design element that you like. Be sure to include at least one gradient fill and a drop shadow.

a. Start Illustrator, open the file AI E-5.ai from the location where you store your Data Files, then save it as **my card_AI-E**. (*Hint*: The rectangle on the artboard represents the business card.)

b. Use the Type tool to create text for the card.

c. Display the Character panel, then format the text as you wish.

d. Create a simple design or logo for the card.

e. Create a new gradient, then save it as **My Gradient** on the Swatches panel.

f. Apply the My Gradient swatch to the text, graphics, or both.

g. Create a drop shadow for one piece of text.

h. Save your work, then close my card_AI-E.ai.

Visual Workshop

Start Illustrator, open the file AI E-6.ai, then save it as **atoms_AI-E**. Using Figure E-34 as a guide, use the shape tools and the Gradient panel to recreate the artwork shown in the figure. (*Hint*: Use the Rounded Rectangle tool to create the yellow connectors with the rounded edges.) Save your work, compare your screen to Figure E-34, then close atoms_AI-E.ai.

FIGURE E-34

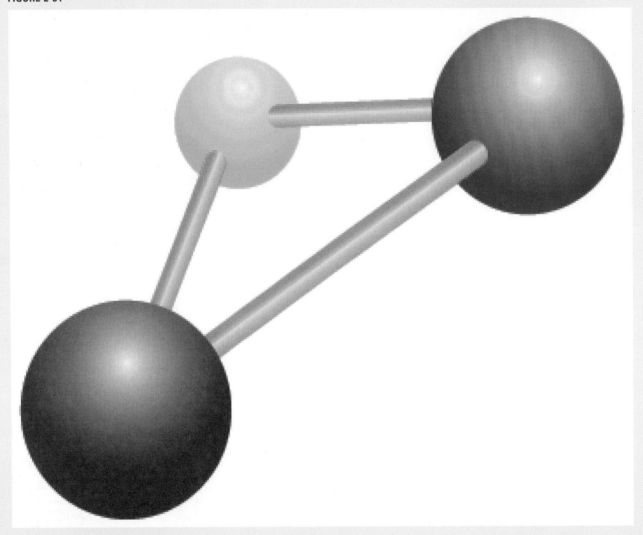

Drawing in Illustrator

Files You Will Need:

To view a list of files needed for this unit, see the Data Files Grid in the back of the book.

Illustrator is essentially a drawing program, and any time you create an object, you're drawing. If you make a circle, you're drawing a circle. However, when designers refer to "drawing" in Illustrator, they're talking about creating original, unique shapes, and that type of work is done with the Pen tool. The Pen tool is the primary drawing tool in Illustrator; with it, you can create straight and curved paths, and thus create all types of unique objects. Illustrator offers a number of other great features to help you draw complex and visually interesting graphics. Use the Image Trace feature to trace photographs or your own hand-drawn sketches as Illustrator artwork. Once you're done drawing, you'll find that the brushes on the Brushes panel offer some of the most exciting options for bringing your drawings to life. Jon asks you to create a series of exercises demonstrating how to trace placed images and how to use the Pen tool to modify paths and to create original shapes.

OBJECTIVES

Trace artwork with Image Trace

Use the Pen tool

Join paths and points

Draw curved paths

Reverse the direction of a path

Outline a stroke

Create an art brush

Apply brushes

Create pseudo strokes

Tracing Artwork with Image Trace

The Image Trace feature in Illustrator is one of the most powerful features in the entire application. Essentially, it allows you to convert a digital image into individual Illustrator objects. Whenever you place an image, the Image Trace feature becomes available on the Control panel. The Tracing Presets menu offers a number of built-in tracing presets that will trace the artwork with a variety of results. Some will create black-and-white artwork. Some will trace the artwork based on color and reproduce the image with colored objects. And the most powerful presets will create thousands of Illustrator objects to reproduce the artwork with the appearance of a continuous tone photograph. Jon gives you a piece of low-resolution clip art that he wants to use on a poster. He asks that you trace the digital image to recreate it as a resolution-independent vector graphic.

STEPS

1. **Start Illustrator, create a new 8" × 8" document, save it as image trace_AI-F, click the Window menu, then verify that Control is checked**

2. **Click the File menu, click Place, navigate to the location where your Data Files are stored, click the file named Ram.tif, then click Place**
    As shown in Figure F-1, the Image Trace feature is available on the Control panel when a placed file is selected. Ram.tif is a digital image that was created in Photoshop.

3. **On the Control panel, click the Tracing Presets list arrow (next to the Image Trace button) to expose the list of tracing presets, then click Black and White Logo**
    The Control panel changes to show the default settings at which the artwork is traced. The artwork does not appear to change, even though it has been traced.

4. **Click the Expand button on the Control panel, then compare your screen to Figure F-2**
    When you click the Expand button, the bounding box disappears and the traced artwork becomes selected as an Illustrator object. The object is fully editable, just like any Illustrator object.

5. **Deselect all, then click the Direct Selection tool**

6. **Click the image of the ram**

7. **Apply a fill of CMYK Red and a stroke of None to the selected artwork**

8. **Save your work, then close image trace_AI-F.ai**

Expanding in Illustrator

You can think of the term "expand" in Illustrator as being a synonym for "make it selectable." Expand is used for a number of different procedures, but in most, if not all cases, the result is that objects that weren't selectable become selectable. For example, if you create a blend between two objects, the intermediary objects are not selectable. But if you expand the blend, all the intermediate objects can then be selected. Similarly, if you create a rectangle with a red fill and a black stroke, you can use the Expand command on the Object menu to select the fill independently from the stroke as though they were two separate objects. When you trace with the Image Trace utility, the traced image remains in the same bounding box that appears when the image is first placed. If you want to select the paths and points of the traced object, you must first expand the traced path. So, in general, if there's an object you want to select but can't, click the Object menu to see if the Expand command is available.

FIGURE F-1: **Image Trace on the Control panel**

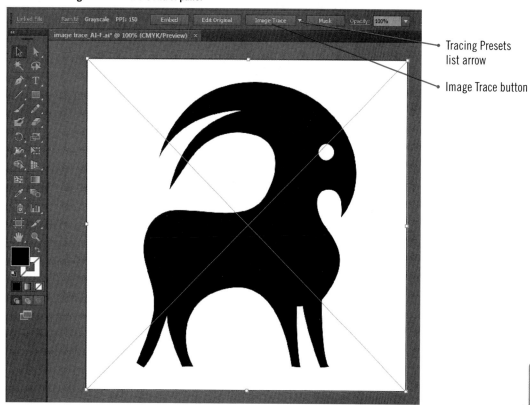

Tracing Presets
list arrow

Image Trace button

FIGURE F-2: **Expanding the traced artwork**

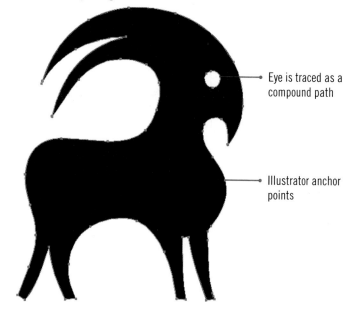

Eye is traced as a
compound path

Illustrator anchor
points

Using the Pen Tool

Ultimately, mastering Illustrator involves mastering the Pen tool. When you draw with the Pen tool, you create two types of paths: straight paths and curved paths. Similarly, you create two types of anchor points: **corner points** and **smooth points**. Corner points join path segments at an angle. Smooth points join curved paths with a smooth arc. When you click to create anchor points with the Pen tool, straight paths appear, automatically connecting the points. To create curved paths, you click and drag with the Pen tool to create smooth points. Curved paths will be created as you drag with the Pen tool, and the smooth point will show direction handles. **Direction handles** determine the length and arc of the curved paths associated with the smooth point. You can use the Add Anchor Point or Remove Anchor Point tool to add or remove anchor points from a path. You can also use the Convert Anchor Point tool to convert an anchor point from a corner point to a smooth point, or vice versa. ▨▨▨ Jon asks you to demonstrate how to create straight paths with the Pen tool, add an anchor point to a path, then convert the added anchor point from a corner point to a smooth point.

STEPS

1. **Open the file AI F-1.ai from the location where your Data Files are stored, save it as flower sketch pad_AI-F, click the Selection tool ▶, then click the image on the artboard to select it**

   The sketch is a drawing that we will re-create as Illustrator artwork using the Pen tool.

2. **Click the Object menu, point to Hide, then click Selection to hide the selection**

   The artboard shows various sketch components of the flower illustration for you to trace.

3. **Click the View menu, then click Vase at the bottom of the View menu**

   The Vase view of the artboard fills the screen.

4. **Click the Pen tool ✒, set the fill color to None, set the stroke color to CMYK Red, then set the stroke weight to 2 pt**

5. **Click the blue X beside the number 1, click the blue X at number 2, click the blue X at number 3, then compare your artwork to Figure F-3**

   Each time you click, you add an anchor point, and straight paths are automatically drawn between the anchor points. A description of the four types of Pen tools is on the facing page in Table F-1.

6. **Position the Pen tool over the path halfway between points 2 and 3 until you see a plus sign appear beside the tool ✒₊, then click the path**

   A new anchor point is added to the path where you click.

7. **Click the Direct Selection tool ▶, then drag the new anchor point left to the pink star, as shown in Figure F-4**

   The new point is a **corner point**. Attached to it are two straight paths that meet at an angle at the anchor point.

8. **Press and hold ✒ to expose the hidden tools, select the Convert Anchor Point tool ▶, position it over the new corner anchor point, then click and drag toward the bottom of the artboard until your path resembles Figure F-5**

   The corner anchor point is converted to a **smooth point**. Attached to it are two curved paths that meet at the anchor point at a smooth curve. The anchor point shows direction handles that define the arc of the curved paths attached to the anchor point.

9. **Save your work**

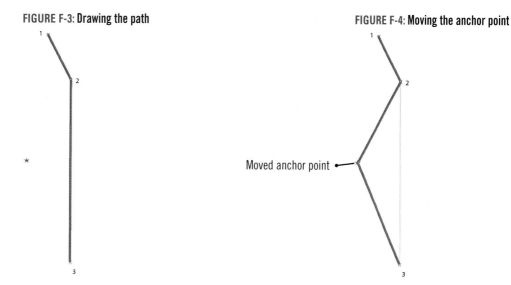

FIGURE F-3: Drawing the path

FIGURE F-4: Moving the anchor point

Moved anchor point

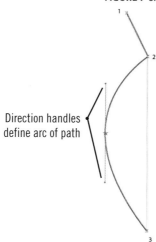

FIGURE F-5: Converting the anchor point to a smooth point

Direction handles
define arc of path

TABLE F-1: Four types of Pen tools

tool name	tool icon	tool function
Pen tool		Creates anchor points and paths. Click to create corner points and straight paths. Click and drag to create smooth points and curved paths.
Add Anchor Point tool		Appears when you position the Pen tool over a selected path. Click the path to add an anchor point.
Delete Anchor Point tool		Appears when you position the Pen tool over an anchor point. Click the point to remove it.
Convert Anchor Point tool		Converts anchor points from corner to smooth or vice versa. Click a smooth point and it becomes a corner point. Click and drag a corner point, and it becomes a smooth point. Click and drag a direction handle on a smooth point, and the point becomes a corner point; the two direction handles associated with the point will move independently of one another.

Joining Paths and Points

Use the Join command to join any two open anchor points. If the two anchor points are positioned in the same location, the Join command will unite them as one point. If the two points are not in the same location, the Join command will draw a straight path between them to join them. The Join command often plays a role when you are using the "draw/flip" technique. With this technique, you draw only half of an object. For example, let's say you are drawing a peppermill. Rather than draw the whole object, simply draw the left half of the object. Then, create a reflected copy and join the two paths with the Join command. Jon asks that you demonstrate the "draw/flip" technique to quickly draw the vase, even though it's not a symmetrically balanced object.

STEPS

TROUBLE
The Reflect tool may be hidden beneath the Rotate tool on the Tools panel.

1. Click the Selection tool, select the entire path, then click the Reflect tool

2. Verify that the rulers are showing, then press and hold [Alt] (Win) or [option] (Mac), then click approximately ½" to the right of the number 2

   The Reflect dialog box opens, offering options for reflecting, or "flipping," a copy of the path.

3. In the Axis section, click the Vertical option button, then click Copy

   As shown in Figure F-6, a copy of the path is reflected across the Vertical axis at the point you clicked.

4. Click the Direct Selection tool, then draw a selection marquee to select just the top anchor points on each of the paths

5. Click the Object menu, point to Path, then click Join

6. Select the bottom two anchor points, then press [Ctrl][J] (Win) or ⌘[J] (Mac) to join the two bottom anchor points and create one closed path, as shown in Figure F-7

7. Click, select the entire path, then reposition it over the sketch of the vase to the right labeled Vase End

8. Deselect, click, click one edge of the vase, then drag each anchor point into place to reshape your path to match that of the sketch, as shown in Figure F-8

9. Save your work

FIGURE F-6: **Reflected path**

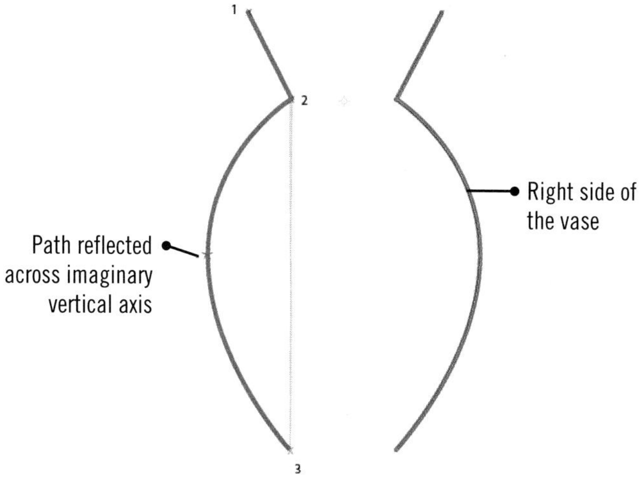

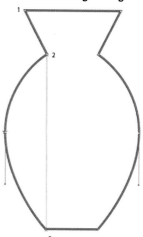

Path reflected across imaginary vertical axis

Right side of the vase

FIGURE F-7: **Viewing the single closed path**

FIGURE F-8: **Reshaping the object**

Using the Average command

The Average command is listed with the Join command on the Object/Path menu because the two work hand in hand. Many times, when joining two points, you're going to want to verify their position. For example, you might want to be sure that they're aligned on the horizontal or vertical axis. Or, if you're joining two paths at a corner, you might want to verify that the two anchor points being joined are in the exact same location. This is where the Average command comes in. Select two points and, before joining them, open the Average dialog box and choose how you want the points to be aligned. It's a great technique for keeping your illustrations in perfect alignment.

Drawing Curved Paths

UNIT F

Illustrator CS6

You draw curved paths by clicking and dragging the Pen tool to create smooth points. You can then manipulate the direction handles to modify the curved paths. The technique is not difficult, but what does require some practice and experience is developing a sense of where to place anchor points to draw a desired curve. This lesson is designed to help you develop that sense. As you follow along, note where you are placing the anchor points vis-à-vis the curves you are drawing, and how far you are dragging the direction handles to position the curve. Jon instructs you to develop a tracing exercise to help the designers develop a sense of how and where to place anchor points to trace a curved path.

STEPS

TROUBLE

The Pen tool may be hidden beneath the Convert Anchor Point tool.

1. Click the View menu, click Petal at the bottom of the menu, then click the Pen tool 🖊

2. Click the blue X at #1

3. Position the Pen tool over the blue X at #2, then in one move, click and drag to the first pink star, as shown in Figure F-9

   You have drawn a curved path between two points.

4. Position the Pen tool over the next blue X, then in one move, click and drag to the next pink star

5. Using this method, continue drawing until you finish point #8 and your path resembles Figure F-10

6. Position the Pen tool over the blue X at #9, then in one move, click and drag to the pink star

7. Position the Pen tool over the anchor point you created at #1

   A small circle appears beside the Pen tool, indicating that you will close the path when you click this point.

8. In one move, click and drag to the black star above #1, as shown in Figure F-11

   The path is closed. The handle you drag to the black star will not be visible.

9. Save your work

Restarting a path

Inevitably, when working with the Pen tool, the time will come when you'll need to restart a path that's been deselected. It sounds simple, but it can get a little bit tricky. For example, if you select the last point on the path with the Direct Selection tool then start drawing with the Pen tool, the Pen tool will start a new path that is not connected to the original. If you click the last point on the path with the Pen tool, the point's direction handle will be removed. So, the best method for restarting a deselected path is to click and drag the last point of the path. When you do so, click and drag a handle in the direction that you want to continue, then keep on drawing.

FIGURE F-9: Drawing the first path

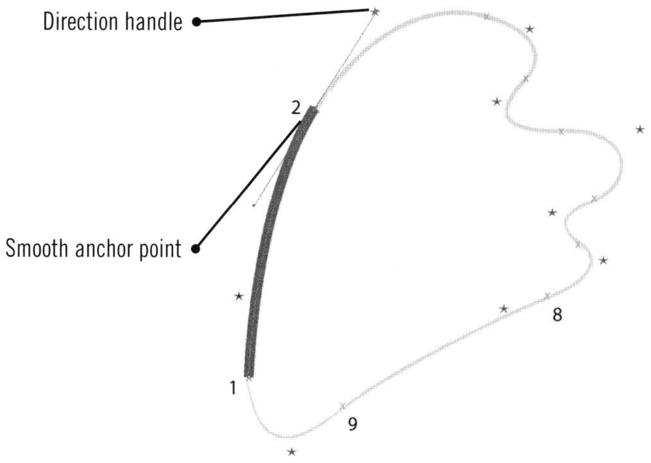

Direction handle
2
Smooth anchor point
8
1
9

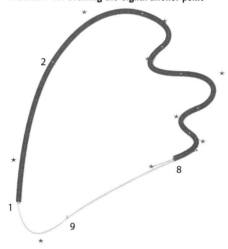

FIGURE F-10: Drawing the eighth anchor point

2
8
1
9

FIGURE F-11: Closing the path

2
Black star
8
1
9

Illustrator CS6

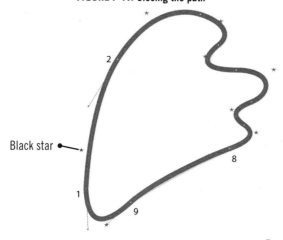

Reversing the Direction of a Path

When you draw a smooth point, it's important that you understand that the direction handles determine the "flow" of the path. In other words, when you click and drag a direction handle in a specific direction, that direction handle actually directs the path to continue moving in that direction. In some cases, that's exactly what you'll want to do, but in other cases, you'll want the path to continue in an entirely different direction. In order to redirect the path, you'll need to change the position of the direction handle so that it points in the new direction that you want to continue toward. To do so, you use the Convert Anchor Point tool to move the direction handle. When you do, the smooth point is converted to a corner point, and the direction handle moves independently from the other handle associated with the anchor point. ▨▨▨▨ Jon wants you to demonstrate how to use the Convert Anchor Point tool to trace a path that suddenly reverses direction.

STEPS

1. **Click the View menu, click Blades at the bottom of the menu, then click the blue X at #1**

2. **Position the Pen tool ✐ over the blue X at #2, then in one move, click and drag to the first pink star, as shown in Figure F-12**

   The direction handle points the path in a northeast direction, but the gray "sketch" calls for the path to change direction drastically. You need to move the direction handle to point the path toward a new direction.

3. **Press and hold [Alt] (Win) or [option] (Mac) to change the Pen tool to the Convert Anchor Point tool ⌐**

   Pressing [Alt] (Win) or [option] (Mac) is the fastest and easiest way to access the Convert Anchor Point tool while drawing with the Pen tool.

4. **Position the Convert Anchor Point tool ⌐ over the direction handle at the pink star, then click and drag it to the green star, as shown in Figure F-13**

   Moving the direction handle with the Convert Anchor Point tool converts the anchor point to a corner point. The two direction handles attached to point #2 are now independent of one another, and the move did not affect the arc of the first path you drew. The moved direction handle now directs the path to arc toward point #3.

5. **Position the Pen tool ✐ over the blue X at point #3, then in one move, click and drag to the pink star below point #3**

   The point #3 direction handle directs the path to continue downward, but the gray "sketch" path goes directly to the left. Since it goes left in a straight line—not an arc—there's no need for a direction line.

6. **Position the Pen tool over the anchor point at point #3, then note that a small upside-down V appears next to the Pen tool**

   The upside-down V refers to the Convert Anchor Point tool icon. The anchor point will be converted when clicked.

7. **Click the anchor point at the #3 point**

   The direction handle is removed. The previous path—from point #2 to point #3—is not affected.

8. **Click the anchor point at the #1 point to close the path, compare your result to Figure F-14, then save your work**

FIGURE F-12: Viewing the second anchor point and direction handle **FIGURE F-13: Repositioning the direction handle**

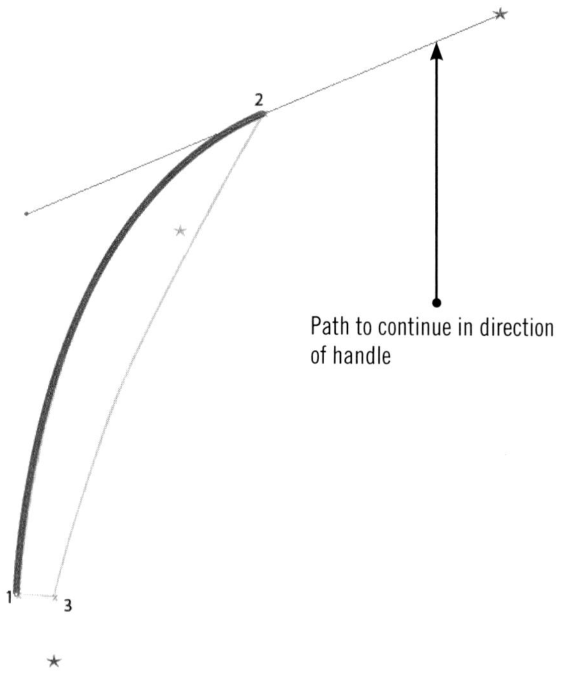

Path to continue in direction
of handle

Moved direction handle points
path in a new direction

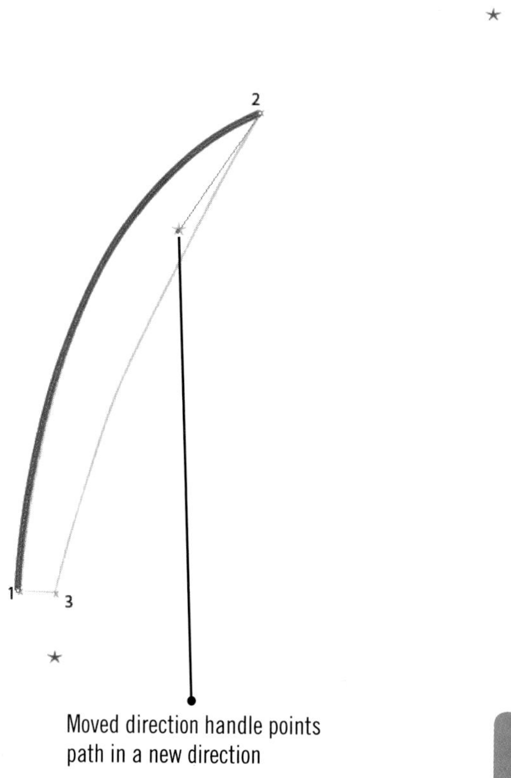

FIGURE F-14: Closing the path

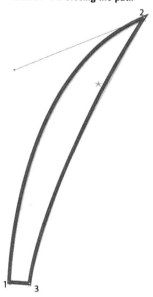

"Breaking" the direction handles

Remember that if you move a direction handle with the Convert Anchor Point tool, you convert the smooth point to a corner point. This is referred to as "breaking the handles." Even though the handles remain, the smooth point becomes a corner point, and the two direction handles will now function independently of one another. This is very useful for abrupt changes in the path you are drawing. However, if you want to convert the corner point back to a smooth point, simply click and drag with the Convert Anchor Point tool on the anchor point itself to create new "unbroken" handles.

Outlining a Stroke

The Outline Stroke command converts a path with a stroke into a filled object. The command traces the outline of the stroke at its current stroke weight, then converts the stroke into a filled object with that size. This can be especially useful if you're tracing a curved object: rather than draw both sides of the object, draw a single curved stroke, then outline it. ██████ Looking at the flower exercise, Jon suggests that you should demonstrate the Outline Stroke command as the quickest and easiest method for drawing the thin stem component of the illustration.

STEPS

1. Click the View menu, click Stem at the bottom of the menu, then click the Selection tool ▸

2. Select the red curved path, click the Stroke panel icon ▤ to open the Stroke panel, then increase the Weight to 6 pt

3. Click the Object menu, point to Path, click Outline Stroke, then compare your screen to Figure F-15

    The stroke is converted to a filled object.

4. Deselect, click the Direct Selection tool ▸, then reposition the anchor points on the red stem and manipulate the direction lines to align the object with the gray "sketch," as shown in Figure F-16

5. Using the skills you have learned, trace the remaining wisps, petals, blades, and centers using the appropriate views on the View menu

6. Save your work, then close flower sketch pad_AI-F.ai

FIGURE F-15: Outlined stroke

Stem

FIGURE F-16: Modifying the object

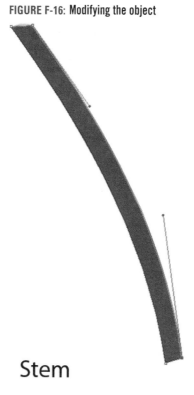

Stem

Outlining dashed and dotted strokes

Sometimes it's interesting to see how Illustrator features overlap. Let's say you create a 10-step blend between two circles of the same size. If you expand the blend, you're left with a row of 12 selectable circles. You can achieve the same result outlining a stroke. If you are working with a dotted stroke, the dots become independently selectable circles if you apply the Outline Stroke command to the stroke. This is a fine example of using two entirely different methods to achieve the same result.

Creating an Art Brush

In Illustrator, brushes are Illustrator objects that you paint with or apply to other objects as strokes. If you create an oval object, for example, you can save it to the Brushes panel as a new brush style. You could then use any of the brush tools to paint with the oval. You could also apply the oval brush as a stroke for an object—let's say a square. When you do so, the oval would be stretched around the square object to create a rounded stroke. Things get more interesting when you capture real artistic strokes—like a charcoal line, for example—as a digital image and then trace it in Illustrator. You can then use that traced object as a brush and apply a charcoal effect as an edge for your drawing. When you learn to work with them, you'll see that brushes are an important method for creating interesting and classic drawing effects. The design team is tasked with creating lots of original Illustrator artwork, and Jon asks that you demonstrate how to save a real-world texture as an art brush.

STEPS

1. Open the file AI F-2.ai from the location where your Data Files are stored, save it as flower brushes_AI-F, click the File menu, then click Place

2. Navigate to where your Data Files are stored, click the file named Pencil Lead.tif, then click Place

   As shown in Figure F-17, Pencil Lead.tif is a digital image of a line drawn with a pencil. The line has varying widths. The image was taken with a smartphone camera, brightened in Photoshop, then saved.

3. Click the Tracing Presets list arrow (next to the Image Trace button), then click Line Art

4. Click Expand on the Control panel

   The artwork is traced and converted to filled Illustrator objects.

5. Click the Brushes panel icon ▦, click the Brushes panel menu button ▤, verify that Thumbnail View is selected, then drag the bottom of the panel down until you see all the brushes in the panel

6. Click the Selection tool ▶, use Figure F-18 as a guide to drag the traced artwork over the empty gray area of the Brushes panel, then release the mouse button

   When the mouse pointer touches the Brushes panel, a plus sign appears next to the pointer, indicating that you are adding a new brush to the panel. When you release the mouse button, the New Brush dialog box opens.

7. Click the Art Brush option button, then click OK

   The Art Brush Options dialog box opens. In this dialog box, you can choose a name for the new brush, as well as other options, such as the direction of the brush stroke.

8. Type Pencil Lead in the Name text box, click the Method list arrow in the Colorization section, then click Tints and Shades

   Your dialog box should resemble Figure F-19. The Tints and Shades option allows you to apply different colors to the art brush after it's applied. For more information about colorization options, see the information in the next lesson called *Changing the color of brush strokes*.

9. Click OK to close the Art Brush Options dialog box

   The Pencil Lead brush appears on the Brushes panel. The brush thumbnail image is distorted to fit in the panel.

QUICK TIP
When you point to a brush on the Brushes panel, a tool tip appears showing the brush's name.

10. Verify that the traced brush artwork on the artboard is selected, click the Edit menu, click Cut, then save your work

    You no longer need the pencil lead artwork on the artboard.

FIGURE F-17: Viewing the placed image

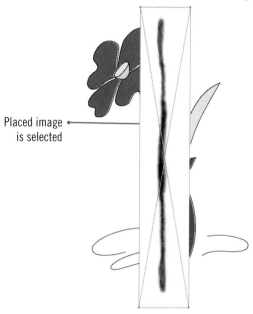

Placed image ●
is selected

FIGURE F-18: Dragging the traced artwork to the Brushes panel

FIGURE F-19: Art Brush Options dialog box

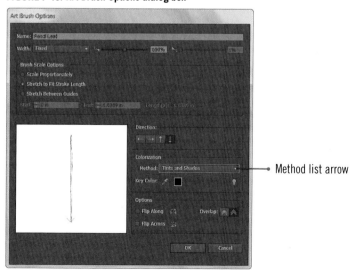

Method list arrow

UNIT
F

Illustrator CS6

Applying Brushes

There are five types of brushes in Illustrator: Calligraphic, Scatter, Art, Bristle, and Pattern. Of these, the Calligraphic and Art brushes are the most commonly used. To apply an art brush as a stroke to an object, you select the object and on the Brushes panel click the art brush you want to use. The brush artwork will stretch and wrap around the entire object, like a stroke. Use the Stroke panel to specify the weight of brush stroke. Jon asks you to demonstrate how the lead pencil texture you traced and saved as a brush can be applied to the artwork.

STEPS

1. **Evaluate the artwork in terms of shape, color, dimension, and its overall effect**

   The artwork has interesting shapes, and the colors work well together, but overall, the illustration is boring. It looks like what it is: a few Illustrator objects with color fills and a thin black stroke. The illustration is flat—it is not dynamic.

2. **Select all of the artwork on the artboard, click the View menu, then click Hide Edges**

3. **Click the Pencil Lead brush thumbnail on the Brushes panel**

   The Pencil Lead brush is applied as a stroke to the selected objects.

> **QUICK TIP**
> You can also change the Stroke properties on the Control panel.

4. **On the Stroke panel, reduce the weight of the stroke to .75 pt**

   The Stroke panel controls the weight of brushes applied as strokes to the artwork.

5. **Compare your artwork to Figure F-20**

   The Pencil Lead stroke, with its uneven and varying width, adds a sense of movement to the artwork. The illustration has come to life—it is dynamic and visually much more interesting.

6. **Click the Charcoal brush thumbnail on the Brushes panel**

   The Charcoal brush, a default brush, is applied to the artwork.

7. **On the Stroke panel, increase the stroke weight to 1 pt, then compare your screen to Figure F-21**

8. **Click the View menu, then click Show Edges**

9. **Save your work**

Drawing in Illustrator

FIGURE F-20: Evaluating the Pencil Lead brush applied

FIGURE F-21: Viewing the Charcoal brush applied

Illustrator CS6

Changing the color of brush strokes

Generally speaking, you change the color of an applied art brush stroke just like you do any other stroke: make the Stroke button active on the Tools panel, select the object, then choose the color you want for the brush stroke. However, your ability to change the color of an art brush stroke depends on how the art brush was created. If you find that you can't change the color of a brush stroke, you need to modify its formatting. Double-click the brush stroke on the Brushes panel to open the Art Brush Options dialog box. In the Colorization section, click the Method list arrow, choose Tints and Shades, then click OK. A dialog box will appear, asking if you want to apply the change to existing brush strokes. Click Apply to Strokes. Any time you apply the brush in the future, you'll be able to modify its color.

Drawing in Illustrator   **Illustrator 143**

Creating Pseudo Strokes

Sometimes the best stroke choice is not really a stroke at all. One classic method for making Illustrator artwork more visually interesting is to create a false stroke effect. A "pseudo" stroke is a black copy of the artwork pasted behind the original artwork. You then modify that black copy so that it shows from behind the artwork in varying amounts, thus creating interesting varying width stroke effects. This is a classic look that still works very well, and you'll find that your skills with the Offset Path command and the Unite shape mode will come in handy for creating pseudo strokes. Jon asks you to create an exercise showcasing the classic pseudo strokes effect behind the artwork.

STEPS

1. **Select all, copy, paste in front, click the** Object menu, **point to** Hide, **then click** Selection
   A copy of the artwork is hidden.

2. **Delete the three black "wisps" on either side of the vase, then select all of the artwork**

3. **Click the** Brushes panel menu button 🔻, **then click Remove Brush Stroke**

4. **Click the** Object menu, **point to** Path, **click** Offset Path, **type** .12 **in the Offset text box, then click** OK

5. **Select all, open the Pathfinder panel, then click the** Unite button 🔲 **on the Pathfinder panel**

6. **Set the stroke color to** None, **then set the fill color to** Black
   Figure F-22 shows the artwork with selection marks hidden. Note that the point of the middle "blade" has been squared off. This happens sometimes when you use the Offset Path command, especially on very acute angled paths. You're going to add an anchor point to this path to restore the point for the blade.

7. **Click the** Pen tool 🖊, **add an anchor point to the squared off blade part of the path, click the** Direct Selection tool 🔺, **then drag the** new anchor point **up to add the point back into the blade, as shown in Figure F-23**
   Figure F-23 shows the artwork with selection marks hidden.

8. **Click the** Object menu, **click** Show All **to show the hidden artwork, then lock it**

> **QUICK TIP**
> Selecting and moving multiple anchor points will make it easier to move some curved paths.

9. **Using the Direct Selection tool, manipulate the black offset path by moving anchor points and segments to vary how much of the path appears behind the locked artwork, as shown in Figure F-24**

10. **Save your work, then close flower brushes_AI-F.ai**

FIGURE F-22: Viewing the offset, united path

Blade point
is squared off
when offset

FIGURE F-23: Making a point for the blade

Added anchor
point moved to
create point

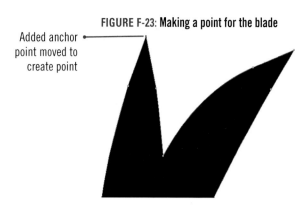

FIGURE F-24: Viewing the final artwork

The pseudo strokes effect

What's great about the pseudo strokes effect is that it's unique because the stroke appears to be hand-drawn. When you modify the black back object, you can create interesting relationships of varying widths between the foreground art and the black object.

Note, too, that the final artwork in this lesson was a combination of pseudo strokes and the Charcoal brush: the Charcoal brush strokes were still visible on the *inside* of the flower artwork.

Practice

Concepts Review

Label the elements of the Illustrator screen shown in Figure F-25.

FIGURE F-25

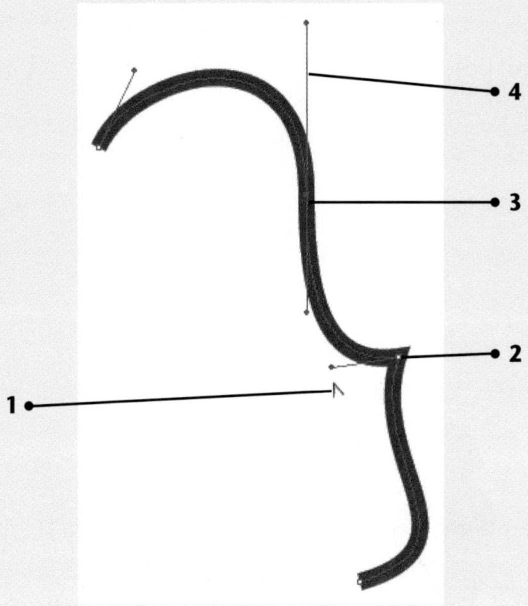

Match each term with the statement that best describes it.

5. Smooth point
6. Convert Anchor Point tool
7. Image Trace button
8. Direction handle
9. Outline Stroke command
10. Art brush
11. Place command
12. Tints and Shades

a. Defines the arc of a curved path
b. Creates an object with a closed path
c. Can be applied as a stroke
d. Joins curved paths
e. Command used to import images
f. Art brush option
g. Available on the Control panel when a placed image is selected
h. "Breaks" direction handles

Select the best answer from the list of choices.

13. Which of the following is not true about smooth points?

    a. They are used to draw curved paths.

    b. They sometimes have direction lines.

    c. They can be created with the Convert Anchor Point tool.

    d. All of the above

14. Which of the following is not an option in the Tracing Presets menu?

    a. Shades of Gray

    b. 16 Colors

    c. Grayscale

    d. Technical Drawing

15. Which option do you use to select the components of a traced image?

    a. Extend

    b. Export

    c. Expand

    d. Outline

16. Which of the following commands do you use to convert a stroke into a filled object?

    a. Offset Path

    b. Trace Stroke

    c. Outline Mode

    d. Outline Path

17. Which of the following is not available on the Brushes panel?

    a. Art brushes

    b. Pseudo brushes

    c. Calligraphic brushes

    d. Scatter brushes

Skills Review

1. Trace artwork with Image Trace.

FIGURE F-26

    a. Create a new 8.5" × 8" document, save it as **skills trace_AI-F**, click the Window menu, then verify that Control is checked.

    b. Click the File menu, click Place, navigate to where your Data Files are stored, click the file named Fruit.tif, then click Place.

    c. Click the Tracing Presets list arrow (next to the Image Trace button), then click Low Fidelity Photo

    d. Click the Expand button on the Control panel.

    e. Deselect, then compare your result to Figure F-26.

    f. Save your work, then close skills trace_AI-F.ai.

2. Use the Pen tool.

    a. Open AI F-3.ai, then save it as **drawing skills_AI-F**.

    b. Click the View menu, then click Panel 1 at the bottom of the menu.

    c. Click the Pen tool, set the Fill color to None, then set the Stroke color and size to CMYK Red, 2 pt.

    d. Click the small gray circle beside the number 1, click the circle at number 2, click the circle at number 3, then click the circle at number 4.

    e. Float the Pen tool over the path between points 2 and 3 until you see a plus sign appear beside the tool, then click the path.

    f. Click the Direct Selection tool, then drag the new anchor point up to the purple star.

    g. Select the Convert Anchor Point tool, position it over the anchor point, then click and drag until the path aligns with the light blue path you're tracing. (*Hint*: The Convert Anchor Point tool may be hidden beneath the Pen tool.)

    h. Save your work.

3. Join paths and points.

    a. Click the Selection tool, select the entire path, then click the Reflect tool.

    b. Press and hold [Alt] (Win) or [option] (Mac), then click approximately ³/₄" below the path.

    c. In the Axis section of the Reflect dialog box, click Horizontal, then click Copy.

    d. Click the Direct Selection tool, then draw a selection marquee to select just the farthest right anchor points on each of the paths.

Skills Review (continued)

    e. Click the Object menu, point to Path, then click Join.

    f. Select the two farthest left anchor points, then press [Ctrl][J] (Win) or ⌘[J] (Mac) to join the points and create one closed path.

    g. Save your work.

4. Draw curved paths.

    a. Click the View menu, click Panel 2 at the bottom of the menu, then click the Pen tool.

    b. Position the Pen tool over the first gray circle, then click and drag up to the first purple star.

    c. Position the Pen tool over the second gray circle, then click and drag down to the red star.

    d. Using the same method, trace the remainder of the path.

    e. Click the Direct Selection tool, select each anchor point, then adjust the direction handles to improve the alignment of the red path with the light blue path.

    f. Save your work.

5. Reverse the direction of a path.

    a. Click the View menu, click Panel 3 at the bottom of the menu, then click the Pen tool.

    b. Position the Pen tool over the first gray circle, then in one move, click and drag down to the purple star.

    c. Position the Pen tool over the second gray circle, then click and drag up to the red star.

    d. Press and hold [Alt] (Win) or [option] (Mac) to access the Convert Anchor Point tool.

    e. Position the Convert Anchor Point tool over the direction handle at the red star, then click and drag it down to the center of the second purple star.

    f. Position the Pen tool over the third gray circle, then click and drag it up to the second red star.

    g. Press and hold [Alt] (Win) or [option] (Mac) to access the Convert Anchor Point tool.

    h. Position the Convert Anchor Point tool over the direction handle at the second red star, then click and drag it down to the third purple star.

    i. Using the same method, trace the remainder of the blue path.

    j. Save your work.

6. Outline a stroke.

    a. Click the View menu, click Panel 4 at the bottom of the menu, then click the Selection tool.

    b. Select the red path, open the Stroke panel, then increase the point size to 20 pt.

    c. Click the Object menu, point to Path, then click Outline Stroke.

    d. Fit the artboard in the window, then compare your artboard to Figure F-27.

    e. Save your work, then close drawing skills_AI-F.ai.

7. Create an art brush.

    a. Open AI F-4.ai, save it as **brush skills_AI-F**, click the File menu, then click Place.

    b. Navigate to the location where your Data Files are stored, click the file named Skinny Pencil.tif, then click Place.

    c. Click the Tracing Presets list arrow (next to the Image Trace button), then click Sketched Art.

    d. Click the Expand button on the Control panel, open the Brushes panel, then drag the traced brush into the Brushes panel.

    e. Click the Art Brush option button, then click OK.

    f. Type **Skinny Pencil** in the Name text box, click the Method list arrow in the Colorization section, then click Tints and Shades.

    g. Click OK.

    h. Verify that the traced brush artwork on the artboard is selected, click the Edit menu, then click Cut.

    i. Save your work.

FIGURE F-27

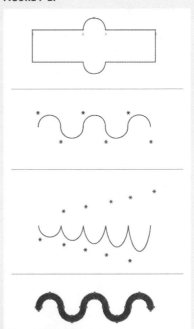

Skills Review (continued)

8. **Apply brushes.**

   a. Select all the artwork on the artboard, click the View menu, then click Hide Edges, if necessary.

   b. Click the Skinny Pencil brush thumbnail on the Brushes panel.

   c. Open the Stroke panel, then reduce the weight of the stroke to .4 pt.

   d. Compare your result to Figure F-28.

   e. Click the View menu, then click Show Edges.

   f. Save your work.

FIGURE F-28

9. **Create pseudo strokes.**

   a. Select all, copy, paste in front, click the Object menu, point to Hide, then click Selection.

   b. Select all, click the Brushes panel menu button, then click Remove Brush Stroke.

   c. Click the Object menu, point to Path, click Offset Path, type **.15** in the Offset text box, then click OK.

   d. Select all, open the Pathfinder panel, then click the Unite button.

   e. Set the Stroke color to None, then fill the object with Black.

   f. Show the hidden artwork, then lock it.

   g. Using the Direct Selection tool, manipulate the black offset path to vary how much of it appears behind the locked artwork.

   h. Save your work, then close brush skills_AI-F.ai.

Independent Challenge 1

You're designing a logo for a children's television show. You sketch a design in blue ink, scan it or photograph it with a digital camera, place the file in Illustrator, then decide to trace it with the Pen tool.

   a. Open AI F-5.ai, save it as **elephants_AI-F**, click the View menu, then click Big Trunk at the bottom of the menu.

   b. Click the Pen tool, set the Fill color to None, then set the Stroke color to CMYK Red and the stroke weight to 2 pt.

   c. Click the Pen tool on the small gray circle beside the number 1.

   d. Position the Pen tool over the second gray circle, then click and drag to the right to align the path with the guide.

   e. Position the Pen tool over the third gray circle, then click and drag up to align the path.

   f. Position the Pen tool over the fourth gray circle, then click and drag up to align the path.

   g. Position the Pen tool over the fifth gray circle, then click and drag to the red star to align the path.

   h. Press and hold [Alt] (Win) or [option] (Mac) to access the Convert Anchor Point tool, then click and drag the handle from the red star to the purple star.

   i. Position the Pen tool over the sixth gray circle, then click and drag down to align the path.

   j. Position the Pen tool over the seventh gray circle, then click and drag to finish the path.

   k. Click the Ellipse tool, then draw a circle to trace the eye.

Independent Challenge 1 (continued)

l. Compare your result to Figure F-29.

m. Trace the remainder of the blue paths for the elephant and the baby elephant. (*Hint*: You may need to zoom out to see the baby elephant.)

n. Save your work, then close elephants_AI-F.ai.

Independent Challenge 2

You're designing a logo for a children's television show. You've traced your own ink sketch with the Pen tool; now you decide to create and apply a brush stroke to make the line art interesting. Since the subject of the television show is elephants, you decide to create a playful brush stroke for the logo that starts out narrow and gets increasingly wider.

FIGURE F-29

a. Open AI F-6.ai, save it as **brushed elephants_AI-F**, click the Selection tool, then select the two black circles at the top of the artboard.

b. Double-click the Blend tool to open the Blend Options dialog box.

c. Click the Spacing list arrow, click Specified Steps, type **512** in the text box, then click OK.

d. Click the Object menu, point to Blend, then click Make.

e. Click the Object menu, point to Blend, then click Expand.

f. Open the Pathfinder panel, then click the Unite button.

g. Open the Brushes panel, click the Selection tool, then drag the united artwork into the Brushes panel.

h. Click the Art Brush option button, then click OK.

i. Type **Elephant** in the Name text box, click the Method list arrow in the Colorization section, then click Tints.

j. Click OK.

k. Delete the united artwork from the artboard.

l. Select all, then click the Elephant brush on the Brushes panel.

m. Reduce the point size to .5 pt.

n. Deselect all, then compare your screen to Figure F-30.

o. Save your work, then close brushed elephants_AI-F.ai.

FIGURE F-30

Independent Challenge 3

You really enjoy scrapbooking, and you're putting together a keepsake album of your trip to Seattle—where it rained every day you were there. To brighten up your rather drab collection, you decide to create some colorful illustrations to go with the pictures. You start with, appropriately, an umbrella.

a. Open AI F-7.ai, then save it as **umbrella_AI-F**.

b. Show the Brushes panel, if necessary.

c. Select all, then apply the Charcoal brush to the umbrella artwork.

d. Double-click the Charcoal brush on the Brushes panel to open the Art Brush Options dialog box.

e. Click the Preview check box, then drag the Width slider to 300%.

f. Click OK to close the dialog box then click the Apply to Strokes button.

Independent Challenge 3 (continued)

g. Click the Object menu, then click Show All.

h. Deselect all, save your work, then compare your screen to Figure F-31.

Advanced Challenge Exercise

- Select just the three color triangles.
- Apply the Gothic brush stroke.
- Verify that the Stroke color is active on the Tools panel.
- Apply a 1 pt. black stroke.

l. Save your work, then close umbrella_AI-F.ai.

Real Life Independent Challenge

You're working on an advertisement for kitchen products that requires you to draw a peppermill. Your art director e-mails you an Illustrator file with a traced path of the first half. She tells you to complete the other half.

a. Open AI F-8.ai, then save it as **peppermill_AI-F**.

b. Click the Brushes panel menu button, then click New Brush.

c. In the New Brush dialog box, click the Bristle Brush option button, then click OK.

d. Type **My Bristle Brush** in the Name text box, then click OK to accept the default settings.

e. Click the Selection tool, select the path, then click the Reflect tool.

f. Press and hold [Alt] (Win) or [option] (Mac), then click the top anchor point on the path to open the Reflect dialog box.

g. In the Axis section, click Vertical, then click Copy.

h. Click the Direct Selection tool, then draw a selection marquee to select the top anchor point of each path so that two points are selected.

i. Click the Object menu, point to Path, then click Join.

j. Join the two bottom anchor points of the two paths.

Advanced Challenge Exercise

- Click the artboard to deselect the peppermill object.
- Using the Direct Selection tool, then drag a small selection marquee around the lower-middle part of the path where the two anchor points were joined.
- Click the Object menu, point to Path, then click Average.
- In the Axis section, click Vertical, then click OK.

k. Click My Bristle Brush on the Brushes panel to apply the brush.

l. Deselect, then compare your artwork to Figure F-32.

m. Save your work, then close peppermill_AI-F.ai.

FIGURE F-32

Visual Workshop

Open AI F-9.ai, then save it as **lsat_AI-F**. Use the pencil artwork at the top of the artboard to create a new art brush. After you've made the art brush, delete the pencil artwork from the artboard, then select the red path and apply the pencil art brush so that your screen resembles Figure F-33. Save your work, then close lsat_AI-F.ai.

FIGURE F-33

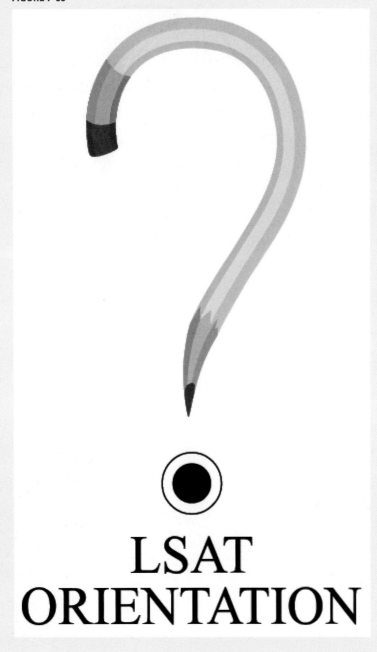

Working with Advanced Techniques

**Files You
Will Need:**

To view a list of
files needed for
this unit, see
the Data Files
Grid in the back
of the book.

Having gone through the first six units in this book, you're ready to take a tour of some of the more advanced features in Illustrator. By advanced, we don't mean difficult. Instead, we are referring to those features that go beyond the basic uses of Illustrator. Now that you've become familiar with the architecture of Illustrator, you'll be able to understand these features in the context of the application as a whole. Ultimately, that's the route to mastering any software application: learn the basic architecture, then incorporate more subtle or specific features within the context of that basic architecture. Jon asks you to prepare a series of lessons showcasing some of the more advanced features of Illustrator, focusing especially on layers, patterns, distortions, and 3D objects.

OBJECTIVES

Layer artwork

Create a pattern swatch

Apply and edit a pattern swatch

Use the Shear tool

Distort with the Free Transform tool

Apply Warp effects

Extrude a 3D object

Revolve a 3D object

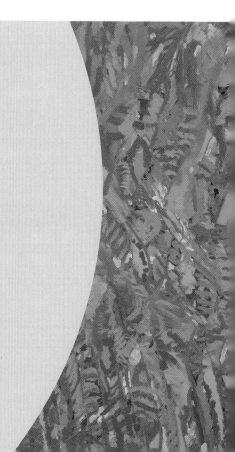

Layering Artwork

The Layers panel offers many options for layering artwork. When you're working with complex illustrations composed of multiple objects, segregating components on different layers helps you to organize the artwork and make working with it easier. With layered artwork, you can quickly hide and show all the artwork on a layer, making it easier to work on other components without distraction. You can also quickly lock and unlock artwork on a layer, and with just one click, you can select all the artwork on a single layer. So when it comes to complex illustrations, working with layers is often a smart approach. ▰▰▰▰ Jon asks you to segregate the ATLAS artwork onto individual layers on the Layers panel to make it easier to work with.

STEPS

QUICK TIP
Choose the Essentials workspace, then reset the workspace, if necessary.

1. **Open the file AI G-1.ai from the location where your Data Files are stored, save it as atlas layers_AI-G, then click the Layers panel button** ▨ **to open the Layers panel**

2. **On the Layers panel, click the word Globe to select the layer, click the Layers panel menu button** ▤, **then click New Layer**

3. **Type Event TV in the Name text box, click the Color list arrow, click Magenta, then click OK**

   A new layer named Event TV is added above the Globe layer. All objects on the Event TV layer will have magenta selection marks when they are selected.

QUICK TIP
All of the artwork in this document is on the Background layer.

4. **Click the Selection tool** ▸, **click the globe artwork on the artboard to select it, then compare your Layers panel to Figure G-1**

   The Background layer becomes selected, informing you that the globe artwork is on the Background layer. The Indicates Selected Art button appears, indicating that an item on this layer is selected.

QUICK TIP
The Indicates Selected Art button is the tiny square on a layer that appears when an object on that layer is selected.

5. **Click and drag the Indicates Selected Art button on the Background layer up to the same location on the Globe layer, then compare your result to Figure G-2**

   Moving the Indicates Selected Art button moves the selected art onto the Globe layer. The globe artwork is now above all the other artwork, because the Globe layer is above the Background layer.

6. **Select both instances of the *EVENT TV* text on the artboard, then click and drag the Indicates Selected Art button on the Background layer up to the Event TV layer**

   The text is moved to the Event TV layer.

7. **Select the *ATLAS* text on the artboard, then drag the Indicates Selected Art button up to the Atlas layer**

   The *ATLAS* text is moved to the Atlas layer.

8. **As shown in Figure G-3, click and drag the Atlas layer on the Layers panel above the Globe layer, then release the mouse button when the white line appears above the Atlas layer**

   The *ATLAS* text is above the globe artwork because the Atlas layer is above the Globe layer on the Layers panel.

QUICK TIP
You can hide and show all artwork on a layer by clicking the Toggles Visibility icon (eyeball), and lock all of the artwork on a layer by clicking the empty gray square next to the eyeball icon.

9. **Click the empty gray square next to the eyeball icon on the Atlas layer**

   A padlock icon appears indicating that all objects on the Atlas layer are locked.

10. **Click the Target button on the Event TV layer to select all of the artwork on the Event TV layer, then compare your artwork to Figure G-4**

    All the artwork on the Event TV layer is selected.

11. **Apply a 1-pt Black stroke to the selection, save your work, then close atlas layers_AI-G.ai**

FIGURE G-1: Viewing the Indicates Selected Art button

Indicates Selected
Art button

Selected art

FIGURE G-2: Moving artwork between layers

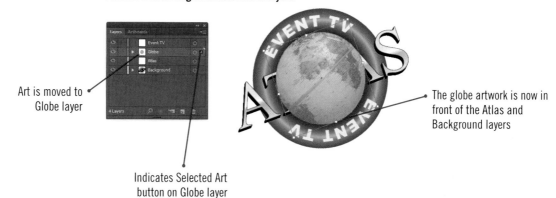

Art is moved to
Globe layer

The globe artwork is now in
front of the Atlas and
Background layers

Indicates Selected Art
button on Globe layer

FIGURE G-3: Moving the Atlas layer above the Globe layer

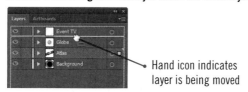

Hand icon indicates
layer is being moved

FIGURE G-4: Selecting all objects on a layer

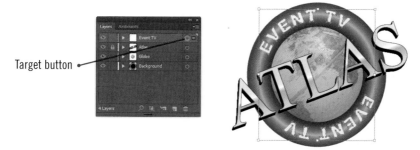

Target button

About layers and the stacking order

Each layer on the Layers panel has its own stacking order. In other words, if a layer contains multiple objects, the objects are stacked in a particular order, with various objects in front of or in back of other objects. The Arrange commands—Bring to Front, Bring Forward, Send to Back, and Send Backward—are applied to objects within the confines of the layer. For example, if you select an object on a layer named "Layer 3" and choose the Bring to Front command, the object will become the front-most object in the stacking order *on Layer 3*. That doesn't necessarily mean that it will be the front-most artwork on the artboard. Artwork on any layers above Layer 3 will by definition be above any artwork on Layer 3.

Creating a Pattern Swatch

Patterns are powerful features in Adobe Illustrator, and they have many practical real world uses: creating background artwork, wallpaper, designs for fabric, and so on. To create a pattern, you first create artwork for the pattern. When the artwork is ready, simply drag it into the Swatches panel to create a pattern swatch. You can modify many settings about your pattern in the Pattern Options panel and then use it to fill an object. A pattern fills an object by repeating a single original pattern in a process called **tiling**. When the artwork is ready, simply drag it into the Swatches panel to create a pattern swatch. When you fill an object with a pattern, you can transform the pattern—scale it, rotate it, and so on—within the object. Jon asks you to design a pattern for a new client that specializes in selling gift wrap.

STEPS

QUICK TIP
You can also make a new pattern by selecting the artwork, clicking Object on the Menu bar, pointing to Pattern, then clicking Make.

1. **Open the file AI G-2.ai from the location where you save your Data Files, save it as patterns_AI-G, then show the Swatches panel**

2. **Click the Selection tool 🔲, select the "B" artwork, then drag the artwork into the Swatches panel**

   The artwork is automatically defined as a pattern swatch on the Swatches panel.

3. **Select the artwork on the artboard, then delete it**

   Once you have created a pattern swatch, you no longer need the artwork on the artboard. If the artwork remains selected on the artboard, it will be filled with the new pattern swatch.

4. **Double-click New Pattern Swatch 1 on the Swatches panel to open the Pattern Options panel, then type Busy B in the Name text box**

   A pattern tile appears around the selected artwork and a dimmed sample of the pattern surrounds it. As shown in Figure G-5, the Pattern Options panel offers several options for further defining your pattern. You can change the width and height, the vertical and horizontal offset, and the number of copies that appear in the example. Next you will make changes to the pattern and watch it update automatically.

5. **Click the Type tool 🔲 on the Tools panel, then double-click the B inside the pattern tile**

6. **Click the Fill button ☐ on the Tools panel, then click CMYK Blue**

   The pattern tile and the dimmed sample updates to CMYK Blue automatically.

7. **Click the Ellipse tool 🔲 on the Tools panel, then draw a small circle inside the top of the letter B, as shown in Figure G-6**

QUICK TIP
You can also click the Exit Pattern Editing Mode button to save the pattern and leave pattern editing mode.

8. **Click CMYK Red on the Swatches panel to change the color of the circle to CMYK Red, then click Done, as shown in Figure G-7**

   The Busy B pattern is updated in the Swatches panel and you are no longer in Pattern Editing Mode.

9. **Save your work**

Creating a pattern swatch

Patterns do not necessarily need to be created from rectangles or squares. Any basic Illustrator object can be dragged into the Swatches panel and used as a pattern swatch for a pattern fill. For example, if you drag a circle into the Swatches panel, you will create a pattern fill of repeating circles. If you're making a pattern of just lines, that's when you need to place an unfilled, unstroked square or rectangle behind the line artwork to define the tile for the line pattern. Remember, an unfilled, unstroked square or rectangle behind any artwork crops the artwork when it's used as a pattern swatch. The following items can be used in a pattern: text, compound paths, blends, gradients, and brush strokes.

FIGURE G-5: Viewing the pattern and the Pattern Options panel

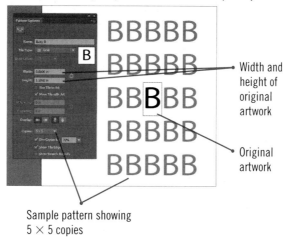

Width and height of original artwork

Original artwork

Sample pattern showing
5 × 5 copies

FIGURE G-6: Modifying the pattern

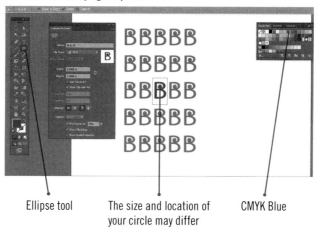

Ellipse tool

The size and location of
your circle may differ

CMYK Blue

FIGURE G-7: Saving changes to the pattern

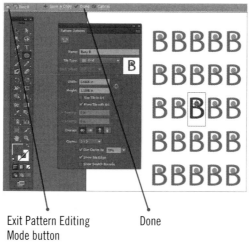

Exit Pattern Editing
Mode button

Done

Working with Advanced Techniques

Applying and Editing a Pattern Swatch

When you fill an object with a pattern, you can transform the pattern—scale it, rotate it, and so on—within the object. The Scale dialog box allows you to scale the contents of the selected object without scaling the object itself. You can also scale an object and the pattern inside the object uniformly. Jon asks you to create a sample 5 × 5 square of the new gift wrap and scale the pattern 25%.

STEPS

1. **Double-click the Hand tool** 🖐 **on the Tools panel to fit the artboard in the window**

2. **Press and hold the Ellipse tool** 🔵 **on the Tools panel, then click the Rectangle tool** 🔲

3. **Click the artboard, type 5 in the Width text box, press [Tab], type 5 in the Height text box, then click OK**

   A 5 × 5 square filled with CMYK Red appears on the artboard.

4. **Click the Busy B pattern swatch on the Swatches panel, then compare your screen to Figure G-8**

   Next you will scale the pattern artwork inside the square.

5. **Double-click the Scale tool** 🔲 **on the Tools panel**

   As shown in Figure G-9, the Scale dialog box offers options for transforming the object, the pattern, or both.

6. **Click the Uniform option button in the Scale dialog box, then type 25 in the Uniform text box**

7. **Click the Transform Objects check box to remove the check mark, then verify that the Transform Patterns check box is checked**

8. **Click the Preview check box, then compare your filled object and your Scale dialog box to Figure G-10**

9. **Click OK to close the dialog box, then save your work**

10. **Close patterns_AI-G.ai**

FIGURE G-8: The Busy B pattern used as a fill

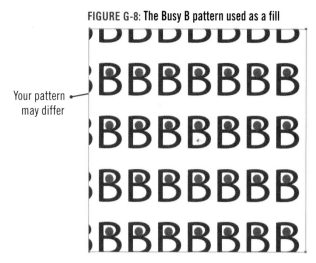

Your pattern
may differ

FIGURE G-9: Options in the Scale dialog box

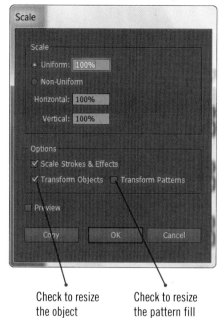

Check to resize
the object

Check to resize
the pattern fill

FIGURE G-10: Scaling the pattern 25%

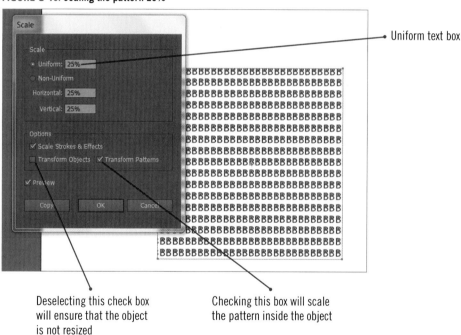

Uniform text box

Deselecting this check box
will ensure that the object
is not resized

Checking this box will scale
the pattern inside the object

Using the Shear Tool

The Shear tool is a transform tool that you use to distort artwork along a horizontal or vertical axis. Shear is a tool you're likely to use less often than the other transform tools, but it's particularly useful for creating the effect of one object casting a shadow on a different plane. As with every transform tool, you can specify a point of origin for the transformation. Jon's design team is designing a headline for a game box. He asks you to demonstrate how to create the effect that the headline text is casting a shadow on the imaginary plane that it sits on.

STEPS

QUICK TIP

The Shear tool is hidden behind the Scale tool.

1. Open the file AI G-3.ai from the location where your Data Files are stored, save it as shear_AI-G, click the Selection tool ▶, then select the text

2. Copy the text, click the Edit menu, click Paste in Front, change the fill color to C=0 M=0 Y=0 K=30 (light gray), then select the Shear tool 🗗

3. Press and hold [Alt] (Win) or [option] (Mac), then click the lower-right anchor point of the letter *W*

   The lower-right anchor point of the W becomes the point of origin for the transformation and the Shear dialog box opens.

4. Type 45 in the Shear Angle text box, verify that the Horizontal option button is selected, then click OK

   As shown in Figure G-11, the gray text is sheared at a 45° angle across an imaginary horizontal axis.

5. Click the Scale tool 🗗, press and hold [Alt] (Win) or [option] (Mac), then click the bottom anchor point of the first letter *S*

   The Scale dialog box opens.

6. Click the Non-Uniform option button in the Scale dialog box, verify that 100% appears in the Horizontal text box, type 50 in the Vertical text box, then click OK

7. Click the Object menu, point to Arrange, then click Send to Back

8. Click ▶, select the blue letters, apply a 1-pt Black stroke, deselect, then compare your screen to Figure G-12

9. Save your work, then close shear_AI-G.ai

Art skewed at 45° angle from
imaginary horizontal axis

Illustrator CS6

FIGURE G-12: **Viewing the final effect**

Working with Advanced Techniques

Distorting with the Free Transform Tool

The Free Transform tool is a quick alternative to the Scale and Rotate tools: simply select an object, and a bounding box appears, allowing you to quickly resize and rotate the object by dragging the selection handles. You'll be pleased to learn that the Free Transform tool also offers the ability to distort selected artwork to create interesting and practical perspective effects. **⬛⬛⬛⬛** A new job is going to call for lots of perspective effects. Jon asks you to demonstrate for the design team the "hidden" ability of the Free Transform tool to distort artwork and create such effects.

STEPS

1. **Open the file AI G-4.ai from the location where you store your Data Files, save it as impact_AI-G, click the Selection tool** 🔳**, then select all**
   The letter forms are outlines created from the font Impact. The selection edges are hidden.

2. **Click the Free Transform tool** 🔳**, then position the mouse pointer over the upper-left handle of the bounding box**

3. **Press and hold the mouse pointer on the anchor point**

4. **Press and hold [Ctrl] (Win) or ⌘ (Mac), drag straight down to the bottom of the letter *F*, release the mouse button and [Ctrl] (Win) or ⌘ (Mac), then compare your result to Figure G-13**
   The objects are distorted. Pressing and holding [Ctrl] (Win) or ⌘ (Mac) while dragging with the Free Transform tool distorts the text.

5. **Press and hold the mouse pointer over the lower-right handle of the bounding box**

QUICK TIP
Show the rulers, if necessary.

6. **Press and hold [Ctrl] (Win) or ⌘ (Mac), then drag the handle down until it is about one inch from the bottom edge of the artboard**

7. **Click** 🔳**, deselect the artwork, then compare your artwork to Figure G-14**

8. **Save your work, then close impact_AI-G.ai**

FIGURE G-13: Viewing the first transformation

FIGURE G-14: Viewing the perspective effect

The "free" in the Free Transform tool

One of the great reasons to use the Free Transform tool to distort objects is the fact that it's a freehand operation. You're making the move by hand, and to a degree, that makes it more unique to you and your drawing style. Illustrator offers many ways to distort objects. Warp, distort, and transform effects are all capable of producing cool and interesting results. However, those results are only achieved using dialog boxes, dragging sliders, and choosing options—basically, something anybody could repeat exactly. So there's something a little more interesting about distorting with the Free Transform tool because the result is just a bit more unique.

Applying Warp Effects

Warps are a series of preset distortion effects that produce fun and often practical results for distorting artwork. **Effects** are operations that you can apply to objects to alter their appearance without actually altering the object itself. You can apply effects that distort, transform, warp, outline, and offset a path—among others—without changing the original size, anchor points, and shape of the object. When you apply an effect to an object, the effect is listed on the Appearance panel, where it can be hidden or shown, reordered with other effects, and deleted. The term **appearance** refers to what an object looks like when an effect has been applied to it. Working with effects offers you the ability to edit your artwork at any time, because each effect can be quickly modified or removed without disturbing other effects that may be applied. You can also edit the original artwork at any time, regardless of which effects have been applied. ▰▰▰▰ You're using an image of the American flag for a layout. Jon tells you to keep it interesting; he suggests that you apply a Warp effect to the flag illustration so that it appears to be waving.

STEPS

1. **Open the file AI G-5.ai from the location where you store your Data Files, then save it as flag warp_AI-G**

TROUBLE
If you do not see the Appearance panel button, refresh the Essentials workspace by selecting Reset Essentials from the Workspace switcher on the Menu bar.

2. **Click the Appearance panel button ▦ to open the Appearance panel**

3. **Select all, click the Object menu, then click Group**
   Because the artwork is grouped, the Warp effect will be applied to the artwork as though it were a single object.

4. **Click the Effect menu, point to Warp, then click Flag**
   The Warp Options dialog box opens.

5. **Check the Preview check box, verify that the Horizontal option button is selected, drag the Bend slider to 40, then click OK**
   As shown in Figure G-15, the Warp effect is applied to the artwork, but the selection marks show the original object before the effect was applied. The Warp effect is listed on the Appearance panel as Warp: Flag.

QUICK TIP
When working with effects, it's a good idea to work with edges hidden.

6. **Click the View menu, then click Hide Edges**
   You will now modify the Warp effect.

7. **Click Warp: Flag on the Appearance panel**
   The Warp Options dialog box opens, showing the settings you first applied. You can continue to modify these settings. For more information about modifying effects, see the *Modifying effects* box in this lesson.

8. **Drag the Bend slider to -40, click OK, deselect, then compare your artwork to Figure G-16**
   With a negative value applied, the bend is reversed.

9. **Save your work, then close flag warp_AI-G.ai**

Modifying effects

When you first apply an effect to an object, you do so by choosing an effect from the Effect menu, opening the effect's dialog box, choosing settings, then clicking OK. However, if you later want to modify that effect, you don't go back to the Effect menu. Instead, you go to the Appearance panel, where any and all effects applied to the object are listed. When you click the effect on the Appearance panel, the effect's dialog box opens, showing you the settings that were applied when the effect was created or last modified. That's the whole point of working with effects: at any time, you can modify or remove them.

FIGURE G-15: Viewing the applied warp

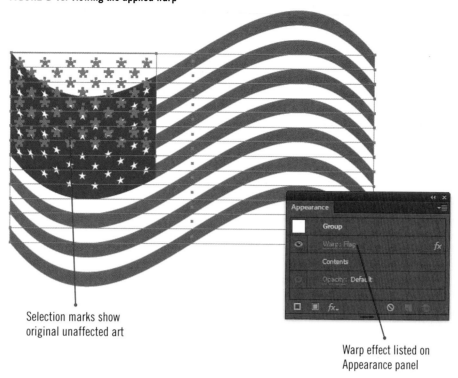

Selection marks show
original unaffected art

Warp effect listed on
Appearance panel

FIGURE G-16: Viewing the change in the Bend value

Working with Advanced Techniques

Extruding a 3D Object

Creating 3D objects is one of the more exciting features in Illustrator. The Extrude & Bevel effect applies a three-dimensional effect to a two-dimensional object. A two-dimensional object has two axes: an X-axis, representing its width; and a Y-axis, representing its height. When you **extrude** an object, you create a third dimension by extending the object on its Z-axis, which represents the object's depth. You then determine the degree of extrusion in the 3D Extrude & Bevel Options dialog box. The 3D effect automatically applies shading to enhance the sense of depth and dimension. ▆▆▆▆ Jon asks you to teach the designers how to add a 3D effect to artwork using the Extrude & Bevel effect.

STEPS

1. **Open the file AI G-6.ai from the location where you store your Data Files, save it as 3d extrude_AI-G, select all, group the selection, then click Hide Edges on the View menu**
   When applying a 3D effect to an illustration composed of multiple objects, it's suggested and sometimes necessary that you group the objects to produce the desired effect.

2. **Click the Effect menu, point to 3D, then click Extrude & Bevel**
   The 3D Extrude & Bevel Options dialog box opens.

TROUBLE
If you cannot drag the slider to 150, type 150 in the Extrude Depth text box.

3. **Click the Preview check box, click the arrow next to Extrude Depth, drag the slider to 150, click OK, then compare your result to Figure G-17**
   A three-dimensional appearance is applied to the artwork, and 3D Extrude & Bevel is listed on the Appearance panel. You will now modify the effect.

4. **Verify that the artwork is still selected, then click 3D Extrude & Bevel on the Appearance panel**
   The 3D Extrude & Bevel Options dialog box opens with the setting you applied previously.

5. **Click the Preview check box, click and drag the rotation cube in various directions, then release the mouse button**
   The rotation cube represents the selected artwork. As shown in Figure G-18, the rotation cube can be rotated across the X-axis (horizontal axis), the Y-axis (vertical axis), and the Z-axis (axis showing depth).

6. **Type 28 in the Specify rotation around the X axis text box, type 18 in the Specify rotation around the Y axis text box, type -3 in the Specify rotation around the Z axis text box, then click OK**

7. **Click the Object menu, click Expand Appearance, click the View menu, then click Show Edges**

8. **Deselect all, click the Direct Selection tool ▶, select the number 3, click the Select menu, point to Same, then click Fill Color**

9. **Fill the selection with CMYK Yellow, deselect, then compare your screen to Figure G-19**

10. **Save your work, then close 3d extrude_AI-G.ai**

Beveled edges

The Bevel menu provides the Bevel component of the Extrude & Bevel effect. A **beveled edge** is an angled or indented edge, like you would see on a picture frame or on a mirror. The Bevel menu, located in the 3D Extrude & Bevel Options dialog box, using the Bevel list arrow, contains a list of preset beveled edges that you can apply to objects as part of a 3D effect. This can add some visual complexity to 3D objects and can be especially useful to decorate extruded text. Use the Height slider beneath the menu to control the size of the beveled edge.

FIGURE G-17: Viewing the extruded appearance

FIGURE G-18: 3D Extrude & Bevel Options dialog box

FIGURE G-19: Final artwork

Revolving a 3D Object

In addition to extruding, **revolving** is another method that Illustrator provides for applying a three-dimensional effect to a two-dimensional object. Imagine taking a large hardcover book and opening it so much that its front and back covers touch. The pages would fan out from one cover to the other. This example is similar to what happens when the Revolve effect is applied to an object. Revolving an object creates multiple duplicates of the object, "sweeping" around the Y-axis. Then, as with the Extrude & Bevel effect, surface shading is applied automatically to enhance the effect. By default, an object is revolved around a vertical axis that represents its leftmost point. If the artwork that you're revolving is composed of multiple objects, you must group the artwork so that all the objects will revolve together around one axis. If not grouped, each object will revolve independently around its own left axis. Jon likes your Extrude & Bevel exercise and asks that you demonstrate how to create a 3D effect with the Revolve effect.

STEPS

1. **Open AI G-7.ai, save it as** 3d revolve_AI-G, **then locate the gray object on the artboard**
   The gray object is a single Illustrator object created by tracing half of the bishop chess piece with the Pen tool.

2. **Click the** Selection tool , **select the photograph of the bishop chess piece, hide the selection, select the** gray object, **then hide edges**

3. **Click the** Effect menu, **point to** 3D, **then click** Revolve
   The 3D Revolve Options dialog box opens.

4. **Click the** Preview check box, **click** OK, **then compare your result to Figure G-20**
   The artwork is revolved around its left edge to create the three-dimensional effect.

5. **Click** 3D Revolve **on the Appearance panel, click the** Preview check box, **click and drag the** rotation cube **in various directions, then release the mouse button**

6. **Type** -49 **in the Specify rotation around the X-axis text box, type** -2 **in the Specify rotation around the Y-axis text box, type** 52 **in the Specify rotation around the Z-axis text box, then click** OK
   Your screen should resemble Figure G-21.

7. **Show edges, select the** yellow half circle, **click the** Effect menu, **point to** 3D, **then click** Revolve

8. **Click the** Preview check box, **click the** arrow **next to Offset, drag the slider to approximately** 135, **click** OK, **then compare your result to Figure G-22**
   The object is revolved around the object's left edge with an offset radius of 135 points, creating the effect of a negative circular space around which the object revolves.

9. **Save your work, then close 3d revolve_AI-G.ai**

FIGURE G-20: Revolving the artwork

FIGURE G-21: Rotating the revolved artwork

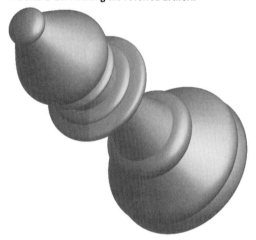

FIGURE G-22: Revolving a 135 pt offset

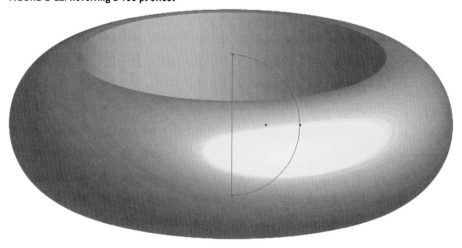

Practice

Concepts Review

Label the elements of the Illustrator screen shown in Figure G-23.

FIGURE G-23

Match each term with the statement that best describes it.

6. Warps
7. Shear tool
8. Revolve
9. Extrude
10. Layers panel
11. Tiling

a. Separates artwork
b. Extend an object on its Z-axis
c. Repeating a single original pattern
d. Distorts artwork along a horizontal or vertical axis
e. Creates multiple duplicates of an object that sweep around the Y-axis
f. Create fun and practical results

Select the best answer from the list of choices.

12. When you are ready to create a pattern, drag it to the _____ panel.

   a. Styles   **c.** Swatches

   b. Pattern brushes   **d.** Patterns

13. The following dialog box allows you to scale a pattern without scaling the object that is filled by the pattern _____.

   a. Scale   **c.** Resize

   b. Pattern Options   **d.** Scale Pattern

14. The Z-axis represents the _____ of the object.

   a. height   **c.** angle

   b. depth   **d.** width

15. When you apply an effect to an object, it is listed on the _____ panel.

   a. Appearance   **c.** Effects

   b. Layers   **d.** None of the above

Skills Review

1. Layer artwork.

   a. Open the file AI G-8.ai from the location where you store your Data Files, save it as **new earth layers_AI-G**, then click the Layers panel button to open the Layers panel. (*Hint*: Choose the Essentials workspace, then reset the workpace, if necessary.)

   b. On the Layers panel, click Globe to select the Globe layer, click the Layers panel menu button, then click New Layer.

   c. Type **New Earth** in the Name text box, click the Color list arrow, click Gold, then click OK.

   d. Click the Selection tool, then click the globe artwork on the artboard to select it.

   e. Click and drag the Indicates Selected Art button on the Background layer up to the same location on the Globe layer.

   f. Select the *GREEN* text on the artboard, then click and drag the Indicates Selected Art button on the Background layer on the Layers panel up to the Green Text layer.

   g. Click and drag the Green Text layer on the Layers panel above the Globe layer, then release the mouse button.

   h. Select both instances of the *A NEW EARTH* text on the artboard, then drag the Indicates Selected Art button on the Background layer up to the New Earth layer. (*Hint:* Select one instance at a time, if necessary.)

FIGURE G-24

   i. Click the Target button on the New Earth layer on the Layers panel to select all of the artwork on the New Earth layer.

   j. Change the stroke color of the selection to CMYK Blue, then save your work.

   k. Deselect, compare your screen to Figure G-24, then close new earth layers_AI-G.ai.

2. Create a pattern swatch.

   a. Open the file AI G-9.ai from the location where you store your Data Files, save it as **star pattern_AI-G**, then verify that the Swatches panel is visible.

   b. Click the Selection tool, select all of the artwork to the left of the green rectangle, then drag the artwork onto the Swatches panel.

   c. Delete the selected artwork from the artboard, double-click the new pattern swatch on the Swatches panel to open the Pattern Options panel, then replace the existing name with **Star** in the Name text box.

    d. Double-click the small white star in the center of the pattern artwork inside the pattern tile to select just the star.

    e. Verify that the Fill button is active on the Tools panel, then click C=0 Y=35 M=85 B=0 (orange) on the Swatches panel.

    f. Double-click the white circle around the orange star inside the pattern tile.

    g. Click the Effect menu, point to Distort & Transform, then click Pucker & Bloat.

    h. In the Pucker & Bloat dialog box, drag the slider to -13, then click OK.

    i. Click Done below the Control panel, then click OK in the warning box to expand the artwork.

    j. Save your work.

3. Apply and edit a pattern swatch.

    a. Double-click the Hand tool on the Tools panel to fit the artboard in the window.

    b. Click the Selection tool, select the green square on the artboard.

    c. Click the Star pattern swatch on the Swatches panel.

    d. Double-click the Scale tool on the Tools panel.

    e. Click the Uniform option button in the Scale dialog box, then type **25** in the Uniform text box.

    f. Click the Transform Objects check box to remove the check mark, then click the Transform Patterns check box to add a check mark, if necessary.

    g. Click the Preview check box, click OK to close the dialog box, then save your work.

    h. Close star pattern_AI-G.ai.

4. Use the Shear tool.

    a. Open the file AI G-10.ai from the location where you store your Data Files, save it as **shear review_AI-G**, click the Selection tool, then select the text.

    b. Copy the text, paste in front, change the fill color to C=0 M=0 Y=0 K=30 (light gray), then select the Shear tool. (*Hint*: The Shear tool is hidden behind the Scale tool.)

    c. Press and hold [Alt] (Win) or [option] (Mac), then click the bottom anchor point of the letter *S*.

    d. Type **45** in the Shear Angle text box, verify that the Horizontal option button is selected, then click OK.

    e. Select the Scale tool, press and hold [Alt] (Win) or [option] (Mac), then click the bottom anchor point of the letter *S*.

    f. Click the Non-Uniform option button in the Scale dialog box, type **100** in the Horizontal text box, type **50** in the Vertical text box, then click OK.

    g. Click the Object menu, point to Arrange, then click Send to Back.

    h. Click the Selection tool, select the black letters, fill the black letters with CMYK Red, apply a 1-pt Black stroke, deselect, then compare your screen to Figure G-25.

    i. Save your work, then close shear review_AI-G.ai.

FIGURE G-25

5. Distort with the Free Transform tool.

    a. Open the file AI G-11.ai from the location where you store your Data Files, save it as **change_AI-G**, click the Selection tool if necessary, then select all. (*Hint*: The selection edges are hidden.)

    b. Click the Free Transform tool, then position the mouse pointer over the upper-left handle of the bounding box.

    c. Click and hold the mouse pointer on the anchor point.

    d. Press and hold [Ctrl] (Win) or [⌘] (Mac), drag straight down to the top of the letter *P*, then release the mouse button and [Ctrl] (Win) or [⌘] (Mac).

    e. Position the mouse pointer over the lower-right handle of the bounding box, then click and hold the mouse pointer on the anchor point.

    f. Press and hold [Ctrl] (Win) or [⌘] (Mac), then drag the handle down approximately 1 1/2 inches.

    g. Save your work, then close change_AI-G.ai.

Skills Review (continued)

6. **Apply Warp effects.**

   a. Open the file AI G-12.ai, save it as **warp text_AI-G**, then open the Appearance panel.

   b. Select all, group the selection, click the Effect menu, point to Warp, then click Arc.

   c. Click the Preview check box, verify that the Horizontal option button is chosen, drag the Bend slider to 40, then click OK.

   d. Click the View menu, then click Hide Edges.

   e. Click Warp: Arc on the Appearance panel.

   f. Drag the Bend slider to 35, click the Vertical option button, then click OK.

   g. Save your work, then compare your screen to Figure G-26.

   h. Close warp text_AI-G.ai.

7. **Extrude a 3D object.**

   a. Open the file AI G-13.ai from the location where you store your Data Files, save it as **extrude review_AI-G**, select the green circle, then hide its edges.

   b. Click the Effect menu, point to 3D, then click Extrude & Bevel.

   c. Click the Preview check box, set the Extrude Depth value to 125, then click OK. (*Hint*: If you cannot drag the slider to 125, type **125** in the Extrude Depth text box.)

   d. Click 3D Extrude & Bevel on the Appearance panel.

   e. Click the Preview check box, click and drag the rotation cube in various directions, then release the mouse button.

   f. Type **60** in the Specify rotation around the X-axis text box, type **25** in the Specify rotation around the Y-axis text box, type **30** in the Specify rotation around the Z-axis text box, then click OK.

   g. Click the Object menu, click Expand Appearance, click the View menu, then click Show Edges.

   h. Use the Direct Selection tool to select various areas of the artwork and change their color for better effect.

   i. Deselect all, then compare your artwork to Figure G-27.

   j. Save your work, then close extrude review_AI-G.ai.

8. **Revolve a 3D object.**

   a. Open the file AI G-14.ai from the location where you store your Data Files, then save it as **revolve_AI-G**.

   b. Click the Selection tool, select the letter *E*, hide the edges, then hide the bounding box, if necessary.

   c. Click the Effect menu, point to 3D, then click Revolve.

   d. Click the Preview check box, then click OK.

   e. Click 3D Revolve on the Appearance panel, click the Preview check box, click and drag the rotation cube in various directions, then release the mouse button.

   f. Type **-20** in the Specify rotation around the X-axis text box, type **21** in the Specify rotation around the Y-axis text box, type **30** in the Specify rotation around the Z-axis text box, then click OK.

   g. Show edges, select the purple object, then click 3D Revolve on the Appearance panel.

   h. Click the Preview check box, click the arrow next to Offset, drag the slider to 20, then click OK.

   i. Save your work, compare your screen to Figure G-28, then close revolve_AI-G.ai.

Independent Challenge 1

You're designing gift wrap for a major department store. You use the Pattern feature in Illustrator to create your ideas.

a. Open the file AI G-15.ai from the location where you store your Data Files, then save it as **gift wrap_AI-G**.

b. Select the red circle on the artboard, then apply a Pucker & Bloat effect with a value of 12.

c. Drag the artwork to the Swatches panel to create a new pattern swatch.

d. Delete the artwork from the artboard.

e. Double-click the new pattern swatch, then rename the pattern **Gift Wrap**.

f. In the Pattern Options panel, change the Copies value to 3×3.

g. Using the shape tools, add some colorful shapes to the pattern, then click Done.

h. Create a 7×7 rectangle on the artboard, then fill it with the Gift Wrap pattern.

i. Deselect, save your work, then compare your screen to Figure G-29.

j. Close gift wrap_AI-G.ai.

FIGURE G-29

Independent Challenge 2

You are a web site designer. Your client wants to create an icon that suggests making a note of something important. She wants something different, not your everyday sticky note. You decide to create a pushpin.

a. Open the file AI G-16.ai, then save it as **push pin_AI-G**.

b. Select all, then group the objects.

c. Apply the 3D Revolve effect to the object.

d. Manipulate the rotation cube in any direction that you like.

e. Save your work, then compare your screen to Figure G-30, which shows one possible result.

FIGURE G-30

Advanced Challenge Exercise

■ Click the Selection tool, then drag the pushpin artwork onto the Swatches panel to create a new pattern.

■ Delete the pushpin artwork from the artboard.

■ Create a large rectangle, then fill it with the pushpin pattern.

f. Close push pin_AI-G.ai.

Independent Challenge 3

You are preparing a test for your art design students. The test is designed to challenge your students' ability to visualize simple paths and how they will appear when the 3D Revolve effect is applied. You have created six graphics, all of which are simple paths to which the 3D Revolve effect has been applied. (No rotation or offset has been applied.) Students will be asked to draw the simple path that is the basis for each graphic.

    a. Open AI G-17.ai, then save it as **revolve shapes_AI-G**.

    b. Look at the first graphic, then try to visualize what it would look like if the 3D Revolve effect were removed.

    c. Using a pencil and paper, draw the original path that was used to create the graphic.

    d. Do the same for the remaining five graphics on the artboard.

    e. Select each graphic, then click 3D Revolve on the Appearance panel to view the original shape.

    f. Compare your pencil drawings to the graphics in the file.

    g. Save your work, then close revolve shapes_AI-G.ai.

Real Life Independent Challenge

The birthday gift you've picked out for a friend is on backorder and won't be here in time for his birthday. You decide to create a card showing him what his gift will be: a lava lamp.

    a. Open AI G-18.ai, then save it as **lava lamp_AI-G**.

    b. Click the Selection tool, then drag the three path segments so that they are aligned with the guide.

    c. Click the View menu, point to Guides, then click Hide Guides.

    d. Select all, click the Effect menu, point to 3D, then click Revolve.

    e. Click the Preview check box, note the results, then click Cancel.

    f. Group the three paths, select the Revolve effect again, then click the Preview check box.

    g. Click OK.

Advanced Challenge Exercise

    ■ Show the Appearance panel, if necessary.

    ■ Select the lava lamp on the artboard.

    ■ Click 3D Revolve on the Appearance panel.

    ■ Click the Preview check box.

    ■ Change the Perspective value to 80°, then click OK.

    h. With the artwork selected, click the Object menu, then click Expand Appearance.

    i. Modify any areas of the artwork that you want to fix or improve, then compare your result to Figure G-31.

    j. Close lava lamp_AI-G.ai.

FIGURE G-31

Visual Workshop

Open AI G-19.ai, then save it as **fish warp_AI-G**. Use the Fish warp effect and the Bend slider to recreate the approximate result shown in Figure G-32. Save your work, then close fish warp_AI-G.ai.

FIGURE G-32

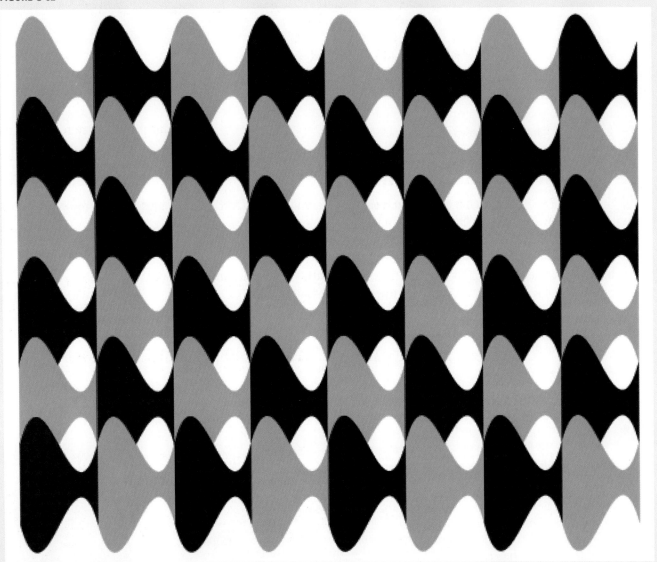

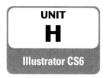

UNIT
H
Illustrator CS6

Enhancing Artwork and Creating Web Graphics

Files You Will Need:

To view a list of files needed for this unit, see the Data Files Grid in the back of the book.

You are now ready to take your artwork "to the next level," meaning you're ready to create an illustration that is a cohesive, integrated piece of artwork—one that is visually dynamic and unique. The Width tool is an excellent resource for quickly resizing the width of stroked artwork, creating dramatic arcs of varying widths. A Bristle brush allows you to apply brush strokes or to paint an object with the effect of traditional media, like a watercolor brush. You can also use the Shape Builder tool to create unique, complex objects as part of your illustration. When you're really ready to go to the next level, you can use the Export to SWF option to export Illustrator blends and non-blend Illustrator artwork as an animation for the web. Megapixel asks you to explore tools and techniques for creating more complex, unique and cohesive illustrations, including animations for the web.

OBJECTIVES

Use the Width tool

Create a new Bristle brush

Paint with a Bristle brush

Create objects with the Shape Builder tool

Export artwork for the web

Export a blend as an animated SWF

Create an animation from non-blend artwork

Export non-blend artwork as an animated SWF

UNIT
H

Illustrator CS6

Using the Width Tool

The Width tool offers you a method for quickly altering the width of a stroke by clicking and dragging the stroke itself. With the Width tool, you simply position the tool over the stroke, then click and drag to increase or decrease the width of the stroke. What's really great about the Width tool is that you can click and drag any area of a path, not just over an already-existing anchor point. This makes the entire path available to you to modify. You email Jon an illustration that you've done of a flower, and he asks you to use the Width tool to make your illustration more visually dynamic.

STEPS

1. **Open AI H-1.ai, then save it as** width tool_AI-H

2. **Click the** Selection tool **, select the vase, then click the** Width tool

> **TROUBLE**
> Zoom in on the vase if necessary.

3. **Position the Width tool over the path of the vase, then click and drag to alter the width of different areas of the vase**

   Figure H-1 shows one possible outcome.

4. **Continue clicking and dragging every path in the illustration to create various widths and new shapes**

   Figure H-2 shows one example of the finished illustration.

5. **Save your work, then close width tool_AI-H.ai**

Expanding strokes modified with the Width tool

When you modify strokes with the Width tool, the Width tool does not change the nature of the stroke—it remains a stroke. The Stroke panel will list the stroke weight at its largest width. In other words, the largest width that you create when dragging with the Width tool is the width that will be listed for the stroke in the Stroke panel.

As with any other stroke, the modified stroke can be converted to an object using the Outline Stroke command. Even though the modified stroke is not applied as an appearance, you can select an object with a modified width and apply the Expand Appearance command. This will convert the stroke to a separate filled object.

Enhancing Artwork and Creating Web Graphics

FIGURE H-1: Width tool applied to the vase

FIGURE H-2: Illustration enhanced by the Width tool

Enhancing Artwork and Creating Web Graphics

Creating a New Bristle Brush

A Bristle brush is a type of brush that you can create in the Brushes panel then use to paint or stroke artwork. A Bristle brush creates a natural brush stroke with the streaks and varying opacities you would find with an actual paint brush, allowing you to mimic the look and feel of traditional disciplines like watercolor or paint. Just like the Paintbrush tool, a Bristle brush creates stroked paths. The color you apply to objects with a Bristle brush is applied as a stroke color. To use the Bristle brush, you first create a new brush in the Brushes panel and choose Bristle Brush as the definition. This opens the Bristle Brush Options dialog box, where you can choose from different brush shapes, like Round Fan or Round Point, and you can specify the stiffness, opacity, thickness, and length of the bristles. With the Bristle brush though, you'll find that the many options are best experienced and understood by giving them a try. For an alternative piece, Jon asks that you use the same basic flower illustration, but that this time you modify it by painting with a Bristle brush.

STEPS

1. Open AI H-2.ai, then save it as bristle flower_AI-H
2. Click the Brushes panel button to open the Brushes panel
3. Click the Brushes panel menu button , then click New Brush
   The New Brush dialog box opens.
4. Click the Bristle Brush option button, then click OK
   The Bristle Brush Options dialog box opens.
5. Type Flower Bristle Brush in the Name text box
6. Enter the settings shown in Figure H-3, then click OK
7. Select all the artwork on the artboard, then change the fill color to white
8. Click the Flower Bristle Brush on the Brushes panel
9. Deselect all, save your work, then compare your artwork to Figure H-4

FIGURE H-3: Moving the Atlas layer above the Globe layer

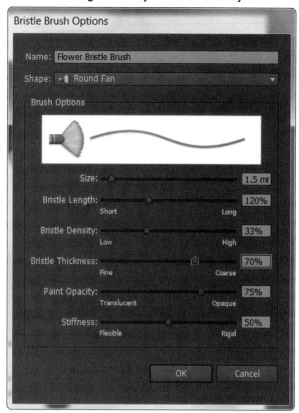

FIGURE H-4: Bristle brush applied to strokes

Painting with a Bristle Brush

Adobe has strived to make Illustrator more and more of a drawing and painting tool, to devise and develop "computer tools" that mimic traditional art tools like pens, brushes, crayons, chalk, and so forth. The Bristle brush represents a real step forward toward that goal. To get the most effect out of working with the Bristle brush, use a Wacom or other brand of pen tablet device. Depending on the device and the features available, the pen will incorporate factors like pressure, angle, and rotation. If you use a mouse or non-tablet device, you can still use the Bristle brush, but it will be like working with a brush fixed at a 45-degree angle. The key when working with the Bristle brush is to experiment. There are no best sets of steps or specific approaches—you simply need to try a variety of techniques and find the ones that work best for your needs. Jon likes the Bristle brush stroke that you've applied to the artwork, but he tells you that you can really "kick it up a notch" by actually painting the illustration with the Paintbrush tool armed with a Bristle brush.

STEPS

1. Verify that the flower artwork is deselected, then open the Layers panel
2. Click the Create New Layer button 🔲 on the Layers panel
   You will paint with the Bristle brush on the empty new layer.
3. Click the Paintbrush tool 🖌, then verify that the Flower Bristle Brush is selected on the Brushes panel
4. Set the Stroke color to one of the green swatches on the Swatches panel
5. Paint the leaves and the stem of the flower artwork, setting your stroke color to various shades of green, then compare your results to Figure H-5
   Feel free to set the Paintbrush tool size and opacity in the Control panel as you like. Your results, obviously, will be unique. You can use the figure as one example of what can be done.
6. Continue painting with various colors to finish the illustration
7. Paint with a black stroke to strengthen the outlines of the artwork, as shown in Figure H-6
8. Paint with a white stroke to add highlights to the artwork, as shown in Figure H-7
9. Save your work, then close the file

TROUBLE
If a warning dialog box appears when you save the file, click the "Don't show again while working on this file in the current session" check box, then click OK.

Using the Multiply blending mode with the Bristle brush

When you work with a Bristle brush using the methods in this lesson, you can first apply the brush as a dark outline to the artwork, then you can paint the interior with the brush. One issue that can develop is that when you paint the interior, the color overlaps and covers the outline. To resolve this, place the outlined artwork on a layer above the painted interior artwork. When you do so, all you'll see is the outlined artwork around objects with a white fill. Select all the outlined objects, then apply the Multiply blending mode in the Transparency panel. Multiply makes all white fills and strokes transparent. Thus, all you'll see is the black outline over the painted interior artwork. You can test this out in the Skills Review and Independent Challenge 3 at the end of this unit.

FIGURE H-5: Painting the green areas

FIGURE H-6: Painting with black

FIGURE H-7: Painting with white

Creating Objects with the Shape Builder Tool

The Shape Builder tool is designed to help you create new objects by creating new closed paths from overlapping objects. Closed objects are highlighted when you drag the Shape Builder tool across them. After doing so, the objects are united into a single object with the current fill and stroke color. In addition to creating new objects, the Shape Builder tool also deletes closed paths from overlapping objects. To delete an object with the Shape Builder tool, press and hold [Alt] (Win) or [option] (Mac) then click or drag over the objects you want to delete.  You sketch a design for a logo and decide that the best way to create it would be to use the Shape Builder tool.

STEPS

1. Open AI H-3.ai, from the drive and folder where your Data Files are stored, then save it as shape builder_AI-H

2. Select all, then click the Shape Builder tool 🔘

3. Set the fill color to CMYK Yellow and the stroke color to None

    Even though the pink circles are selected, when you set the foreground color to a different color, the circles don't change color when you're using the Shape Builder tool.

4. Using Figure H-8 as a guide, click and drag the Shape Builder tool pointer ▶₊ over the objects

    When you release the mouse button, the objects are united as a single object and filled with CMYK Yellow.

5. Click and drag ▶₊ to highlight the objects shown in Figure H-9

    Because you included the first yellow object, the objects are united into a single object.

6. Change the fill color to CMYK Cyan

7. Repeat Step 5 to create the objects shown in Figure H-10

8. Press and hold [Alt] (Win) or [option] (Mac), click or drag over one of the remaining pink objects, then click and drag over the other

9. Deselect all, compare your results to Figure H-11, save your work, then close the file

FIGURE H-8: Creating the first yellow shape

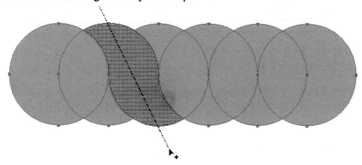

FIGURE H-9: Creating the second yellow shape

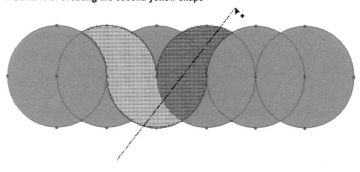

FIGURE H-10: Two cyan objects

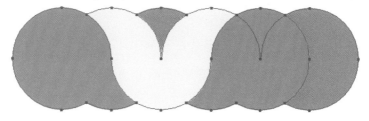

FIGURE H-11: Artwork with pink objects removed

UNIT
H
Illustrator CS6

Exporting Artwork for the Web

SWF is an acronym for Shockwave Flash, Adobe's Flash Player. For Illustrator graphics, SWF will be your export format of choice for exporting to graphics for the web. With SWF, you can export your file to be placed and used in Adobe Flash, or the file can be opened directly by web browser software like Internet Explorer or Mozilla Firefox. You can also upload an SWF file as content on a website. Jon tells you that he wants to use your illustration on the company's website and asks you to export it for the web.

STEPS

1. **Open AI H-4.ai, then save it as** web umbrella_AI-H

2. **Click the** File menu, **then click** Export

   The Export dialog box opens.

3. **Click the** Save as type list arrow, **then click** Flash (*.SWF) **or** Format list arrow, **then click** Flash (swf) **(Mac)**

4. **Click** Save

   The SWF Options dialog box opens.

> **TROUBLE**
> If your dialog box looks different than the figure, click the Basic button in the dialog box.

5. **Apply the settings shown in Figure H-12**

6. **Click** OK

   The file is now available to be used in Adobe Flash.

7. **Launch your browser software, then navigate to where you exported the SWF file**

> **QUICK TIP**
> There are different ways to open a SWF file. You can right-click the .swf file, point to Open with Internet Explorer (Win) or [Ctr][click], point to Open With, click Other, then choose Safari in the Applications folder (Mac). The default for opening a .swf on Mac or Windows is Flash player.

8. **Open the** web umbrella_AI-H.swf **file**

   As shown in Figure H-13, the file opens in your web browser, in this case Internet Explorer.

9. **Close the browser window, save your work, then close the file**

FIGURE H-12: SWF Options dialog box

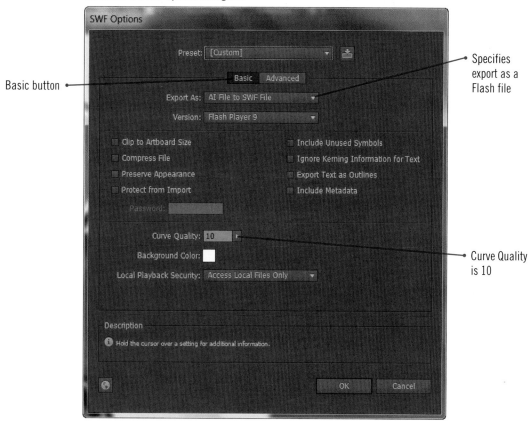

Basic button •

Specifies export as a Flash file

Curve Quality is 10

FIGURE H-13: Artwork in a web browser

Exporting a Blend as an Animated SWF

Illustrator allows you to export a blend as an animation. To export any illustrator artwork—blend or no blend—as an animation, you must choose AI Layers to SWF Frames in the Export As dialog box. When you do, the Advanced SWF Options dialog box offers controls for animations. If the artwork you're exporting is a blend, be sure to check the Animate Blends check box; Illustrator will export each object in the blend as its own frame in the animation. You can also choose between the Sequence and Build options. Choosing **Sequence** means that each subsequent frame will contain the next object in the blend. Choosing **Build** means that each subsequent frame will add the next object in the blend, with each frame "building." With blended artwork, generally speaking, you'll want to choose the Sequence option.  You recently designed a blend in Illustrator, and Jon asks you to export it as an animated SWF for the company's website.

STEPS

1. **Open AI H-5.ai, then save it as** animated blend_AI-H

   The artwork is a five-step blend between the circle and the flower.

2. **Click the** File menu, **then click** Export

3. **Click the** Save as type list arrow, **then if necessary, click** Flash (*.SWF) **or** Format list arrow, **then click** Flash (swf) (Mac)

4. **Click** Save **(Win) or** Export **(Mac)**

   The SWF Options dialog box opens.

5. **Choose the settings shown in Figure H-14**

   Note that AI Layers to SWF Frames is chosen for the Export As option. The file will be exported as an animated SWF, with each object in the blend a different frame in the animation.

6. **Click the** Advanced button, **then enter the settings shown in Figure H-15**

   Note the Frame Rate is set to 12 fps (frames per second). The Animate Blends check box is checked and will be animated in sequence, meaning each object in the blend will appear in sequence. Note too that the animation has been set to Looping—it will play continuously.

7. **Click** OK

8. **Launch your browser software, then navigate to where you exported the SWF file**

9. **Open the animated blend_AI-H.swf file**

   The animation will play in the browser window.

10. **Close the browser window, save your work, then close the file**

TROUBLE

You may need to temporarily disable security measures installed with your browser software that might inhibit your ability to play the animation.

FIGURE H-14: Choosing to export AI Layers to SWF Frames

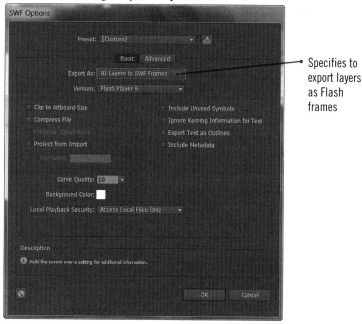

Specifies to
export layers
as Flash
frames

FIGURE H-15: Advanced options for specifying animation

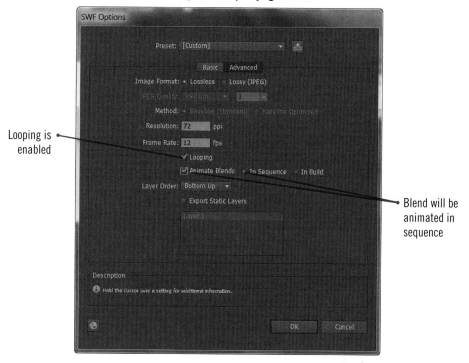

Looping is
enabled

Blend will be
animated in
sequence

Setting the frame rate

All animations play at a specific frame rate. The frame rate measures the number of frames that will play in a second, thus it is specified as frames per second (fps). When you export a blend, each object in the blend will be one frame. The frame rate directly affects the speed of the animation. If you had a blend with six objects and you set the frame rate to six fps, the animation would complete from start to finish in one second; each object would appear for $1/6$ second. It follows logically that if you reduced the frame rate to one fps, the animation would play more slowly; with each frame appearing for one second, the total run time for the animation would be six seconds.

Creating an Animation from Non-Blend Artwork

Illustrations that you create in Illustrator without blends can be exported as animations. To do so, you must first put the components of the artwork on separate layers. Rather than do this by hand, you can use the Release to Layers command on the Layers panel. This will move each object onto an individual layer, from bottom to top, in the order they were created. You always have the option of reordering the layers by hand if you want to manipulate that order. ▰▰▰ You've created an illustration that doesn't contain a blend, and Jon asks that you set up the file so that it can be exported as an animated SWF for the company's website.

STEPS

1. **Open AI H-6.ai, save it as** animated flower_AI-H, **then select all the artwork**

   The artwork was created using the red petal as the start object and rotating it around a fixed point.

2. **Open the Layers panel, click the** Layers panel menu button ▣, **then click** Release to Layers (Build)

   As shown in Figure H-16, each object is moved to its own layer. The layers are created in sequence, from bottom to top, in the order that objects were created. The first object created—the top red petal—is the bottom-most layer. The next layer up is the red petal plus the maroon petal. With each subsequent layer, from bottom up, a new petal is added. Thus the illustration "builds" from the bottom up.

3. **On the Layers panel, select all of the layers except for Layer 1**

4. **Click** ▣, **then click** Duplicate Selection

   New duplicate layers are created. They all have the word *copy* in their names. No layers are selected on the panel.

5. **Select all the layers with the word** *copy* **in their name**

6. **Click** ▣, **then click** Reverse Order

7. **Save your work**

FIGURE H-16: Objects released to layers

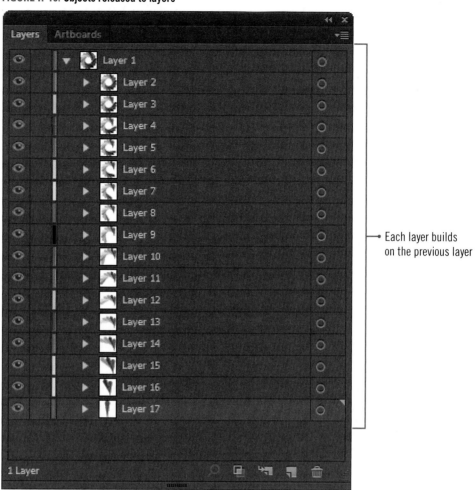

Each layer builds
on the previous layer

Illustrator CS6

Exporting Non-Blend Artwork as an Animated SWF

When you export non-blend artwork as an animated SWF, you have the option to loop the artwork so that it plays repeatedly. You can also choose the layer order to determine the sequence of the animation.  Jon asks that you export the non-blend artwork as an animated SWF for the company's website.

1. **Click the** File menu, **then click** Export

2. **Click the** Save as type list arrow, **click** Flash (*.SWF) **or** Format list arrow, **then click** Flash (swf) **(Mac), then click** Save **(Win) or** Export **(Mac)**

3. **Enter the settings shown in Figure H-17**

4. **Click the** Advanced button, **then enter the settings shown in Figure H-18**
   Note that the Animate Blends check box is not checked—this is not blended artwork. The Layer Order option is set to Bottom Up.

5. **Click** OK, **then open the exported .SWF file in your web browser**
   The illustration builds counter-clockwise, then reverses direction and the petals disappear clockwise.

6. **Close the browser window, save your work, then close the file**

FIGURE H-17: Choosing to export AI Layers to SWF Frames

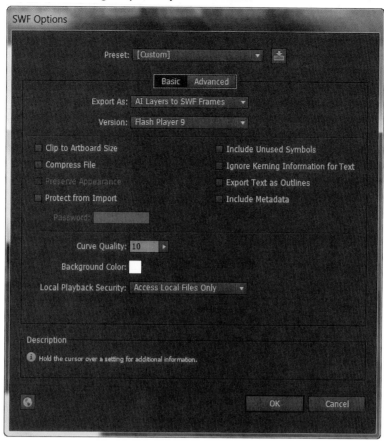

FIGURE H-18: Advanced Options in the SWF Options dialog box

Animate
Blends not
checked

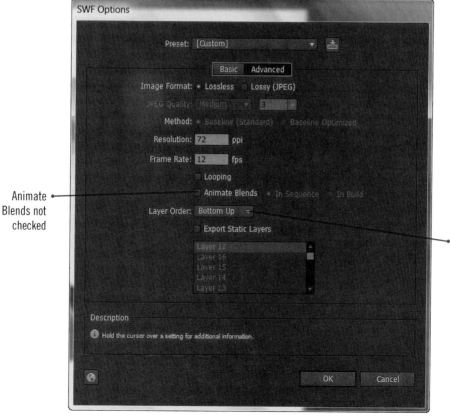

Layer Order set to
animate from
bottom layer up

Practice

Concepts Review

Label the elements of the Illustrator screen shown in Figure H-19.

FIGURE H-19

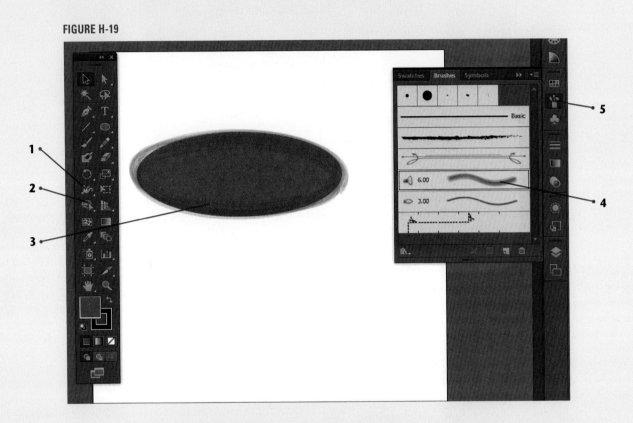

Match each term with the statement that best describes it.

6. SWF
7. Bristle brush
8. Browser
9. Width tool
10. Looping
11. Reverse Order

a. Mimics traditional media
b. Repeats an animation
c. Changes stroke appearance
d. File format used for web graphics
e. Software used to view web pages
f. Controls the sequence of frames in an animation

Select the best answer from the list of choices.

12. **The Shape Builder tool** _____.
    a. creates objects
    b. deletes objects
    c. duplicates objects
    d. a and b

13. **To view Illustrator artwork in web browser software, you must first** _____.
    a. position all objects on a separate layer
    b. save the file as an SWF
    c. save layers as frames
    d. none of the above

14. **Illustrator artwork** _____.
    a. can always be animated
    b. can sometimes be animated
    c. can be animated only when blended
    d. none of the above

15. **Blended Illustrator artwork** _____.
    a. can be saved
    b. can be exported
    c. can be animated
    d. all of the above

Skills Review

1. **Use the Width tool.**
   a. Open AI H-7.ai, then save it as **width tool skills_AI-H**.
   b. Select the red scalloped circle, then click the Width tool.
   c. Click and drag different areas of the stroke with the Width tool to alter the width. Figure H-20 shows one possible outcome.
   d. Save your work, then close width tool skills_AI-H.ai.

2. **Create a new Bristle brush.**
   a. Open AI H-8.ai, then save it as **snowball bristle_AI-H**.
   b. Open the Brushes panel, click the Brushes panel menu button, then click New Brush.
   c. Click the Bristle Brush option button, then click OK.
   d. Type **Snowball Bristle** in the Name text box.
   e. Accept the default settings, then click OK.
   f. Select all of the artwork on the artboard, then change the fill color to White.
   g. Click the Snowball Bristle brush on the Brushes panel.
   h. Deselect all, then save your work.

3. **Paint with a Bristle brush.**
   a. Verify that the artwork is deselected, then open the Layers panel.
   b. Click the Create New Layer button on the Layers panel. (*Hint*: You will paint with the Bristle brush on the empty new layer.)
   c. Click the Paintbrush tool on the Tools panel, then verify that the Snowball Bristle brush is selected on the Brushes panel.
   d. Paint with various stroke colors to finish the illustration.
   e. On the Layers panel, drag Layer 1 to the top of the Layers panel.
   f. Select all objects on Layer 1.
   g. In the Transparency panel, set the blending mode to Multiply.
   h. Figure H-21 shows one example of a finished illustration.
   i. Save your work, then close snowball bristle_AI-H.ai.

FIGURE H-20

FIGURE H-21

Skills Review (continued)

4. **Create objects with the Shape Builder tool.**
   a. Open AI H-9.ai, then save it as **shape builder skills_AI-H**.
   b. Select all, then click the Shape Builder tool.
   c. Set the fill color to **C=50 M=0 Y=100 K=0 (green)** and the stroke color to Black.
   d. Click and drag the Shape Builder tool to highlight the objects as shown in Figure H-22.
   e. Press and hold [Alt] (Win) or [option] (Mac), then drag over the bottom row of yellow diamonds.
   f. Press and hold [Alt] (Win) or [option] (Mac), then drag over the top row of yellow diamonds.
   g. Deselect, compare your results to Figure H-23, then save your work.

FIGURE H-22

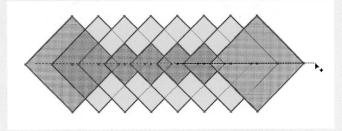

FIGURE H-23

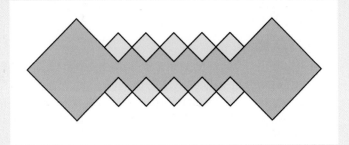

5. **Export artwork for the web.**
   a. Click the File menu, then click Export.
   b. Click the Save as type list arrow, then click Flash (*.SWF) or Format list arrow, then click Flash (swf) (Mac).
   c. Click Save (Win) or Export (Mac).
   d. Click the Export As list arrow, then click AI File to SWF File. (*Hint*: Click the Basic button in the dialog box, if necessary.)
   e. Click OK.
   f. Launch your browser software, then open the exported SWF file.
   g. Close the browser window, save your work, then close shape builder skills_AI-H.ai.

6. **Export a blend as an animated SWF.**
   a. Open AI H-10.ai, then save it as **animated blend skills_AI-H**.
   b. Click the File menu, then click Export.
   c. Click the Save as type list arrow, then choose Flash (*.SWF) or Format list arrow then click Flash (swf) (Mac).
   d. Click Save (Win) or **Export** (Mac).
   e. Click the Export As list arrow, then click AI Layers to SWF Frames. (*Hint*: Click the Basic button in the dialog box, if necessary.)
   f. Click the Advanced button, then set the frame rate to 72.
   g. Verify that Looping is checked.
   h. Verify that the Animate Blends check box is checked and that the In Sequence option is chosen.
   i. Click OK.
   j. Launch your browser software, then open animated blend skills_AI-H.swf. Close the browser window save your work, then close animated blend skills_AI-H.ai.

7. **Create an animation from non-blend artwork.**
   a. Open AI H-11.ai, save it as **splash page sequence_AI-H**, then select all of the artwork.
   b. Open the Layers panel, click the Layers panel menu button then click Release to Layers (Sequence).
   c. On the Layers panel, select all the layers except Layer 1.
   d. Open the Layers panel menu, then click Duplicate Selection.
   e. Select all the layers with the word *copy* in their name.
   f. Click the Layers panel menu button, then click Reverse Order.
   g. Save your work.

Skills Review (continued)

8. Export non-blend artwork as an animated SWF.

a. Click the File menu, then click Export.

b. Click the Save as type list arrow, then choose Flash (*.SWF) or Format list arrow, then click Flash (swf) (Mac).

c. Click Save (Win) or Export (Mac).

d. Click the Export As list arrow, then click AI Layers to SWF Frames. (*Hint*: Click the Basic button in the dialog box, if necessary.)

e. Click the Advanced button, then enter the settings shown in Figure H-24.

f. Click OK.

g. Open the exported SWF file in your web browser.

h. Close the browser window, save your work, then close the file.

FIGURE H-24

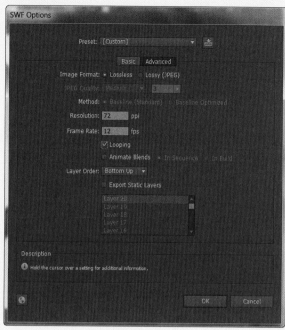

Independent Challenge 1

You've just completed the drawing of a character for a logo and you show it to your creative director. She asks you to modify the line weights of the strokes to make the illustration more dynamic.

a. Open AI H-12.ai, then save it as **web logo_AI-H**.

b. Click the Width tool.

c. Click and drag to select different areas of each object to alter the stroke width.

d. Compare your screen to Figure H-25. The figure shows the logo before and after the Width tool was applied.

Advanced Challenge Exercise

- Click the Selection tool, then select the pompom on the hat.
- Click the Object menu, then click Expand Appearance.
- Select all the other objects with modified strokes and expand their appearance.

e. Save your work, then close web logo_AI-H.ai.

FIGURE H-25

Before   After

Independent Challenge 2

You've created an animation in which a circle becomes a star while it moves across the screen. Your creative director asks that you change the animation so that the circle morphs to a star and back, but without moving across the screen.

FIGURE H-26

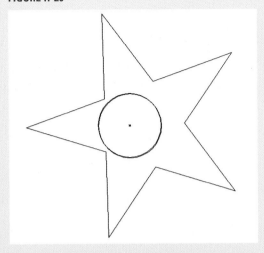

a. Open AI H-13.ai, then save it as **morph_AI-H**. (*Hint*: The blend is composed of 512 objects.)

b. Switch the view to Outline mode, then click the Direct Selection tool.

c. Drag the center points of each object so that the blended objects are aligned as shown in Figure H-26.

d. Export the file as a SWF using the AI Layers to SWF Frames setting, and then using the Advanced settings shown in Figure H-27.

e. Click OK.

f. View the animation in your browser.

Advanced Challenge Exercise

- Click the File menu, then click Export.
- Export the blend with a frame rate of 120 fps.
- View the animation in your browser and note the change in speed.

g. Save your work, then close morph_AI-H.ai.

Independent Challenge 3

You're a designer and you're exploring Illustrator as a venue for producing traditional watercolor effects. You create a Bristle brush, then paint an illustration to create the effect.

FIGURE H-27

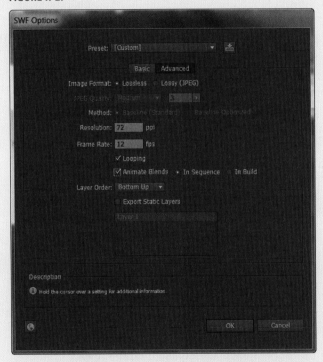

a. Open AI H-14.ai, then save it as **bristle brush practice_AI-H**.

b. Use the View menu to verify that Edges are showing, click the Brushes panel menu button, then click New Brush.

c. Click Bristle Brush, then click OK.

d. Type **Montag Bristle** in the Name text box.

e. Set the size to 2mm, then click OK.

f. Select all the artwork on the artboard, then change the fill color to white.

g. Click the Montag Bristle brush on the Brushes panel.

h. Deselect all, then save your work. (*Hint*: If you get a warning about multiple Bristle Brush paths, click the Don't show again while working on this file in the current session check box, and then click OK to close the dialog box.)

i. Verify that the artwork is deselected, then open the Layers panel.

j. Click the Create New Layer button on the Layers panel. You will paint with the Bristle brush in this new empty layer.

k. Target the new layer.

l. Click the Paintbrush tool on the Tools panel, then verify that the Montag Bristle brush is selected on the Brushes panel.

Independent Challenge 3 (continued)

m. Paint with various stroke colors throughout the illustration.

n. On the Layers panel, drag Layer 1 to the top of the Layers panel.

o. Select all objects on Layer 1.

p. On the Transparency panel, set the blending mode to Multiply.

q. Select layer 2, continue painting to finish the illustration.

r. Compare your artwork to Figure H-28.

s. Save your work, then close bristle brush practice_AI-H.ai.

FIGURE H-28

Real Life Independent Challenge

Your friend has asked you to design a morph animation for her website. She tells you that you are free to choose as many different shapes as you like.

a. Create a new Illustrator file at any size, then name it **my morph_AI-H**.

b. Create the objects that you want to be part of the morph.

c. Create a 256-step blend between each object.

d. Switch to Outline mode.

e. Align the center points of each object.

f. Export the file as a 120-fps animated SWF file.

g. Preview the animation.

h. Save your work, then close my morph_AI-H.ai.

Visual Workshop

Open the file AI H-15.ai, then save it as **montag_AI-H**. Using Figure H-29 as a guide, use the Width tool to make the artwork more dynamic. Save your work, then close montag_AI-H.ai.

FIGURE H-29

Data Files for Illustrator CS6 Illustrated

To complete the lessons and practice exercises in this book, students need to use Data Files that are supplied by Cengage Learning. Below is a list of the Data Files that are supplied and the unit and practice exercise to which the files correspond. For information on how to obtain Data Files, please refer to the inside front cover of this book.

Data File Supplied	Used In	Student Saves File As
UNIT A		
Lessons/ new document AI A-1.ai	Lessons 4-5 Lessons 6-9	double artboards_AI-A.ai workspace basics_AI-A.ai
Skills Review/ new document AI A-2.ai	Skills Review	four artboards_AI-A.ai workspace review_AI-A.ai
IC1/new document	Independent Challenge 1	consignment cards_AI-A.ai
IC2/AI A-3.ai	Independent Challenge 2	exercise_AI-A.ai exercise_ACE_AI-A.ai
IC3/new document	Independent Challenge 3	dinner party_AI-A.ai dinner party_ACE_AI-A.ai
Real Life IC	Real Life Independent Challenge	No solution file
VW/new document	Visual Workshop	guides_AI-A.ai
UNIT B		
Lessons/ AI B-1.ai	Lessons 1-8	basic shapes_AI-B.ai
Skills Review/ AI B-2.ai	Skills Review	shape review_AI-B.ai
IC1/new document	Independent Challenge 1	eyecare vision design_AI-B.ai
IC2/new document	Independent Challenge 2	checkerboard_AI-B.ai
IC3/AI B-3.ai	Independent Challenge 3	on the move_AI-B.ai
Real Life IC/AI B-4.ai	Real Life Independent Challenge	business card_AI.B.ai
VW/new document	Visual Workshop	shape stack_AI-B.ai
UNIT C		
Lessons/ AI C-1.ai AI C-2.ai AI C-3.ai AI C-4.ai	Lesson 1 Lessons 2-5 Lessons 6-7 Lesson 8	transform each_AI-C.ai direct selections_AI-C.ai just chillin_AI-C.ai pucker & bloat_AI-C.ai

Data File Supplied	Used In	Student Saves File As
Skills Review/AI C-5.ai AI C-6.ai AI C-7.ai AI C-8.ai	Skills Review	triangles_AI-C.ai selection review_AI-C.ai wow_AI-C.ai distort skills_AI-C.ai
IC1/new document	Independent Challenge 1	comb_AI-C.ai comb_ACE_AI-C.ai
IC2/AI C-9.ai	Independent Challenge 2	spade_AI-C.ai spade_ACE_AI-C.ai
IC3/AI C-10.ai	Independent Challenge 3	intersect_AI-C.ai
Real Life IC/AI C-11.ai	Real Life Independent Challenge	card redesign_AI-C.ai
VW/new document	Visual Workshop	club_AI-C.ai
UNIT D		
Lessons/ AI D-1.ai AI D-2.ai AI D-3.ai AI D-4.ai AI D-5.ai AI D-6.ai AI D-7.ai AI D-8.ai	Lesson 1 Lesson 2 Lesson 3 Lesson 4 Lessons 5-6 Lesson 7 Lesson 8 Lesson 9	divided star_AI-D.ai simple compound path_AI-D.ai complex compound paths_AI-D.ai blend tutorial_AI-D.ai clockwise blend_AI-D.ai draw inside_AI-D.ai arrows_AI-D.ai complex dashed strokes_AI-D.ai
Skills Review/ AI D-9.ai AI D-10.ai AI D-11.ai AI D-12.ai AI D-13.ai AI D-14.ai AI D-15.ai AI D-16.ai	Skills Review	kaleidoscope_AI-D.ai purple paths_AI-D.ai complex circle_AI-D.ai blend review_AI-D.ai jagged blend_AI-D.ai draw inside skills_AI-D.ai caps review_AI-D.ai complex stroke review_AI-D.ai
IC1/AI D-17.ai	Independent Challenge 1	eyeball stroke_AI-D.ai eyeball stroke_ACE_AI-D.ai
IC2/AI D-18.ai	Independent Challenge 2	mask_AI-D.ai mask_ACE_AI-D.ai
IC3/AI D-19.ai	Independent Challenge 3	train tracks_AI-D.ai
Real Life IC/AI D-20.ai	Real Life Independent Challenge	landscape card_AI-D.ai
VW/AI D-21.ai	Visual Workshop	stroke challenge_AI-D.ai
UNIT E		
Lessons/ AI E-1.ai	Lessons 1-8	atlas_AI-E.ai
Skills Review/AI E-2.ai	Skills Review	green_AI-E.ai
IC1/AI E-3.ai	Independent Challenge 1	tigers_AI-E.ai tigers_ACE_AI-E.ai

Data File Supplied	Used In	Student Saves File As
IC2/AI E-4.ai	Independent Challenge 2	gradient lesson_AI-E.ai gradient lesson_ACE_AI-E.ai
IC3/new document	Independent Challenge 3	thin ice_AI_E.ai
Real Life IC/AI E-5.ai	Real Life Independent Challenge	my card_AI-E.ai
VW/AI E-6.ai	Visual Workshop	atoms_AI-E.ai
UNIT F		
Lessons/ new document AI F-1.ai AI F-2.ai	Lesson 1 Lessons 2-6 Lessons 7-9	image trace_AI-F.ai flower sketch pad_AI-F.ai flower brushes_AI-F.ai
Skills Review/ AI F-3.ai AI F-4.ai	Skills Review	skills trace_AI-F.ai drawing skills_AI-F.ai brush skills_AI-F.ai
IC1/ AI F-5.ai	Independent Challenge 1	elephants_AI-F.ai
IC2/ AI F-6.ai	Independent Challenge 2	brushed elephants_AI-F.ai
IC3/ AI F-7.ai	Independent Challenge 3	umbrella_AI-F.ai umbrella_ACE_AI-F.ai
Real Life IC/ AI F-8.ai	Real Life Independent Challenge	peppermill_AI-F.ai peppermill_ACE_AI-F.ai
VW/ AI F-9.ai	Visual Workshop	lsat_AI-F.ai
UNIT G		
Lessons/ AI G-1.ai AI G-2.ai AI G-3.ai AI G-4.ai AI G-5.ai AI G-6.ai AI G-7.ai	Lesson 1 Lessons 2-3 Lesson 4 Lesson 5 Lesson 6 Lesson 7 Lesson 8	atlas layers_AI-G.ai patterns_AI-G.ai shear_AI-G.ai impact_AI-G.ai flag warp_AI-G.ai 3d extrude_AI-G.ai 3d revolve_AI-G.ai
Skills Review/ AI G-8.ai AI G-9.ai AI G-10.ai AI G-11.ai AI G-12.ai AI G-13.ai AI G-14.ai	Skills Review	new earth layers_AI-G.ai star pattern_AI-G.ai shear review_AI-G.ai change_AI-G.ai warp text_AI-G.ai extrude review_AI-G.ai revolve_AI-G.ai
IC1/ AI G-15.ai	Independent Challenge 1	low price_AI-G.ai

Data File Supplied	Used In	Student Saves File As
IC2/ AI G-16.ai	Independent Challenge 2	push pin_AI-G.ai push pin_ACE_AI-G.ai
IC3/ AI G-17.ai	Independent Challenge 3	revolve shapes_AI-G.ai
Real Life IC/ AI G-18.ai	Real Life Independent Challenge	lava lamp_AI-G.ai lava lamp_ACE_AI-G.ai
VW/ AI G-19.ai	Visual Workshop	fish warp_AI-G.ai
UNIT H		
Lessons/ AI H-1.ai AI H-2.ai AI H-3.ai AI H-4.ai AI H-5.ai AI H-6.ai	Lesson 1 Lessons 2-3 Lesson 4 Lesson 5 Lesson 6 Lessons 7-8	width tool_AI-H.ai bristle flower_AI-H.ai shape builder_AI-H.ai web umbrella_AI-H.ai web umbrella_AI-H.swf animated blend_AI-H.ai animated blend_AI-H.swf animated flower_AI-H.ai animated flower_AI-H.swf
Skills Review/ AI H-7.ai AI H-8.ai AI H-9.ai AI H-10.ai AI H-11.ai	Skills Review	width tool skills_AI-H.ai snowball bristle_AI-H.ai shape builder skills_AI-H.ai shape builder skills_AI-H.swf animated blend skills_AI-H.ai animated blend skills_AI-H.swf splash page sequence_AI-H.ai splash page sequence_AI-H.swf
IC1/ AI H-12.ai	Independent Challenge 1	web logo_AI-H.ai web logo_ACE_AI-H.ai
IC2/ AI H-13.ai	Independent Challenge 2	morph_AI-H.ai morph_ACE_AI-H.ai morph_AI-H.swf
IC3/ AI-H-14.ai	Independent Challenge 3	bristle brush practice_AI-H.ai
Real Life IC/ new document	Real Life Independent Challenge	my morph_AI-H.ai my morph_AI-H.swf
VW/AI-15	Visual Workshop	montag_AI-H.ai

Glossary

Artboard The area on which you create artwork. You may have more than one artboard in a document.

Average Command that aligns selected anchor points.

Baseline shift Specifies how far above or below the path the text is positioned.

Blend A series of intermediate objects between two objects.

Bounding box A rectangle whose size matches the width and height of the selected object. When the bounding box is visible, it shows selection handles, small white squares that you can drag to resize the object.

Brushes Illustrator objects that you paint with or apply to other objects as strokes.

Clipboard A temporary virtual storage location. The Copy command copies the selected object to the clipboard. The Cut command cuts a selected object to the clipboard.

Clipping mask Any object that you use to "clip" other objects so that only the parts of the objects that are clipped are visible and the parts that are not clipped are not visible.

Compound path Occurs when a single object is composed of two or more paths.

Concentric circles Circles that have a common center.

Corner points Points that join path segments at an angle.

Direction handles Small boxes that appear on the anchor points of a curved path. The length of the direction handles and the angle at which they are positioned from the path determine the arc of the curved path.

Drop shadows A classic effect used to enhance type.

Effects Operations that you can apply to objects to alter their appearance without actually altering the object itself.

End caps Determine the appearance at the ends of a path. The Stroke panel offers three end caps to choose from: a butt cap (the default) is a blunt cap that ends at the anchor points; a round cap creates an oval at the ends of the path; and a projecting cap extends the stroke past the anchor points to a distance that is equal to $1/2$ the point size of the stroke itself.

Fill The color that you apply to the interior of an object.

Gradient A type of fill that provides a transition between colors. You design gradients using the Gradient panel.

Image trace Feature that allows you to take any placed digital image and convert it into a tracing object.

Join Command that joins any two selected anchor points.

Kerning Increasing or decreasing the space between any two pairs of letters to improve the overall visual appearance of text.

Landscape Alternate page orientation; wider than it is tall.

Layers Panel that offers many options for working with artwork in layers, including locking/unlocking and hiding/showing.

Line segment Part of a path. Line segments fall within each set of two anchor points.

Linear gradient A gradient in which color gradates in one straight direction.

Opacity How opaque the fill or stroke of an object is. You specify an object's opacity on the Transparency panel.

Outline mode Shows only the vector outline of objects.

Pasteboard The white space surrounding the artboard.

Pathfinders Operations in the bottom row of the Pathfinder panel.

Patterns A powerful feature that repeats artwork as a fill for an object.

Point of origin The point from which a transformation is executed.

Portrait Default page orientation, taller than it is wide.

Preview mode Shows artwork with its fill and stroke colors.

Radial gradient A gradient in which color radiates outward from a central point.

Radius A straight line extending from the center of a circle to its outer edge. A star has two radii; the first is from the center of the star to the inner point, and the second is from the center to the outer point.

Shape modes Operations in the top row of the Pathfinder panel.

Smart guides Appear as you drag the mouse pointer over the artboard. Words such as *center*, *anchor*, *path*, and *intersect* appear when the mouse pointer touches one of those items. Smart guides are also useful for moving objects in Illustrator. If you want to align two objects by their center points, the word "center" will appear once the two are aligned.

Smooth points Points that join curved paths with a smooth arc.

Stacking order Refers to the order of how objects are arranged in front of and behind other objects on the artboard.

Stroke The color that you apply to the outline of an object.

Tile The base artwork for a pattern.

Tiling The process by which patterns repeat tiles to create artwork for a pattern fill.

Transform Refers to tools and operations that modify objects. Moving, scaling, rotating, reflecting, and shearing are all examples of transformations.

Transform panel Shows you specific height and width values for a selected object.

Vector graphics Created with lines and curves and are defined by mathematical objects called vectors. Vector graphics consist of anchor points and line segments, together referred to as paths.

Warps Preset distortion effects that produce fun and often practical results for distorting artwork.

Index

transforming and coloring, 34–35

transforming and distorting, 2

Offset Path command, 64, 67

offsetting paths, 67

opacity, defined, 116

operations

objects

creating, 28–29

duplicating, 32–33

resizing, 30–31

transforming and coloring, 34–35

overview, 27

point of origin, 38–39

Polygon tool, 42–43

Transform Again command, 36–37

using Star and Reflect tools, 40–41

outline mode, 12

Outline Stroke command, 138, 178

outlining strokes, 138–139

P

painting. *See* drawing

pasteboard feature, 6

Paste command, 37

Paste in Front option, 52, 60

pathfinders, 62

paths

Compound, creating, 78–79

creating text on, 118–119

joining points and, 132–133

overview, 2

restarting, 134

reversing direction of, 136–137

scaling versus offsetting, 67

patterns, creating with Compound paths, 80–81

pattern swatches

applying and editing, 158–160

creating, 156–157

Pen tool, 130–131

pixels, 112

Place command, 112

point of origin, 38–39

points

joining paths and, 132–133

overview, 130

Polygon tool, 42–43

portrait orientation, 8

preferences, for units, 42

preference settings, 4–5

press and hold action, 39

preview mode, 12

processes, applying, 2

profiles of documents, 9

Projecting Cap option, 90

pseudo strokes, 144–145

Q

quick keys, 37

R

radial gradients, 104, 114–115

radius, defined, 40

Rectangle tool, 28

Redo command, 37

reference points, 53

Reflect tool, 40–41, 132

Reset Essentials option, 104

resizing objects, 30–31

restarting paths, 134

Reverse Gradient button, 114

Reverse Order option, 190

reversing direction of paths, 136–137

revolving 3D objects, 166–167

Rotate tool, 34

Round Cap option, 90

ruler guides, 16–17

S

saving documents, 8–9

Scale section, 52

Scale tool, 34, 40, 67

scaling paths, 67

selecting within groups, 54–55

selection handles, 30

Send Backward command, 59

Send to Back command, 58–60

Sequence option, 188

Shape Builder tool, 184–185

vectors, 2

views

    changing, 12–13

    creating, 13

    workspace, 6–7

W

warp effects, 164–165

warps, defined, 164

watches panel, 28

web graphics

    animation

        creating from non-blend artwork, 190–191

        exporting blends as SWF files, 188–189

        exporting non-blend artwork as animated SWF files, 192–193

    Bristle brush

        creating, 180–181

        painting with, 182–183

    creating objects with Shape Builder tool, 184–185

exporting artwork as, 186–187

    overview, 177

    using Width tool, 178–179

weight of strokes, 34

Width tool, 178–179

workspace, viewing, 6–7

workspace switcher, 6

Z

Zoom tool, 12